Publication description

Socialism was never a part of Mormon doctrine, but internal and external proponents of socialism have nonetheless been able convince many members (and outsiders), through perpetuating myths and legends, that it has been or is a part of church doctrine.

The Mormon Church (The Church of Jesus Christ of Latter-day Saints) was organized in 1830 and immediately began moving westward from New York to Kirtland, Ohio, and Independence, Missouri, and, later, from about 1838 to 1845, to Nauvoo, Illinois. The next move was to Utah beginning in 1847. Numerous cooperative efforts were necessary at each stage to help the poorer and weaker members of the Church move along with the others. Some of its first converts had been members of communal societies before their contacts with the Mormons. Also, the enemies of the Church found an untrue but effective epithet against "those sheep-stealing Mormons" by calling their new organization "common stock" communalism or socialism, a damning charge in the political atmosphere of the time.

Joseph Smith went to great efforts to speak and write against this falsehood, declaring that it had nothing to do with the church. His successor Brigham Young continued the practice of denouncing this false claim, declaring that such a doctrine could destroy the church, especially in its precarious Utah setting. Nonetheless, it appears that the external enemies of the church and some of its politically leftwing members have, by sheer weight of repetition, made it part of the unofficial lore of the church.

The term "united order" came from the "united firm," one name for the early church business partnerships. The term "united order" also comes from the Brigham Young era of the church's history, and needs to be further explained in that unique context, as is done in the subsequent book, Brigham Youngs United Order. With no powers of self-government granted the Mormons for the first 22 years of their time in Utah, some unusual and creative temporary substitutes were invented.

The official history of the church makes it clear that various practical methods were used to solve problems as they arose, many involving cooperation, as one might expect of any tight-knit religious body, but none required any doctrinaire overriding of the principle of private ownership of property, as the centralizing socialists would like to see. For one thing, that would be severely inconsistent with the church's reverence for the constitution of the United States.

In the first 8 years of the church's existence, it was not legally possible to organize it as a corporation as it is today. As an unsatisfactory but necessary stop-gap measure, a common-law business partnership was organized to carry on church business of all kinds. (The partners also constituted a temporary Quorum of the Twelve for ecclesiastical purposes.) In the normal accounting practices of partnerships, all partners are assumed to be agents of all the others, and also to share equally in the both the liabilities and profits of the business, including being personally liable for all the partnership's debts. There is thus no escape from full liability, but the use of silent (unknown) partners can give those unknown partners a small amount of financial protection. It is strange to see that misunderstandings of the British common law (and misunderstandings of many other events and circumstances as well) have been used in political and polemical efforts to justify pressing socialism into the canon of church doctrine, but socialism (centralized ownership and control of nearly everything) can never be part of a value system that emphasizes individual responsibility. It is no accident that Utah is mostly a conservative, Republican state.

This apparent inconsistency deep within the doctrines of the church will likely lead to a whole set of difficulties as the church grows in size and influence. At some point in time, this issue must be cleared up unequivocally, and this book should help.

Dust Cover, front flap

JOSEPH SMITH'S
UNITED ORDER

What is the Law of Consecration? What does living the Law of Consecration mean today? What was the United Order? Why was it disbanded? Was it a failure? If so, why? Will it be reinstated? Is reinstatement of the United Order necessary to fully live the Law of Consecration? What about the U.S. Constitution? Will the principles of private ownership contained in the U.S. Constitution eventually be displaced before or during the second coming of Christ? How will the saints be living in order to accept the economic rule which Christ will bring? Can we live that way now?

Joseph Smith's United Order by Kent W. Huff gives one of the most unique perspectives on early church economic history to ever be published. It provides great insight into tithing history and administration. It also shows that 36 percent of the sections of the Doctrine and Covenants deal with Church economic organization and policy.

Joseph Smith's United Order is indeed a monumental work on Church finance and administration. Its principles should be studied, understood, and considered by every Latter-day Saint.

KENT W. HUFF

JOSEPH SMITH'S UNITED ORDER

A NON-COMMUNALISTIC INTERPRETATION

Copyright (c) 1988 by Kent W. Huff

All rights reserved. This book or any part thereof may not be reproduced in any form whatsoever, whether by graphic, visual, electronic, filming, microfilming, tape recording, or any other means, without the prior written permission of the publisher, except in the case of brief passages embodied in critical reviews and articles.

Paperback: ISBN 978-0-9755831-3-5
July 2020

Hardback: ISBN 1-55517-038-2
First Printing October 1988
Distributed by:
Cedar Fort, Inc.
1182 North Industrial Park Drive
Orem, Utah 84057

Printed in the United States of America

About the Cover

The cover illustration by Richard Holdaway shows various names used for business transactions of the Church under the United Order. Although it depicts the time period no attempt was made to achieve authenticity of location.

**to my
Father**

Table of Contents

Chapter   **Page**

1. Introduction. 1
    a. An Overview of Joseph Smith's United Order
    b. The Brigham Young and Joseph Smith Eras Contrasted
    c. Some Quantitative Aspects of the Gathering
2. Early Leaders Were Firmly Against "Common Stock" Communalism or Socialism; Meaning of Consecration. 20
3. Administrative Arrangements for the Gathering Before the United Order Firm Was Organized. 49
4. Organizing the First United Order Firm or Partnership to Assist in the Gathering 82
5. Transactions of the First United Order Firm. 121
6. The United Order Firm Becomes Two Firms. 147
7. Transactions of the Kirtland United Order Firm 159
8. Transactions in Missouri by the United Order Firm and Other Units 179
9. The United Order Firms Cease Operation 188
10. The United Order Firms Replaced by the Corporate Trustee-in-Trust 202
11. Relationships Among the United Order, Quorum of the Twelve, Kirtland High Council, and Other Early Administrative Bodies 217
12. Communalism Was Not Present in the Ordinary Activities of the Joseph Smith Period 234
13. Tithing and the United Order, Part 1: Tithing Procedure is Adapted to Circumstances. 270
14. Tithing and the United Order, Part 2: Tithing was an Active Doctrine from the Beginning of this Dispensation. 286
15. Tithing and the United Order, Part 3: Sections 119 and 120 Improved Tithing Procedure. 296
16. Joseph Smith's Definition of the Phrase "The Law of the Lord" 322
17. The Principles and Programs Described in D&C Section 42:. The Meaning of the Word "Consecration" 331
18. Summary 357
19. Conclusion. 364

x

PREFACE

Two bodies of information have grown up on the subject of the relationship between economics and the Gospel. One consists of detailed historical materials that generally leave the reader with the impression that communalism or socialism is a definite part of the Gospel, although possibly having been suspended for the moment. The other consists of strong denials by various of the leading brethren that any such philosophies are part of the Gospel. Unfortunately, those denials have not met the more lengthy historical works on their own ground and overcome their communalistic implications.

As part of an effort to resolve the question for myself, I examined the history of the Joseph Smith period in detail. In that search, instead of finding evidence of communalistic doctrines being taught and practiced, I found evidence of very practical, non-doctrinaire, and individualistic solutions to the problems of the day.

This book is the result of that study. It describes the administrative techniques Joseph Smith used in drawing together many thousands of scattered believers, and providing direction and organization as needs arose and leaders could be found to fulfill them. An alternative theory of LDS economic history is presented to explain the meaning of those early events, and to relate the past to the present.

The results of the study are in marked contrast with the later Brigham Young period, and raise many questions concerning our understanding of that era. However, this book does not deal directly with the Brigham Young period, nor does it attempt a comparative study of the various communalistic economic theories applied by other writers to the Joseph Smith and Brigham Young periods. Those significant projects are left to a later time or another writer, or, as they say in many textbooks, it is "left as a student exercise."

Note on content: Chapters 1 through 10 contain large doses of quotations and detailed discussion showing the evolution of the united order partnership, and related policy and practice, from beginning to end including its replacement by the corporate form. Chapter 11 gives a broader view of the development and interplay of most of the major church organizations during the Joseph Smith period. Chapters 12 through 17 cover peripheral issues usually assumed to be related to the united order concept, including tithing and consecration. Chapter 18, included here as a summary, was written as a short magazine article to cover the entire subject in three pages, and thus has a tone different from that found throughout the remainder of the book. Chapter 19 offers some tentative conclusions about the formulation of church economic programs.

Acknowledgements: I owe a special debt to my wife Suzanne Snow Huff for her patience with a hobby that has been almost an obsession for several years. She has been both my most encouraging colleague and toughest critic. Another friend, Dan, has also made a significant contribution to getting this project completed through his encouragement and thoughtful criticism. Nonetheless, I think both would be happy to let me bear the full responsibility for the final product and any future developments.

Note on research philosophy: It seems that religious historians of many faiths are prone to elevate to the level of general doctrine what was only ad hoc adaptation to circumstance in the original instance. I have attempted to avoid that pitfall by looking for the practicalities behind the recorded events and comments. Where it was not possible to extend my practical research as far as I would have liked, I have employed the observation that often "there is nothing so practical as a good theory" and filled the gap as best I could. It could take a lifetime to explore in depth all the questions raised in the study. I can only hope that this book may serve to encourage further work on the topic.

CHAPTER 1

Introduction

The opening remarks of an address given by President J. Reuben Clark, First Counselor in the First Presidency of the Church of Jesus Christ of Latter-day Saints, at an October 3, 1942, session of LDS general conference may serve as a beginning point:

> Brethren:
> I have been trying for a week to relieve you of this experience, but Brother McKay, so kind, so sweet, and so merciful, has been perfectly adamant. So I stand before you here, not to preach, but to counsel with you.
> There is a great deal of misapprehension among our people regarding the United Order.
> I have not been able to believe that the United Order meant what some people have thought it meant, so within the last months I have spent quite a little time reading the revelations thereon, also reading our history, and at the same time giving some consideration to a dissertation which has been written regarding the Order.
> .... So I thought that perhaps if I said just a few words to you tonight regarding the way I interpret the revelations that are printed about this in the Doctrine and Covenants (if there are other revelations about the Order, I do not know of them) ... it might be helpful.[1]

Misapprehension of the united order was once serious enough to concern the First Presidency. It might once again become a problem if Church members do not understand the meaning of their own history.

A Structural and Operational Overview of Joseph Smith's United Order

The term "united order" has been the rubric under which various mild to extreme doctrines of communalism have been said to be associated with the LDS church. The term "united order" does appear in the scriptures revealed through Joseph Smith, the founder and first Prophet of the church. The term also appears in the histories and records of Joseph Smith's administration (1829-1844). However, its meaning during the Joseph Smith period is quite different from that assumed by many. What follows is a brief summary of the theory or interpretation to be developed throughout this book:

The united order at Joseph Smith's time was the equivalent of today's Corporation of the President in that it was organized to hold property and conduct general church business.

The united order group or firm consisted of nine men at its beginning in 1832. Two men were specifically added later. In 1834, when the firm became two firms, a few other men may have been added to meet the growing need for administrators to help the gathering process.

These men constituted a partnership and followed the usual business law rules for conducting a partnership, including those relating to general and limited (or silent) partners, agency, profit sharing, etc. Corporate (limited liability) forms of business organization were relatively rare and required specific action by a state legislature to acquire a charter.[2] That form was also less flexible than the partnership form, a serious deficiency in the early days of quick and dramatic changes.

The Lord's instructions on how to organize and operate a partnership are similar to His later revelations concerning the business arrangements for funding through stock sales a hotel project in Nauvoo, Illinois, known as the Nauvoo House. Both are practical instructions on how to accomplish a particular business or economic objective. Both used standard business organization techniques suited to the time and the task.

The secret names used in various revelations and historical accounts were used only by the members of the united order, and only in their capacity as partners in the united order, order, united firm, firm, or company as it was variously called by them. One purpose of the code names was to allow the church leaders in their business roles to manage and distribute their liabilities without harassment from overanxious creditors. This secrecy made it possible for the concept of limited (or silent) partners to be used effectively. Ironically, for the united order organization to function properly, it was necessary that most members of the Church not even know it existed. If many church members knew of it, it would not be long until outsiders knew as well.

The movement of thousands of saints from eastern United States and European locations to Ohio and Missouri could more easily be accomplished if a few critical administrative functions were centralized. The business dealings of the united order supported the migration plans of the church, especially in purchasing and selling land, making needed supplies available through various mercantile establishments, and printing church periodicals and scriptures. All other functions were handled by the individuals and small groups making the move to Missouri.

The procedures used in settling Kirtland, Ohio, Jackson County, Missouri (sometimes referred to as *Zion*), Far West, Missouri, and Nauvoo, Illinois, were all essentially the same. Wherever possible the brethren first bought or contracted for large tracts of land (one or more square miles of land at a time). The total land purchased in Missouri was probably in the range of two hundred fifty square miles, and included one whole county and parts of others. These tracts were then subdivided into farms and city lots and sold to migrating members. This meant that the debts of the central church business unit were often very high, at times amounting to well over a hundred thousand dollars. Thus the regular concern about debts that is evident in Joseph Smith's journal history was not a small matter. In addition to the land transactions, such things as chapels, temples, stores, printing shops, etc., were needed to sustain the saints in their migration and in their missionary duties. Large amounts of capital were needed for all these activities.

The members were asked to support the brethren (in the sense of following their lead or counsel, rather than in the sense of providing them with a living, although that too was necessary at times) by purchasing land from them and thus allowing the large land contracts to be fulfilled without embarrassing the brethren. When the saints bought other land, that tended to leave the brethren holding tracts of land for which they had no means to pay. In many cases it was appropriate for the saints to buy land on their own, but the brethren wished them to coordinate those purchases ("accept counsel") to avoid conflict and confusion. Some members attempted to benefit personally from the migration by buying up land on their own, waiting a time, and then selling it at a profit as the area filled up with settlers and the land prices went up. This activity and the trouble it caused is the basis for much of the discussion of the need for "consecration." The church wished the members, for very practical real estate development reasons, to buy just the amount of land they needed and to buy it through the church, avoiding speculation, high prices, and confusion.

A related problem occurred when some who had made contributions to the church, whether in money or land, changed their minds, and wished to regain control of their gifts for what they believed would be a more personally profitable use. The "deed that cannot be broken" language was aimed at the very practical goal of making gifts irrevocable and thus forestalling disputes over ownership of land or other property as economic and spiritual conditions changed.

In short, the evidence of economic cooperation in the Joseph Smith period is all directly associated with the actual migration operations of the saints. During those brief periods when they were settled, they followed a pattern of individual freedom. There never was any general involvement of a large number of saints in a structured communalistic society. The concept of individual ownership and management of property was given full sway for all church members, modified only by the practical needs of the gathering process.

The Contrast Between the Brigham Young and Joseph Smith Eras

After Joseph Smith's martyrdom in June, 1844, Brigham Young assumed leadership of the church and guided the saints to Utah. In Utah, he and others speaking on his behalf declared that it was his intention to unite all the property and wealth of all the saints in the intermountain west into a single economic monolith, with all transactions with the external world handled through one centrally controlled channel. Title to all property would be held by a church controlled central body, and would be available to be used as collateral for loans from outsiders. All significant internal trade and investment decisions would be made by the central authority or its designate. Internal competition and redundancy would be eliminated by assignment of personnel to jobs according to talents or the needs of the system. All church members would essentially become employees of a single corporate structure, and would not hold title to any productive property.[3]

Although Brigham Young's sweeping plans were never fully implemented,[4] they deserve extensive study because from them have come a whole set of ideas and traditions that still provide much of the rhetoric of church-related economics, regardless of how much today's applied economics may differ from that rhetoric.

However, before we can deal intelligently with the Brigham Young period, we should first examine the earlier and strongly contrasting Joseph Smith period. With one exception, Joseph Smith was the conduit for all the revelations published as canonized scripture before 1890, including a myriad of revelations dealing with economic topics. Unless we are to abandon canonized scripture and look only to later conference reports or other secondary sources in our search for economic truth, we must deal with the Joseph Smith period, the reasons for his requesting the revelations, and his interpretation and application of these scriptures in his own time. After achieving some understanding of that great body of experience we can better understand and evaluate the economic events and policies of the Brigham Young period.

Materials from the Joseph Smith period will be presented to establish the following main points:

1. Contrary to traditions stemming from the Brigham Young era, any form of socialism, defined here as centralized or common ownership and/or control of property, was not a part of the teachings or practice of the Joseph Smith era; Joseph Smith and other leaders of that time made strong efforts to counter such teachings and practices.

2. The united order organizations of the Joseph Smith era had no elements of socialism, but were simply the administrative forerunners of today's Corporation of the President, with a special function of facilitating the gathering process. Following a natural pattern of progression from the simple and informal to the complex and formal, the administrative processes of the gathering and other central church activities were first carried on by individuals, later by

one or more partnership arrangements, and finally by a single corporate form.

3. During the Joseph Smith era, the term consecration did not imply any socialistic mechanism or behavior, but referred only to contributions of the sort commonly made within the church today. One circumstance, certain land purchase transactions in Missouri related to the gathering process, did involve an extra element of "dedication" of land, which meant that the purchasers intended to use the land in a certain way and would not resell to outsiders, but this was a far cry from any centralized ownership or control of land and labor. There were also some cooperative business efforts, but they were based on principles of common sense economics, not some intervening religious doctrine. Joseph Smith made it clear that participation in the Big Farm organizations was completely optional.[5]

The relationships between these concepts and the teachings of the Brigham Young and other periods invite further exploration in
detail.

Some Statistics of the Gathering

A few statistics may help in understanding the problem that Joseph Smith's united order and its predecessors were organized to deal with. The settling of Jackson County commenced in the summer of 1831.[6] By the time of the attacks of the Jackson County mob in October 1833, there were about twelve hundred saints living there,[7] with about two hundred buildings having been constructed by them.[8] These were the saints that were driven out and the buildings that were destroyed.[9] The saints then directed their gathering efforts to other places including the Far West area, and continued to increase in numbers.

Five years later, in October 1838, when the saints were finally driven completely out of the state of Missouri, there were about fifteen thousand people to be removed.[10] The property value lost was estimated at two million dollars.[11] The purchase price of the land lost was estimated to be about two hundred thousand dollars, with perhaps one hundred fifty thousand dollars having been paid to the United States Government,[12] the remainder going to other sellers.

If we use a purchase price of one dollar and twenty-five cents per acre, the normal sale price of public lands at the time, that means that about one hundred sixty thousand acres were acquired by the saints through various means. At six hundred forty acres per square mile, then about two hundred fifty square miles of land were at issue, or the equivalent of a single plot ten miles wide and twenty five miles long. The saints did hold at least one whole county plus other peripheral land at different times.

Acquiring land on that scale and settling nearly fifteen thousand people on it was a substantial task, and it is only to be wondered how the small united order firm was able to handle the process. In fact, the scope of the undertaking and the smallness of the firm, only four men in Missouri to begin with, is strong evidence that the united order's purpose really was limited to a land sales function. There was simply no manpower available to administer any communal program, beyond welfare assistance to the very poor.[13]

By October 1833 the saints had been gathering to Missouri for two and one-half years, and twelve hundred people had moved there. The united order had been in existence for one and one-half years. The split of the firm into two independent firms occurred in April 1834, about six months after those first saints were expelled from Jackson County. Within the next three years, a ten-fold larger migration occurred than had happened in the first two years of gathering there. Splitting the firm was probably a very necessary thing to enable it to handle that level of activity. Although general church history is not clear on this point, it is possible that other men were added to the ranks of both united order firms as the need arose. The two new bishoprics chosen to aid Edward Partridge, the united order firm partner and first bishop sent to Missouri, would have been good candidates for such positions.

There is an interesting relationship between the numbers and timing of the flow of saints to Missouri, and the number and timing of revelations on economic matters that were received to assist the migration. One might expect that the receipt of new revelations would tend to correlate with the timing of new kinds of church activity, in this case, the acceleration of the gathering and migration process. The revelations would come first to show the way, increase in numbers as new circumstances and complexities needed to be dealt with, and remain constant once the problems were solved. Data representing (1) number of revelations in effect concerning economics and (2) thousands of saints in Missouri are placed together on a graph in figure 1.

With the two curves properly scaled and placed side by side, their similarity in shape is striking, with the revelations leading the way of the increase in "gathered" saints. Data recorded in the *Documentary History* were used to plot the cumulative migration line graph. If more data points were available through some other source, the shape of the migration curve might be further refined, and it is possible that other relationships between the two curves could be detected. Figure 2 gives the year and section number of those revelations dealing with economic matters which are plotted in figure 1.

There is no particular intention to show the existence of a mathematical relationship between the number of revelations and the number of people who migrated. The goal here is simply to show that the revelations were closely related to the activities and problems of the gathering process.

A third relationship is also shown in figure 1. The timing of significant administrative events, related to the gathering and church organization, is indicated by underlining the proper year at the bottom of the graph and describing the event in a note. The sequence of administrative events shows an expansion and maturation of church organizational form paralleling the growth in number of gathered saints and numbers of revelations.

Figure 1.

Graph Showing three aspects of the gathering:

1. Cumulative revelations on economics by year.
2. Cumulative saints gathered in Missouri (or Illinois) by year.
3. Significant administrative events related to the gathering and church organization. (Symbols A through F on the time line)

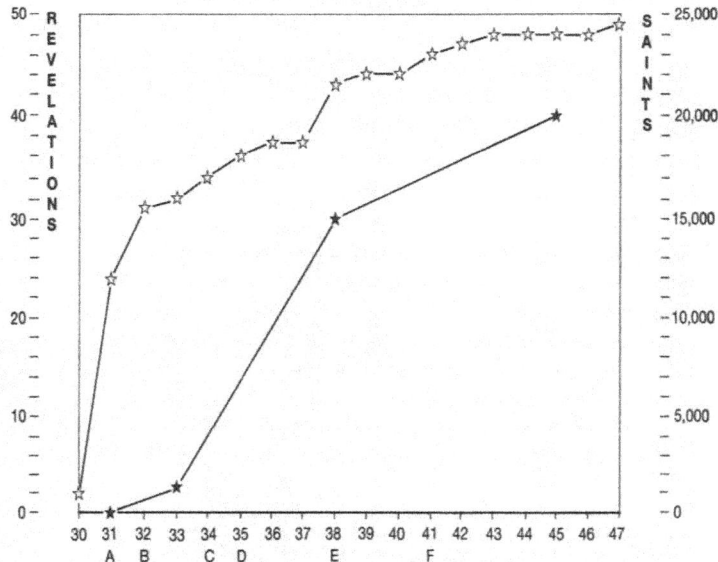

☆ Number of Revelations in effect
★ Thousands of Saints in Missouri (or Illinois, after 1838).

Event Descriptions:

A. 1831 - Migration to Missouri begins.
B. 1832 - United Order firm organized.
C. 1834 - United Order firm is split into two firms.
D. 1835 - The Quorum of the Twelve is organized.
E. 1838 - Tithing procedures regularized; Twelve assume some central church administrative duties; United Order firms cease operation.
F. 1841 - Trustee-in-Trust corporation organized; old partnership forms and debts ended.

Figure 2.
Number and Timing of Revelations Concerning Economic Matters

Year	Total Sections Revealed	Sections Dealing With Economics	Section Numbers
1823	1	0	
1824	0	0	
1825	0	0	
1826	0	0	
1827	0	0	
1828	2	0	
1829	14	0	
1830	19	2	19, 26
1831	37	22	38, 42, 44, 45, 48, 49, 51-58, 60, 61, 63, 66, 68-70, 133. At Kirtland or Independence.
1832	16	7	75, 78, 81, 82, 83, 84, 85
1833	13	1	90
1834	5	2	104, 105
1835	3	2	107, 134
1836	3	1	111
1837	1	0	
1838	8	6	114, 115, 117, 118, 119, 120 At Far West
1839	3	1	123
1840	0	0	
1841	3	2	124, 125
1842	2	1	127
1843	4	1	132
1844	1	0	
1845	0	0	
1846	0	0	
1847	1	1	136
1890	1	1	Official Declaration.
	137	50	(36% of all sections)

Chapter 1 Notes

1. Address by President J. Reuben Clark, Jr., First Counselor in the First Presidency, entitled "Private Ownership Under the United Order," delivered October 3, 1942, during the 113th Annual Conference in Salt Lake City, Utah. Church publication number PGWE0037. Other portions of President Clark's introductory remarks show the nature of his concern:

> There is a growing -- I fear it is growing -- sentiment that communism and the United Order are virtually the same thing, communism being merely the forerunner, so to speak, of a reestablishment of the United Order. I am informed that exbishops, and indeed, bishops, who belong to communistic organizations, are preaching this doctrine. .... I recommend that you, my brethren, read a few of the Sections of the Doctrine and Covenants which cover this matter, beginning with Sections 42 and 51. (See also Sections 70, 78, 82, 83, 85, 90, 92, 96, and 104.)

The positive sentiment toward communism mentioned by President Clark may have been related to the United State's alliance with Russia during World War II. If so, that sentiment has probably long since disappeared as a result of "cold war" conflicts between those two world powers. However, some "misapprehension" still seems to remain.

Some of his assertions about Church history are also of interest here:

Early Deviations

> I may say to begin with, that in practice the brethren in Missouri got away, in their attempts to set up the United Order, from the principles set out in the revelations. This is also true of the organizations set up here in Utah after the Saints came to the Valleys. So far as I have seen there has been preserved only one

> document that purports to be a legal instrument used in connection with the setting up of the United Order, and that document is without date. It is said to have been found among the papers of Bishop Partridge. It was a "lease-lend" document. You may have heard that phrase before. Under this instrument the Church leased to Titus Billings a certain amount of real estate and loaned him a certain amount of personal property. (HC 1:365-367)
> *This instrument is not in accordance with the principle laid down in the revelations touching upon the United Order.* (emphasis supplied)

President Clark challenges the "united order" activities of both the Joseph Smith and Brigham Young periods, and, by implication, also challenges the resulting traditions stemming from those periods. One purpose of this study is to sift the events of both times to more clearly separate the correct from the incorrect, the good from the bad.

On the subject of the Titus Billings deed, the very fact that only one has been found when thousands of deeds must have been executed may tend to show that there were no special Church-created property documents, and that normal land documents were used. Some original research on this point would be most useful.

Comments in a similar vein from a later article are also of interest as we begin a serious study of the united order concept:

> The fundamental principle of this system was the private ownership of property. Each man owned his portion, or inheritance, or stewardship, with an absolute title, which he could alienate, or hypothecate, or otherwise treat as his own. The Church did not own all of the property, and the life under the United Order was not a communal life, as the Prophet Joseph, himself, said. (*History of the Church*, Volume III, p. 28.) The United Order is an individualistic system, not a communal system.
> ....
> In the first place I repeat again, the United Order recognized and was built upon the principle of private ownership of property; all that a man had and lived upon under the United

> Order, was his own. Quite obviously, the fundamental principle of our system today is the ownership of private property.
>
> ....
>
> One very common misapprehension may be corrected here regarding the United Order. The Church never was, and under existing commandments never will be, a communal society, under the directions thus far given by the Lord. The United Order was not communal nor communistic. It was completely and intensely individualistic, with a consecration of unneeded surpluses for the support of the Church and the poor.

President J. Reuben Clark, Jr., "The United Order and Law of Consecration as Set Out In The Revelations of The Lord," pp. 26-27. The article was published some time after the October 3, 1942, talk on a similar topic and printed at pages 15 to 40 in a collection of articles. Available from the Church Historian's Office.

2. A separate act of a state legislature was needed for any new corporation. The saints were not likely to be so favored by men in the legislature who were often their worst enemies. See, for example, the difficulties the saints encountered in obtaining an act of incorporation for the Kirtland Safety Society, see B. H. Roberts, ed, *History of the Church of Jesus Christ of Latter-day Saints* (Salt Lake City: The Deseret Book Company, 1964) 2:468 (hereafter identified as HC).*

For an indication of the historical role and development of limited liability corporations, see "Economic History Since 1500," *Encyclopedia Britannica*, 15th edition, 1981, vol. 6, pp. 234-235.

For more specific information see technical sources such as William L. Cary, *Cases and Materials on Corporations* (Mineola: The Foundation Press, Inc., 1969). A number of pertinent points can be extracted from chapter 1 of that work. In 1780 "there were not more than a few dozen corporations in all of the thirteen colonies combined; and up to 1800 the state legislatures were certainly not enthused to create any more." "The first 'general corporation law for business purposes' is commonly credited to the State of New York, in the year 1811." However, "that act applied only to manufacturing corporations." Between 1818 and 1843 a large number of special charters were issued for business firms. All were severely restricted in powers, in the location of business activities, and in the residences of controlling personnel. "After a classic constitutional struggle, New Jersey, thereby acquiring the title 'Mother of Corporations,' passed a general incorporation act in 1875 giving the widest powers to those who availed themselves of it, and took leadership as an incorporating state."

"General incorporation laws for churches and charities had been known in America since 1784." The Church may have taken advantage of such laws, but the united order would probably not have qualified. It was far too much like a business.

This peek at legal history seems sufficient to establish the rationale for the use of a partnership, but further and more detailed research would undoubtedly prove interesting and would probably verify the wisdom of the organizational choices made.

*This book on Joseph Smith's United Order relies heavily on the seven-volume *History of the Church,* otherwise known as the *Documentary History.* A comment on that source may be appropriate here. In the *Ensign,* July 1985, p. 15, in the "I Have a Question" section, Dean C. Jessee, senior historical associate at the Smith Institute for Church History, Brigham Young University, addresses the authenticity of the *History* and makes this statement:

> The *History,* with its priceless collection of primary documents, remains the most important source of historical information on the life of Joseph Smith and early Latter-day Saint history.

3. *Journal of Discourses,* 26 vols. London: Latter-day Saints Book Depot, 1854-1886. (hereafter referred to as JD) 17:74, 77-78, May 8, 1874; Erastus Snow was discussing the details of the newly announced united order program. JD 21:146, 150, Nov. 1, 1879; Orson Pratt was lamenting the legal barriers to achieving the previously announced united order program.

4. Leonard J. Arrington, Feramorz Y. Fox, and Dean L. May, *Building the City of God* (Salt Lake City: Deseret Book, 1976).

5. Leonard J. Arrington, *The Great Basin Kingdom, An Economic History of the Latter-day Saints, 1830-1900* (University of Nebraska Press, 1966), p. 16.

6. HC 6:84.

7. HC 6:126.

8. HC 6:85.

9. In the Utah period, Brigham Young criticized the saints in Ohio and Missouri for not obeying the law of consecration, which he defined as deeding all their land to the prophet. JD 2:298. (Joseph Smith's definition of that law was substantially different.) Perhaps from this criticism has arisen the impression or tradition that the saints were ejected from their lands in Missouri, at least in part, because of a failure to live the law of consecration and the united order. JD 12:210. This view fails to consider that the united order (partnership) was alive and well and working for one and one-half years before the first expulsion, and continued to function with expanded vigor afterwards. It handled many general church temporal matters and also assisted the poor.

The criticism of the earlier saints was consistent with Brigham Young's recurring theme that strong political, economic, and military power and unity was necessary to maintain the saint's ability to live the gospel and accomplish the church's mission. The saints developed significant temporal power in Nauvoo and were able to greatly expand it in Utah, but during the Missouri period were relatively unprepared for conflict with the world. Weakness that permitted mob action was something Brigham Young hoped never again befell the church. Perhaps his criticisms were actually a reflection of his dismay over the early temporal weakness. In his frame of reference, the deeding of property to the prophet was a way of strengthening the hand of the leader in dealing with the outside world.

Joseph Smith, of course, was greatly disturbed by the expulsion from Jackson County, and sought to understand whether the saints were being punished for some sin or shortcoming such as that later suggested by Brigham Young. However, under persistent questioning from Joseph Smith, the Lord refused to assign that or any other reason as the cause of the saint's forced removal from Missouri. HC 1:453-454.

Section 101 of *The Doctrine and Covenants of the Church of Jesus Christ of Latter-day Saints* (hereafter referred to as D&C) is said to "explain why the saints were driven from Zion." (See HC 1:458n for B. H. Robert's opinion; see also HC 1:402n-403n for Orson Pratt's opinion.). However, there is no indication that the failure to live communally was one of the "transgressions" hinted at. Some "polluted their inheritances," (D&C 101:6), but the use of the word inheritance here does not imply any requirement of communalism or a failure to practice it. It was simply the term used to raise to a level of spiritual significance what would without the gospel have been nothing more than buying and settling cheap western land. The word "inheritance" and similar terms are part of the language of the doctrine of the gathering, but nothing is implied concerning communal economic systems beyond the usual care of the poor and support of the church generally.

D&C 105:3-5 mentions the need for obedience, righteousness, charity, and unity, but says nothing about the necessity of an economic organization.

Considering the final outcome of all the migration activity, and the Lord's likely foreknowledge of all important factors, one might speculate that the Lord found it necessary to apply the carrot of the rich Missouri land to get the saints part way west, and then the stick of the mobs to get them further on to more defensible locations such as Nauvoo, and finally, Utah, in the process teaching them the value and methods of temporal unity so that they would not be dislodged again. Taking this long view of things may be the only way to reconcile the many confusing and upsetting aspects of nineteenth century Mormon history.

10. HC 6:87, 89, 115, 129.

11. HC 6:129, 131.

12. HC 6:89, 99, 131. The U. S. Government took no steps to defend the saints' titles to the land it sold.

13. The early experiences of Brigham City, Utah, provide some interesting support for this idea. The men who accepted the responsibility to make the city's centralized and coordinated economic efforts a success, were finally forced to give up their positions from the sheer fatigue of such a task. See *Building the City of God*, pp. 125-126, 314.

CHAPTER 2.

Early Leaders were Firmly Against "Common Stock" Communalism or Socialism

Meaning of Consecration

The terms "consecration," "stewardship," and "united order," are closely related key terms in the glossary of Mormon economics, and the purpose of this book is to supply enough information to support a detailed and consistent definition of those terms. We will begin the process by presenting some information on the word "consecration," and showing that it does not entail any centralization of property or property management.

To fully understand a word we must know both what it means and what it doesn't mean. The quotations from Joseph Smith's own history which follow, and the associated commentaries, contain information and clues as to both aspects of the word's definition. The continual conflict with the world and the readiness of many to misunderstand the saints made it necessary for Joseph Smith and others to repeatedly define various aspects of the Gospel in painful detail. The definition of the word "consecration" was one of those items. There seemed to be many people willing to spread all manner of falsehood about the church and its teachings, a phenomenon found in every dispensation.

The most explicit definition of the word located thus far comes from Joseph Smith's letter to the church, written

December 16, 1838, while languishing in the Liberty, Missouri, jail:

> We have heard that it is reported by some, that some of us should have said, that we not only dedicated our property, but our families also to the Lord; and Satan taking advantage of this, has perverted it into licentiousness, such as a community of wives, which is an abomination in the sight of God.
>
> When we consecrate our property to the Lord, it is to administer to the wants of the poor and needy, for this is the law of God; it is not for the benefit of the rich, those who have no need; and when a man *consecrates* or *dedicates* his wife and children, he does not give them to his brother, or to his neighbor, for there is no such law: for the law of God is, Thou shalt not commit adultery. Thou shalt not covet thy neighbor's wife. He that looketh upon a woman to lust after her, has committed adultery already in his heart. *Now for a man to consecrate his property, wife and children, to the Lord, is nothing more nor less than to feed the hungry, clothe the naked, visit the widow and fatherless, the sick and afflicted, and do all he can to administer to their relief in their afflictions, and for him and his house to serve the Lord. In order to do this, he and all his house must be virtuous, and must shun the very appearance of evil.*
>
> *Now if any person has represented anything otherwise than what we now write, he or she is a liar, and has represented us falsely - and this is another manner of evil which is spoken against us falsely.* (emphasis supplied).
>
> We have learned also since we have been prisoners, that many false and pernicious things, which were calculated to lead the saints far astray and to do great injury, have been taught by Dr. Avard as coming from the Presidency .... Meantime the Presidency were attending to their own secular and family concerns, weighed down with sorrow, in debt, in poverty, in hunger, essaying to be fed, yet finding [i.e. supporting] themselves. They occasionally received deeds of charity, it is true; but these were inadequate to their subsistence; and because they received those deeds, they were envied and hated by those who professed to be their friends.[1]

Notice that Joseph Smith uses the words "dedicate" and "consecrate" to mean the same thing. He also closely equates the proper treatment of property with the proper treatment of one's family. Just as consecration requires no transfer of possession of one's family and children to another, there is no transfer of one's property to another, except in the event of gifts or donations given to assist the poor or for efforts of common benefit such as constructing a chapel. He defines the rich simply as "those who have no need," as opposed to the poor who do have need. Property is not placed in a common pool for use by those who have no need, but contributed property is only to be used to assist the poor, the same policy as is followed today.

Note that Joseph Smith had no source of help except gifts,[2] and claimed no right to any support. His example shows that no required pooling of property was going on. The Book of Mormon, warning against priestcraft among church leaders, comes to mind as a standard of behavior in this situation, but Joseph Smith avoided even the appearance of evil in this case, like good King Benjamin.[3] A functioning communal system would surely have included a salary for the leader. But note that the "consecration" system was going on all the time, at least in Joseph Smith's estimation,[4] so whatever "consecration" was, it did not include the pooling of property which could have supplied a salary or support for Joseph Smith.

The early brethren had to deal directly and often with the question of communalism versus non-communalism. They consistently denied and rejected communalism, as the following quotations will show. Some entries in the history describe specific beginnings for the communalism falsehood. The logical point to be made here is that if communalism is not a part of the gospel, then it obviously cannot be an aspect of the gospel principle of consecration:

> A few miles from Mr. Rigdon's home in Mentor, at the town of Kirtland, lived a number of the members of his church. They lived together and had all things common - from which circumstance has arisen the idea

that this was the case with the Church of Jesus Christ. To that place the elders immediately repaired, and proclaimed the gospel unto them, with considerable success; for their testimony was received by many of the people, and seventeen came forward in obedience to the Gospel.⁴

As is indicated by the context of this last quote and as is made clear in the next and other quotes, the "idea" that arose was a false one.

> The branch of the Church in this part of the Lord's vineyard, which had increased to nearly one hundred members, were striving to do the will of God, so far as they knew it, though some strange notions and false spirits had crept in among them. With a little caution and some wisdom, I soon assisted the brethren and sisters to overcome them. The plan of "common stock," which had existed in what was called "the family,"* whose members generally had embraced the everlasting Gospel, was readily abandoned for the more perfect law of the Lord; and the false spirits were easily discerned and rejected by the light of revelation.
>
> [The following footnote was added by the editor of Joseph Smith's history, B. H. Roberts]
> *This organization, called "the family," came into existence before the Gospel was preached in Kirtland, through an effort of the people of this neighborhood to live as the early Christians are said to have lived, viz., "and the multitude of them that believed were of one heart and of one soul: neither said any of them that aught of the things which he possessed was his own; but they had all things common." (Acts IV:32.)⁶

Joseph Smith here clearly rejected the communalistic practices of the new converts in Kirtland, equating those practices with "strange notions and false spirits." He later went even further and specifically rejected the scripture on which they based their behavior, at least insofar as that scripture could be applied to the situation in Kirtland.[7] For a definition and discussion of the phrase "the more perfect law of the Lord" contained in the above quote, see chapter 16.

The brethren, including Bishop Partridge, assigned to labor in Missouri to assist in the gathering of the saints to that place, found it necessary to correct a number of errors of doctrine and expectation held by those arriving there. In a long letter to those still in the East, they attempted to disabuse the saints of any misconceptions, and to instruct them in the preparations they should make. One comment relates directly to the meaning of consecration:

> It seems as though a notion was prevalent in Babylon, that the Church of Jesus Christ was a common stock concern. This ought not so to be, for it is not the case. When a disciple comes to Zion for an inheritance, it is his duty, if he has anything to consecrate to the Lord for the benefit of the poor and needy, or to purchase land, to consecrate it according to the law of the Lord, and also according to the law of the land, ...[8]

In the context of the letter it can be seen that the phrase "anything to consecrate to the Lord for the benefit of the poor and needy, or to purchase lands" is a kind of "scriptureze," probably stemming from D&C 42:34-35, which is here intended to mean that every man should pay for the land he gets, and that he will in turn receive the title for the land in the normal way and with the normal rights of ownership. He is also expected to contribute money to help the poor acquire land if he is able. Apparently, many people imagined that they would receive land in Missouri free of charge. That foolish expectation would be very damaging to efforts to make an orderly and expeditious move to the new Missouri area.

The question of how the property of the members was affected by their membership in the Church was an important question to those both in and out of the Church, and there was no lack of specific answers to that general question. The next quote deals directly with an apparently common misconception which existed then and which continues to be a misconception today about the meaning of the word consecration:

> Friday, 30 [October, 1835]. - At home. Mr. Francis Porter, from Jefferson County, New York, a member of the Methodist Church, called to make some inquiry about lands in this place [Kirtland], whether there were any valuable farms for sale, and whether a member of our Church could move into this vicinity and purchase lands and enjoy his own possessions and property without making them common stock. He had been requested to make this inquiry by some brethren who live in the town of Leroy, New York. I replied that I had a valuable farm joining the Temple lot I would sell, and that there were other lands for sale in this place, and that we had no common stock business among us; that every man enjoys his own property, or can, if he is disposed, consecrate liberally or illiberally to the support of the poor and needy, or the building up of Zion. He also inquired how many members there were in this Church. I told him there were about five or six hundred who communed at our chapel, and perhaps a thousand in this vicinity.[9]

As used here the word consecration obviously had nothing to do with how one bought, sold, or used property. The phrase "every man enjoys his own property, or can, if he is disposed, consecrate liberally or illiberally to the support of the poor and needy, or the building up of Zion," makes it clear that the term consecration had the same operational meaning then as the word donation has in the church today - free will offerings. There is no enforcing mechanism or doctrine, just as there is none now.

Here is another quotation defining the economic relationship of the members to the church:

> Tuesday, 8. - I spent the day with Elder Rigdon in visiting Elder Cahoon at the place he selected for his residence, and in attending to some of our private, personal affairs; also in the afternoon I answered the questions which were frequently

asked me, while on my last journey but one from Kirtland to Missouri, as printed in the *Elders Journal,* Vol. I, Number II, pages 28 and 29, as follows:

...Sixth - "Do the Mormons believe in having all things in common?"

No.

...Twelfth - "Do the people have to give up their money when they join his Church?"

No other requirement than to bear their proportion of the expenses of the Church, and support the poor.

...I published the forgoing answers to save myself the trouble of repeating the same a thousand times over and over again.[10]

The comment "no other requirement than to bear their proportion of the expenses of the church, and support the poor," makes it clear that no complicated joinder of property was required. The "thousand times over" comment shows that the whole topic was one which people tediously refused to understand.

The next excerpt again condemns what was then only malicious gossip about communalism, but which has since become widely accepted tradition:

> Letter of Sidney Rigdon to Alfred Stokes - Correcting Misrepresentations of Nauvoo Affairs
>
> Nauvoo, Illinois, February 19, 1843
>
> Mr. Alfred Edward Stokes.
>
> Dear Sir: - In obedience to your request, I send you one number of each of the papers published in this place. I am well aware that designing men, for sinister purposes, have put in circulation reports concerning the people here, which are so monstrous that it is a matter of surprise how any rational being could profess to believe them at all.
>
> ...The old, stale story about common stock, in defiance of fact and truth, it would appear by your letter and that of your friend Evans, is professedly believed by the people in the vicinity of Waynesville, Ohio. This falsehood was invented by an

> ignorant blockhead, by the name of Matthew Clapp, who, for want of any other means to stop the progress of truth in its more incipient stages, invented this falsehood, and finding it took with persons of his own stamp, circulated it with untiring perseverance, in direct opposition to the testimony of his senses, knowing, at the time he commenced circulating it, that it was false. He was a preacher of the Campbellite faith.
>
> It would require the ignorance of barbarians and the credulity of savages to attempt a belief in the falsehoods which are circulated against the saints with great zeal by many....
>
> Yours, with respect,
> Sidney Rigdon, P.M.[11]

Sidney Rigdon, who was involved in the social experiments at Kirtland before the group became church members and received Joseph Smith's corrections, and who was closely involved with the Prophet after that time as well, certainly knew whereof he spoke concerning the common stock question. His strong language leaves little room for guesswork as to what his feelings were on the topic.

The brethren were obviously concerned about these questions, probably because if their enemies were successful at falsely labeling the church as a cult wherein the leaders control the lives and property of fanatical adherents, it would greatly reduce the church's ability to present the real message it has for the world. Complicating things for the saints today is the contrasting rhetoric and practice from the Brigham Young era. The question of why church leaders resisted communal concepts in one era and fostered them in another invites further study. Differences in social and environmental conditions will probably explain many of the policy differences.

During the Joseph Smith period there was a large amount of stir and discussion about various utopian schemes, and the saints were exposed to some of that activity and thought. In fact, after the church left Nauvoo, a socialist group took up residence there.[12] When the topic was raised in Nauvoo, Joseph Smith took the opportunity to refute those theories at length:

> Wednesday, 13. -- I attended a lecture at the grove, by Mr. John Finch, a socialist, from England, and said a few words in reply....
>
> Thursday, 14. -- I attended a second lecture on socialism by Mr. Finch; and after he got through, I made a few remarks, alluding to Sidney Rigdon and Alexander Campbell getting up a community at Kirtland, and of the big fish there eating up all the little fish. *I said I did not believe the doctrine.* (emphasis in original).
>
> Mr. Finch replied in a few minutes, and said -- "I am the voice of one crying in the wilderness. I am the spiritual prophet -- Mr. Smith the temporal...."
>
> Sunday, 24. -- I preached on the stand about one hour on the second chapter of Acts, designing to show the folly of common stock. In Nauvoo every one is steward over his own.[13]

Although not attempted here, an examination of the meaning of the word "socialism" as taught by Mr. Finch might be fruitful to be certain what it means, because whatever it was, Joseph was stoutly against it. He spoke three times against the idea, at least once for about an hour. Notice that the emphasis is his in the italicized statement, *"I said I did not believe in the doctrine."* Notice here that he was refuting the idea expressed in Acts 2:44-45. To him, "all things common' (Acts 2:44-45), "common stock" (HC 6:37), the Kirtland common stock "family" (HC 1:124, 146-147), and socialism were all the same thing, and they are all wrong or folly no matter where they appear, whether in the scriptures or elsewhere. His comment about "the big fish there eating up all the little fish" presumably alludes to one element of society enriching itself at the expense of another as often occurs where control is centralized.[14]

By the term "temporal prophet," apparently Mr. Finch meant to say that Joseph Smith was much too concerned about individual ownership, conservation and improvement or aggrandizement of property. In contrast, Mr. Finch perhaps was saying that one should have no cares about property, but should give it all away or put it into a pool and think only of "spiritual" things. The irresponsibility and inefficiency of this attitude and the related waste leads to the situation where no one has anything, and thus cannot help anyone else. All tend to become beggars by this logic. The gospel concept of freedom or free agency is so closely tied to private property that neither can function properly if separated from the other.

Although the history does not cite any particular verses in Acts chapter 2, presumably Joseph was referring to those containing the phrase "all things in common" or related ideas:

> 44 And all that believed were together, and had all things common;
> 45 And sold their possessions and goods, and parted them to all men, as every man had need.
> 46 And they, continuing daily with one accord in the temple, and breaking bread from house to house, did eat their meat with gladness and singleness of heart.
> 47 Praising God, and having favour with all the people, and the Lord added to the church daily such as should be saved.

Again, it should be obvious to anyone that the sale of property and the distribution and consumption of the proceeds, if continued for any length of time, would quickly reduce a people to beggary and would lead to the economic self-destruction of the group. The church would become the "have-nots" of their society, and would lose the power to help others. In Joseph Smith's eyes such behavior would stop the gathering process and defeat the Lord's plans for the Church's growth in this dispensation. An attempt at a plausible explanation of the Acts 2 economic situation appears at the end of this chapter.[15]

Joseph's statement that "in Nauvoo everyone is steward over his own" is interesting because he is equating the situation in Nauvoo with the correct operation of stewardship principles. And in Nauvoo, from all the other records and comments available to us, everyone purchased and used his own land in the normal way. None of these forms and procedures came from any unique church plan such as a "united order."

The brethren were asked to accept general counsel on where and from whom they purchased land so that an orderly settlement process might go on, but that was the only restraint or control practiced. There was certainly no formalism such as "double-deeding" to enforce any of the brethren's suggestions.[16]

As will be demonstrated below, Joseph also equated the activities of the saints in Nauvoo with living the law of consecration, consecration merely meaning the duty to contribute tithing and other offerings to assist the church building program and the poor. Thus in Joseph's eyes, the full law of consecration and stewardship was operating in Nauvoo, and there were no evidences of any unusual property arrangements.

In trying to construct a definition of the word consecration, it would be helpful to know during what periods of the church's history the law has been said to be in effect. It is the position of this book that it has never ceased to be in effect since the beginning of the church in this dispensation, and that those who tie the practice of the law or doctrine of consecration to a particular social or economic organization simply do not understand the law. The following entry from the history should shed some further light on that question by showing that the law was in full effect a substantial time after many would say it ceased:

> Friday, 6 [March 1840]. -- Attended the meeting of the high council of Iowa, at Brother Elijah Fordham's, Montrose.
>
> Extract from the minutes of the Iowa High Council.
>
> President Joseph Smith, Jun., addressed the council on various subjects, and in particular the consecration law; stating that the affairs now before Congress was the only thing that ought to interest the saints at present; and till it was ascertained how it would terminate, no person ought to be brought to account before the constituted authorities of the church for any offense whatever; and [he] was determined that no man should be brought before the Council in Nauvoo till that time, etc., etc. The law of consecration could not be kept here, and that it was the will of the Lord that we should desist from trying to keep it; and if persisted in, it would produce a perfect defeat of its object, and that he assumed the whole responsibility of not keeping it until proposed by himself.*
>
> He requested every exertion to be made to forward affidavits to Washington, and also letters to members of Congress. The following votes were then passed:
>
> First -- That this council will coincide with President Joseph Smith, Jun.'s decision concerning the consecration law, on the principle of its being the will of the Lord, and of President Smith's taking the responsibility on himself.
>
> Second -- That a committee of three be appointed, consisting of Wheeler Baldwin, Lyman Wight, and Abraham O. Smoot, to obtain affidavits and other documents to be forwarded to the city of Washington.
>
> Third -- That the clerk of this council be directed to inform Judge Higbee, that it is the wish of this council that he should not, upon any consideration, consent to accept of anything of Congress short of our just rights and demands for our losses and damages in Missouri.
>
> [Footnote by editor of the History].
>
> *This is the record of a very important action. The law of consecration and stewardship, with which the action deals, was given to the Church by revelation (Doc. and Cov. sec. xlii). Its fundamental principle is the recognition of God as the possessor of all things, the earth and the fullness thereof. It is

His by right of proprietorship. He created it and sustains it by his power. This recognized, it follows that whatsoever man possesses in it, he holds as a stewardship merely. These principles the Saints were called upon to recognize and act under in the establishment of Zion in Missouri; and apparently the saints in Iowa were disposed to undertake the same order of things in the settlement they were then making, until stopped by the Prophet. The action of the Prophet in this instance demonstrates the elasticity in Church government, and law. The Lord, who commanded to move forward, may also command a halt. He who said take neither purse nor scrip when going to preach the gospel (Matt. x:10) may later say, under other circumstances, "he that hath a purse let him take it, and likewise his scrip" (Luke xxii:35, 36). So, too, in other matters. The Lord commanded the colony of Lehi that there should no man among them "have save it be but one wife, and concubines ye shall have none;" yet reserved the right to command his people otherwise should the accomplishment of His purposes require it. (Book of Mormon, Jacob ii:24-30).[17]

There are many things to be learned from this quote, but the most important is that the law of consecration was still functioning and was a live topic in 1840, two years after section 119 was revealed. Many have supposed that section 119 signaled the termination of the "higher law" of consecration in conjunction with the introduction of the "lesser law" of tithing. However, the above quote shows that no such change occurred. In fact, there are a number of other references to the consecration idea after the 1838 revelation.[18] Many of these references will be discussed in this or other chapters. As discussed at length elsewhere (see Chapters 13, 14 and 15), sections 119 and 120 had only the effect of modifying the existing procedure for collecting and administering tithing.

The actual significance of the high council meeting is simple and straightforward. At this point in time, the saints were engaged in "the suit now before congress, namely the Latter-day Saints versus the state of Missouri,"[19] in which they sought to recover the losses that occurred as a result of the Missouri persecutions. Joseph's main point was that everyone affected should channel resources into winning that action before congress, which was expected to be a costly and time-consuming process.

As had always been the case, any growth in the power of the church was resisted by men of the world. To minimize the political jealousy of the petitioned congressmen, Joseph simply desired to remove as many indicators of church power and current wealth as possible during the proceedings. A rich and powerful petitioner would likely receive less consideration than many weak and poor ones.[20] The efforts of individual voters or non-religious political organizations would be more effective than the actions of church representatives.

Of the changes suggested, the most important item to Joseph seemed to be the need to erase any semblance of a claim by the church to political or civil power through the exercise of the jurisdiction of church courts. Their work is much more like the action of a civil government than alms-giving might be thought to be. His next most significant concern was that contributions to the church would be viewed with jealousy. The relative priority of these two proposals may give us a clue about what they really meant.

If Joseph had been proposing a doctrinal change of the magnitude supposed by B. H. Roberts, it would surely have been treated as of more importance than the operation or non-operation of church courts. Notice that the saints were being asked to "desist" from living the law for a time. This implies that they were already living it. If he had been suspending an "order" in the sense of an integrated organization, economic chaos might have ensued or at least have been feared.[21] We surely would have heard more about it, and the brethren of the high council would have had many more questions on the matter. Something akin to the D&C 104 dissolution and reorganization procedure might have been requested. But no such instructions were sought or given. This implies that the change proposed by Joseph was actually rather a small one, with no expected lasting effect, either doctrinal or temporal.

In any event, the hiatus in courts and contributions was probably a very short one, because within about two weeks of this high council meeting in Iowa, the petition of the saints was finally rejected by the Senate, and any attempts to influence the outcome became useless. A number of historical entries show that both court actions and consecrations or donations resumed within a short time of the Iowa high council's decisions.[22]

The editor's footnote to the high council minutes deserves some examination. The editor of the Documentary History of the Church was B. H. Roberts, who performed those literary labors during the period of 1902 to 1912.[23] Living in that era, he was probably well-acquainted with the teachings of Brigham Young on the question of economic organization. His circumstances may have made it difficult for him to consider another viewpoint. In a series
of footnotes to the history,[24] he attempted to bring the actions of Joseph Smith into conformity with the prevailing ideas of Brigham Young's day. However, in none of the cases do the materials of the Joseph Smith period fit the mold he applied to them.

In this particular case, his use of the word "apparently" shows that the editor is simply guessing at the significance of the action of the Iowa high council. The church had never practiced any property joinder requirement, and the saints in Iowa could not have been "disposed to undertake the same order of things in the settlement they were then making" because there had been no precedents. It must be remembered that this was a stake high council he was addressing, one of the two in the world at that time, and concerned with the actions of a substantial group of people.

This was not some small splinter group of "fundamentalists" he was trying to correct as he had done the early Kirtland Saints.

Joseph and the members of the high council seem to have assumed that the people in the Nauvoo and Montrose area were already living the law of consecration, and that what he proposed was not a major doctrinal change, but merely a practical adjustment to conditions of the moment. We also know from many other comments and events that all property, both land and goods, was held and traded in an almost perfectly free-market way. The only effect of the church on the process was to give council and direction to the locating of newcomers. "Consecration" consisted of tithes and other ordinary offerings to the church to support its building and other programs and to help the poor. To the people of Joseph Smith's time, the term "consecration" had no effect on economic organization.

The footnote reminds us of God's ownership of the world and pursues a line of logic ending with "it follows that whatsoever man possesses in it, he holds as a stewardship merely." This simple conclusion is correct enough. However, what does not necessarily follow is that a man's economic activities must be under the control of another man before he can be said to be in compliance with the stewardship idea. The "stewardship merely" statement is used to justify a formal centralization of control, but that is a not a necessary requirement. Being a steward in relationship to God is quite a different thing from being required to be an essentially propertyless employee of a mortal. We might present the issue in a more general way by asking exactly what functions of temporal government, political or economic, God has authorized men to exercise over one another. The United States Constitution and related and supporting scriptures such as D&C 134 set definite limits to the reach of men's righteous authority over one another, whether in or out of the church.

The footnote tries to stretch this rather small matter of the high council meeting into a major doctrinal affair. Actually, its main importance is to help show that consecration did *not* have the meaning he and others have attributed to it. There were probably some temporary and spontaneous solutions to pioneer and frontier problems as they arose, such as "barn raisings" and the like, but beyond that, none of the processes of the gathering involved any unusual or socialistic property management mechanisms.

The last anecdote for this chapter is a pleasant one. On March 15, 1844, Joseph Smith visited one of the saints in Nauvoo to teach him the doctrine of consecration:

> At two, went to see Brother John Wilkie. He had sent to me to come and see him. He wanted to know what he should do. I told him of the order of tithing, &c., and he wanted I should come again....
>
> John Wilkie. The Blessing of the
> Prophet upon Him.
>
> "This day President Joseph Smith rode over to Brother John Wilkie's at his special request, to give him some instructions relative to his duty in regard to tithing and consecration.
> Brother Wilkie has for a long time back been struggling with his feelings, designing to do right, but laboring under many fears and prejudices, in consequence of having in some degree given way to believe the base reports circulated by individuals for the purpose of injuring the authorities of the church, and also from various other causes. His faithful companion has persevered diligently, and with fervent prayer has called upon God in his behalf, until she has realized her utmost wishes.
> Brother Wilkie now feels anxious to do right in all things, and especially to pay his tithing in full. President Joseph showed him the principles of consecration and the means whereby he might realize the fullness of the blessings of the celestial kingdom; and as an evidence that he desired to do right, he paid over to the Trustee-in-Trust the sum of three hundred

> dollars in gold and silver for the benefit of the temple, and which is now recorded on consecration.
>
> He also signified his intention of paying more as soon as he could get matters properly arranged. The president then pronounced a blessing upon him and his companion, that they should have the blessing of God to attend them in their basket and in their store - that they should have the blessing of health and salvation and long life, inasmuch as they would continue to walk in obedience to the commandments of God.[25]

The action of Brother and Sister Wilkie was simply paying $300 in back tithing and promising to pay more in the future. The joyful spirituality of this event (evidenced by such phrases as "she has realized her utmost desires," "the President then announced a blessing upon him," and "inasmuch as they would continue to walk in obedience") indicates that the Prophet considered them to have complied with the law of consecration. In the members' relationship to the institutional church, tithing essentially equaled the law of consecration in that setting, as it does in ours. He blessed them and promised that a continuation of such behavior would bring further blessings. There is no hint of any further and complex requirement to merge their property and daily economic activity with others.

The definition of consecration implied by this little episode is consistent with all other comments on the subject by Joseph Smith. That should give the modern saints reason to believe that by similar simple compliance with church donation programs, they can feel the same joy of acknowledged obedience to an important principle.

Chapter 2 Notes.

1. HC 3:230-231.

2. HC 5:279-280. Brigham Young later sought food and other provisions for Joseph Smith. See also Robert J. Matthews, "Joseph Smith's Efforts to Publish His Bible Translation," *The Ensign,* January 1983, pp. 57, 61, for other examples of efforts to raise means to support the Prophet through donations. Joseph stated that he had "no means of support whatever." HC 4:137.

3. Mosiah 2:12-17.

4. For example, the short discontinuance of consecration in Nauvoo, for the purpose of calming the fears of the senators in Washington, described later in this chapter, shows that consecration was going on throughout the Joseph Smith period.

5. HC 1:124.

6. HC 1:146-147. Feb. 1831.
Another incident occurred in October and November 1837 in Kirtland which may indicate that some wished to establish a communal arrangement akin to that existing in Kirtland before the Gospel was taught and accepted there:

> On the 30th of October, Brothers Norris, Brewster, and others, presented to the high council a plan for a better organization of the church in temporal affairs, stating that Moroni had appeared to Collins Brewster. The council decided that it was a trick of the devil. HC 2:520.

Later, on November 20, a high council meeting was held to consider the case:

> Brother Sawyer stated that he heard Brother Norris say that those in authority were against him and if he could not establish an order of things here to his mind he would go out among the Gentiles and do it....
> One [witness] ... said ... that he was informed that Brother Norris laid his hands on Collins Brewster and ordained him a prophet....
> ... the council decided that the charge had been fully sustained and withdrew fellowship from those who persisted in their course of conduct as before mentioned. HC 2:526.

The claim of Collins Brewster to receiving revelation and being ordained a prophet by Brother Norris, are indications that he unrighteously sought power over others. That is a common reason for attempts at centralization of control over "temporal affairs," which normally means control of property and its fruits. Although not present at this high council meeting, Joseph Smith always objected to any such seeking of power over others, and the brethren of the high council apparently agreed. This appears to be another instance of a conscious rejection of the principles of socialism which some have assumed were accepted during Joseph Smith's day.

7. HC 6:32, 33, 37, 38. Acts 2, containing part of the story concerning sharing of goods which is continued on into Acts 4, is rejected. See footnote 15 for an explanation of the circumstances in which the Acts 2 sharing comments were applied.

8. HC 1:381. July 1833.

9. HC 2:295-296. October 30, 1835.

10. HC 3:28-29. May 8, 1838, Far West.

11. HC 5:280-281. February 19, 1843, Nauvoo.

12. JD 13:98. April 6, 1869. George Q. Cannon.

13. HC 6:32, 33, 37, 38. September 13, 14, and October 24, 1843. Nauvoo.

At an earlier time, while Elders Heber C. Kimball, Wilford Woodruff, and George A. Smith were performing missionary labors and preaching in London, a local preacher arose and addressed the street meeting then in progress:

> He spoke all manner of evil, and gave the Latter-day Saints a very bad character, and commanded the people not to hear the elders, "as we have got the Gospel, and can save the people, without infidelity, socialism, or Latter-day Saints." HC 4:183. August 30, 1840.

The lies and misconceptions about the Mormons were as bad or worse then as at any other time in the history of the Church. The fact that the Church's enemies, such as the speaker in this case, tried to link the Church with some of the controversial or cultist social teachings of the day, such as communal ownership of wives and property, which were widely condemned by good Christians (including the Mormons), should be a strong clue that the church did not do or teach any of those things. Lest anyone take this quoted statement to mean that Joseph Smith and the Mormons did teach socialism and community of wives, please consider that it would be strange indeed if Joseph Smith included an enemy's derogatory comment in his history for the purpose of showing that the enemy's statement was correct and that the church did espouse those principles. Joseph denied any such connection many times over as already illustrated above.

14. This note deals with three topics related to the contrast between the Joseph Smith and Brigham Young eras.

The phenomenon of the "the big fish eating up all the little fish" in the Kirtland setting, appears to be corroborated to some extent by Israelson's study of Utah towns which had a "united order" mechanism operating, as opposed to those which did not. In the "united order" towns, the disparity between the economic status of citizens increased: people became more unequal rather than less. L. Dwight Israelson, "An Economic Analysis of the United Order," BYU Studies, Summer 1978, pp. 536-562. This is consistent with Brigham Young's goal of maximizing overall concentrated strength, with less concern about individual equality. Although he generally supported "equality" sermons (for example see JD 2:96), in his last year of life, while still advocating large-scale centralization of property, he finally specifically stated that it was not appropriate to enforce equality among individuals. JD 18:354.

However, in the Utah setting, rather than attribute the increased inequality of income to exploitation by the stronger, there is another possibility. It appears from extensive modern studies that the beginning of economic growth in developing countries is always accompanied by an increase in inequality of income: "The first effect of technical progress ... is to increase the inequality of the distribution of income" as skilled engineers and managers begin to appear and to command higher salaries. Everett E. Hagen, *The Economics of Development* (Homewood, Ill.: Richard D. Irwin, Inc., 1980), p. 38. The long-term positive benefits of growth seem to justify Brigham Young's policies, however inconsistent they may have been with the equality question.

It may be worth noticing that Brigham Young was in Boston for a conference held September 9, 1843, and began a return trip home on October 29. HC 6:11, 39. The Nauvoo discussions on socialism happened in the meantime on September 13 and 14 and October 24. He also missed out on the early events concerning the Kirtland "family," because he did not join the church until more than a year after that event, and did not meet the Prophet until nearly another year had passed. He was abroad during most of the time the united order was operating. He surely had some contact with the related concepts, but for the really unequivocal refutations of socialism or common stock, he seemed to be elsewhere. In contrast, he seemed to have had a hand in the "togetherness" times, usually caused by forced migration, such as the movements from Missouri to Illinois. This skewing of experience may account for some of the differences in doctrines taught during the two periods marked by the presidencies of Joseph Smith and Brigham Young.

There are indicators of a substantial loss of data and experience in the transition from the administrators of Joseph Smith's time to the Twelve who carried on afterward. For example, the Twelve discovered for the first time in 1845 (HC 7:412, May 17), and published with fanfare, something that was known to the prior administrators 12 years earlier in 1833 (HC 1:364, June 25). The instructions to Bishop Partridge concerning the Missouri land transactions were ancient and well-worn history, but the Twelve had known nothing of it (see Chapter 11). There is little reason to wonder then at the doctrinal drift that seems to have occurred on matters affecting economics. Without contact with the original sources and experiences, these men were left to relearn on their own, and at great cost, much that was elementary to Joseph Smith when the church was just being organized.

Joseph's journal was probably not available to Brigham Young on a contemporary basis. Joseph had trouble enough compiling and retaining it himself. That material was not published for the first time until well into the Utah period. Brigham Young certainly read the scriptures, but in some cases seemed to lack information concerning the qualifying circumstances behind the receipt of those modern-day revelations. This is information that could probably only be available to him through Joseph's written record.

15. Following is a brief attempt at an explanation of the "all things common" account in Acts 8:

Acts 8:1 tells us that because of persecution, all the saints except the apostles left Jerusalem. First they fled to other Judean and Samarian cities, and then on to Cyprus, Antioch, Damascus, and Alexandria. (New Testament Media Kit, Life of Paul Series Kit, PISI0629, March 1980, Filmstrip #3, "Commitment to Christ," frame #10.) This had essentially been accomplished before the conversion of Saul. The Bible chronology tells us that Saul's conversion occurred in 35 A.D. If we use the date of 33 A.D. as the year of the death and resurrection of Christ, then the large growth spurt of the Church and the exodus from Jerusalem all took place within two years. The Annanias and Sophira episode occurred somewhere during that time, probably near the beginning of the two-year period.

The persecutions would mean that people would have to flee their homes and lands to avoid imprisonment or death. Selling those possessions where possible would be the most sensible thing to do. The money received could be used to help finance a trip to a new location and the establishment of a new home and occupation. Part of those funds could go to assist those who had no means, perhaps because their belongings had been confiscated or destroyed.

In these circumstances it would it probably be important to establish some kind of welfare system. If a person were to turn over all his property to the church, he would then have no property and could logically be classified as "poor." By being a poor person, he could qualify for sharing in the proceeds from other similar donations. Someone such as Joses (Acts 4:36-37) may have set the pattern by donating all his property and then becoming eligible for sharing in the proceeds of other donations.

Apparently Annanias and Sophira decided to take advantage of the system by pretending to give all their property and thus become eligible to be maintained by the church. By secretly keeping back a part of the original sales price, they could have two sources of wealth. They thus became some of the first "welfare cheaters" on record. Their behavior would justify a strong action by the Lord so that no one would be tempted to take advantage of the system made possible by the unselfish acts of others.

Although possibly under a higher level of persecution, these Jerusalem saints were somewhat like those latter-day saints who were asked to leave their homes in the east and migrate to the west as part of the gathering process. They were counseled to do the best they could under the circumstances, that is, to sell their land if they could, or to rent it or simply leave it behind if no other arrangement could be made. D&C 38:37.

Attitudes toward property and its use are likely to be quite different during a time of forced or required migration. There are many parallels between the Jerusalem saints and the saints of Joseph Smith's day. A "use it or lose it" or "give it or lose it" philosophy would become reasonable. It might as well be used to help your friends as be left to your enemies. When people are migrating, they give up and share property easily - if they don't use it, they lose it anyway. Nomadic peoples or others in subsistence economies typify some of these practices for very sensible reasons. See George Dalton, ed., *Tribal and Peasant Economies: Readings in Economic Anthropology* (Garden City, N.Y.: The Natural History Press, 1967), p. 17.

Two other scriptural references to communal situations can be explained in a similar way. The reference in the Book of Mormon to a people with "all things common among them," 4 Nephi 1:3, occurred just after the wholesale destruction of cities in the New World. With supplies and facilities gone, people might well have to band together in a tribal subsistence kind of organization in order to survive. As economic conditions improved through hard work and accumulation of supplies and tools, organization ties could become more casual.

About two hundred years after the gospel-based society originated, the majority of the people rejected the gospel (4 Ne 1:24, 38, 40), and as a consequence, most of the cooperation they had enjoyed was replaced with contention (4 Ne 1:25-49). With only a catch-phrase, "all things common," and a few remarks about the setting to go on, there is little that can be determined about the nature of the society, and we are left almost wholly to speculation. However, it seems clear enough that the peoples' acceptance of the gospel

(4 Ne 1:15, "no contention ..., because of the love of God") was the factor that made possible whatever cooperation there was, rather than the reverse: an economic mechanism does not the gospel bring. In other words, it seems unlikely that the apostasy was a consequence of a change in social structure. It is more likely that the apostasy damaged the social fabric.

The phrase "no poor among them," Moses 7:18, is often assumed to indicate some kind of communal organization. It comes from a time when the armies of the world were attacking the people of Enoch. The Lord protected the people of Enoch through power given to their leader, but they probably found it necessary to help themselves as well by organizing along military lines for defense. This process would include centralized control of many aspects of life, including the army quartermaster functions of acquisition and sharing of supplies, facilities, and equipment.

The common thread running through the New Testament, Book of Mormon, and Pearl of Great Price references to communalism is the hostile, primitive, migratory conditions in which the organizations developed and the survival purpose they served. Brigham Young's united order in Utah and Joseph Smith's in Illinois and Missouri continued the pattern.

16. HC 5:35, 272-273. "Double-deeding" is a phrase used to describe the process of deeding property to the church, and then receiving a deed back from the church.

17. HC 4:93. March 6, 1840.

18. HC 4:589, 592, April 12, 1842. Consecration of old promissory notes. HC 5:44, June 26, 1842. Brigham Young gave a talk on the subject of consecration. There was no implication of any doctrinally required economic joinder, but only suggestions for

voluntary cooperation for certain specific business ventures. HC 6:264, March 15, 1844. Consecration taught by Joseph Smith.

19. HC 4:96.

20. For political reasons, it was probably wise to avoid passing money through the formal church channels. It would best be done by the injured individuals themselves; they should temporarily devote some of their "surplus" to the prosecution of the request for payment for losses and other remedies. In a way, this might be considered a redirection of the flow of "consecration" funds, not a real stoppage of them. This is like the earlier channeling of funds into Missouri land purchases. Funds that were not needed for helping the memorial process could be held for later contribution to the church, or could be applied directly by each individual to the needs of others in the classic alms manner. The only difference is that these resources didn't flow through the church, a relatively small matter. As discussed further below, this involves quite a different kind of flexibility than that described in the editor's footnote to the high council minutes.

The effect of "consecration" was to make it appear that there was an accumulation of wealth by the church through various contributions, and that the church's temporal power was growing. If the saints were only harmless persecuted folks, they might get some recompense. But if they were perceived as any kind of organized political threat, then the politicians would not be willing to thus help their "enemies."

One of the main goals of the law of consecration was to help the poor. But if the church members were to continue in trying to help the poor through the church organization, they might actually and ultimately be injured. The poor might be denied just reimbursement for their Missouri losses.

Organized welfare assistance by the church may appear to some to be in competition with the central government for the control of the hearts, minds, and votes of the people. The same kind of logic probably prevailed among politicians then as well. For these reasons, both the court actions and the pooling of donations needed to be stopped for a time. The changes were made to lower the apparent practical importance of the church in the temporal affairs of the saints.

21. A sudden suspension of the types of economic systems that existed for a time in Brigham city and Orderville, Utah, would have been most chaotic and upsetting, because everyone there was essentially employed and supervised by a single leader or small group of leaders.

22. A number of events show that the stopping of courts and consecration was very short in duration. The memorial to congress was rejected March 24, 1840. HC 4:98. (A second memorial was prepared in December 1843 during Joseph Smith's candidacy for President of the United States. HC 6:63, 116. It was not attended by changes in church courts or donation procedures.)

At the next church conference, April 6, 7, and 8, 1840, "a great part of the time of the conference had been taken up with charges against individuals." These charges were processed, but the saints were told to handle such matters locally in the future. This shows that it was "business as usual" on church courts within two weeks of the end of the memorial process. At the same conference, a request for donations was made to assist the poor getting land in Nauvoo. HC 4:106, April 7, 1840.

The Nauvoo high council was active during that period and dealt with a number of temporal questions. (HC 4:95, March 13, 1840, ferry administrators appointed. HC 4:120, April 19, 1840, decision to meet every week. HC 4:136, June 18, 1840, relieve Joseph Smith of city plot administration.) In the Nauvoo high council minutes of July 3, 1840, bishops are told to get funds from sources other than land sales to pay for the support of the presidency and associated clerks. HC 4:144-145. Those other sources are presumably donations or "consecrations."

On July 17, two men were called and later (July 22 or 23) given a letter of introduction and told to go on a mission to collect donations, subscriptions, and loans to pay for printing scriptures and other church literature. HC 4:161, 164. The funds they were collecting would be considered consecrations.

In July 1840, fellowship was removed from Almon W. Babbitt by the church in Nauvoo, presumably through court action, for his misleading the newer saints in Kirtland in an attempt to benefit himself. HC 4:166.

A high council court was convened on October 11, 1840, to hear extensive charges against an individual, with minutes recorded in the history. HC 4:219.

23. B. H. Roberts, *Comprehensive History of the Church,* 6 vols. (Salt Lake City: Deseret News Press, 1930), p. 1:33n (hereafter identified as CHC).

24. HC 1:124, 146-147, Kirtland communalism before the gospel was taught there. HC 1:180n, the plans, covenants, contracts, and movements of the Colesville, later, Thompson, saints. HC 1:270, the united firm's mercantile companies. HC 1:365-367, the land transactions in Missouri. HC 4:93, the high council minutes under discussion.

25. HC 6:264.

CHAPTER 3

Administrative Arrangements For The Gathering Before The United Order Firm Was Organized.

The nature of the united order organization, created by the revelation known to us as D&C Section 82, can best be understood in the context of the active process of gathering the saints to Missouri via Kirtland. Table 3-1 provides an overview of the revelations which direct or describe the gathering, and shows the main steps in that process. The topics and events mentioned in Table 3-1 will be studied in chapters 3 through 10. This chapter covers the time preceding the organization of the united order firm.

The table indicates that the saints from New York, especially the Fayette and Colesville branches, were the main test case for beginning the gathering process. They left their homes in the spring of 1831, spent only one or two months in Kirtland, Ohio, and arrived in Missouri in August of that year.

Although not all of the saints moved through Kirtland so quickly, one of the themes throughout all these revelations is that the gathering place in Ohio was just a temporary stopping place on the way to a more permanent location. For examples of specific verses see D&C 38:13, 18; 42:62; 44:6; 48:3-5; 54:7. The plan is more explicit in D&C 51:16, May 1831:

Table 3-1. Steps In Organizing the Gathering Process

D&C	Date	Content or Effect
38	Jan 2, 1831	Organize branches to move west to Kirtland and the "land of promise."
42	Feb 9, 1831	Assemble resources in Kirtland to assist incoming migrants.
44	Feb 1831	Directs legal organization of church in Ohio.
48	Mar 1831	Directs acquisition of land in Kirtland area for temporary settlement.
51	May 1831	First migrants, saints from New York, actually arrive in Kirtland and are given temporary accommodations.
52	Jun 7, 1831	Bp. Partridge and others sent to Missouri to purchase lands. Hint at legal organization of church in Missouri.
54	Jun 1831	Saints from New York, temporarily located in Ohio, told to continue on to Missouri (see also D&C 57:15).
57	Jul 20, 1831	Actual location of land to be purchased for permanent settlement is revealed. Sidney Gilbert assigned to buy land and open a store to furnish supplies in Missouri. W. W. Phelps and Oliver Cowdery to do printing.
58	Aug 1831	Saints from New York arrive in Missouri. Sidney Rigdon given assignment to collect money for land. Martin Harris to help finance land purchases.
69	Nov 1831	John Whitmer to accompany Oliver Cowdery to Missouri with revelations to be printed.
78	Mar 1832	Preparations to be made for a formal organization to assist in the gathering.
82	Apr 26, 1832	United order partnership organized to strengthen individuals already conducting the business of the gathering. One branch of the firm is in Kirtland, and the other branch is in Missouri.
104	Apr 23, 1834	The united order partnership's two branches become two separate firms, D&C 104:48 (47-53), to better conduct the widespread affairs of the gathering.
117	Jul 8, 1838	Kirtland is abandoned. (And the united order firms have ceased to function).

> 16 And I consecrate unto them this land for a little season, until I, the Lord, shall provide for them otherwise, and command them to go hence;

and D&C 64:21-22, September 11, 1831:

> 21 ... I, the Lord, will to retain a strong hold in the land of Kirtland, for the space of five years, ...
> 22 And after that day, I, the Lord, will not hold any guilty that shall go with an open heart up to the land of Zion; ....

Section 117, dated July 8, 1838, was a signal to terminate the church's ties with Kirtland. Most of the active members had already moved from there to Far West, Missouri. The remaining church administrators were told to "let the properties of Kirtland be turned out for debts" (verse 5), and to "come up hither unto the land of my people, even Zion" (verse 9).

It is important to realize that the Kirtland settlement was to be a temporary one, that people were expected to move through it quickly, and that, after a limited time, the city was to be abandoned altogether. It makes a great deal of difference in interpreting the revelations whether the society to which they apply is assumed to be static or in turmoil. By becoming aware of the turmoil, we can better appreciate the short-term, limited, and practical purposes of the instructions given.

The remainder of the chapter is divided roughly into four sections: (1) the eastern saints are prepared for the move west, (2) the Kirtland saints make preparations for their arrival, (3) the eastern saints actually arrive in Kirtland, and (4) the eastern saints move on to Missouri. Portions of many quotations are underlined for emphasis.

The Eastern Saints Are to Move West to Kirtland

As will be shown in succeeding chapters, the united order was a business unit created by revelation and charged with conducting many of the affairs associated with the gathering of the saints. However, it did not come on the scene until after the gathering process had already begun and was gaining momentum. In the early activities of the gathering there were a number of precursors of the main organization. For example, section 38, dated January 2, 1831, directs the branch of the church in Fayette, New York, to organize a temporary administrative body to assist in the migration of that branch first to Kirtland, and later to the "land of promise," Missouri:

> 16 And for your salvation I give unto you a commandment, for I have heard your prayers, and the poor have complained before me, and the rich I have made, and all flesh is mine, and I am no respecter of persons.
> 17 And I have made the earth rich, and behold it is my footstool, wherefore, again I will stand upon it.
> 18 And I hold forth and deign to give unto you greater riches, even a *land of promise, a land flowing with milk and honey,* upon which there shall be no curse when the Lord cometh;
> 19 And I will give it unto you for the land of your inheritance, if ye seek it with all your hearts.
> 20 And this shall be my covenant with you, ye shall have it for the land of your inheritance, and for the inheritance of your children forever, while the earth shall stand, and ye shall possess it again in eternity, no more to pass away.
> 21 But, verily I say unto you that in time ye shall have no king nor ruler, for I will be your king and watch over you.
> 22 Wherefore, hear my voice and follow me, and you shall be a free people, and ye shall have no laws but my laws when I come, for I am your law-giver, and what can stay my hand?

....

> 24 And let every man esteem his brother as himself, and practice virtue and holiness before me.
> ....
> 27 ... I say unto you, be one; and if ye are not one ye are not mine.
> ....
> 32 Wherefore, ... I gave unto you the commandment that ye should *go to the Ohio;* and there I will give unto you my law; and there you shall be endowed with power from on high;
> ....
> 34 And now, *I give unto the church in these parts a commandment, that certain men among them shall be appointed,* and they shall be appointed by the voice of the church.
> 35 And they shall *look to the poor* and the needy, and administer to their relief that they shall not suffer; and *send them forth* to the place which I have commanded them;
> 36 And this shall be their work, to *govern the affairs of the property of this church.*
> 37 And they that have farms that cannot be sold, let them be left or rented as seemeth them good.[1]

Note that the revelation is addressed to "the church in these parts (v. 34)," that is, Fayette, New York, and that the term "this church" in verse 36 likewise refers to the single branch. This revelation does not contemplate any central church organization, but only a local organization created for the limited purpose of migration.

After exhortation and promises, the saints of that branch are told to move themselves to Ohio (v. 32). Their ultimate destination, Missouri, had not yet been revealed, but is described in glowing terms in verse 18. Administrators are to be appointed (v. 34) to supervise affairs associated with the migration, including property management and charity.

The duties given those administrators are much like those given later to the united order which handled similar affairs on a church-wide basis rather than just for one branch.[2] They were to arrange to send the people on to their destination (v. 35, 36), and help those who had difficulty in making the journey. As indicated by verse 37, the problem of selling or otherwise transforming land into cash was not a small matter. This device of having a single branch organize itself for the journey west and for the purchase of land was widely recommended and used.[3]

Preparing for the Arrival of the Eastern Saints in Kirtland.

Section 42, dated February 9, 1831, was another step in the process of creating a system for handling the needs of the migrating saints. While section 38 presents the pattern for organizing the saints in the east for movement westward to Kirtland and beyond, section 42 begins the arrangements for temporary settlement of them in Kirtland before the final journey to "the New Jerusalem" (v. 62), later shown to be in Missouri. It deals with care of the poor in the church through donations from those with more ample means. This was a necessary program for the residents of Kirtland, but became especially pressing because of the large numbers of poor saints who would be involved in migrating and would pass through Kirtland. Heeding the dire predictions in verse 64, they had some of the characteristics of refugees fleeing from before a conflict:

> 30 And behold, thou wilt remember the poor, and consecrate of thy properties for their support that which thou has to impart to them, with a covenant and a deed which cannot be broken.
> 31 And inasmuch as ye impart of your substance unto the poor, ye will do it unto me; and they shall be laid before the bishop of my church and his counselors, two of the elders, or high priests, such as he shall appoint or has appointed and set apart for that purpose.
> 32 And it shall come to pass, that after they are laid before the bishop of my church, and after that he has received these testimonies concerning the consecration of the properties of my church, that they cannot be taken from the church,

agreeable to my commandments, every man shall be made accountable unto me, *a steward over his own property, or that which he has received by consecration,* as much as is sufficient for himself and family.

33 And again, if there shall be properties in the hands of the church, or any individuals of it, more than is necessary for their support after this first consecration [donation], which is a *residue* to be consecrated unto the bishop, it shall be kept to administer to those who have not, from time to time, that every man who has need may be amply supplied and receive according to his wants.

34 Therefore, the residue shall be kept in my storehouse, to administer to the poor and the needy, as shall be appointed by the high council of the church, and the bishop and his council;

35 And for the purpose of *purchasing lands* for the public benefit of the church, and building houses of worship, and *building up of the New Jerusalem which is hereafter to be revealed* -

36 That my covenant people may be gathered in one in that day when I shall come to my temple. And this I do for the salvation of my people.

37 And it shall come to pass, that he that sinneth and repenteth not shall be cast out of the church, and shall not receive again that which he has consecrated unto the poor and needy of my church, or in other words, unto me -

38 For inasmuch as ye do it unto the least of these, ye do it unto me.

39 For it shall come to pass, that which I spake by the mouths of my prophets shall be fulfilled; for *I will consecrate of the riches of those who embrace my gospel among the Gentiles unto the poor of my people who are of the house of Israel.*

40 And again, thou shalt not be proud in thy heart; let all thy garments be plain, and their beauty the beauty of the work of thine own hands;

41 And let all things be done in cleanliness before me.

42 Thou shalt not be idle; for he that is idle shall not eat the bread nor wear the garments of the laborer.

....

53 Thou shalt stand in the place of thy stewardship.

54 Thou shalt not take thy brother's garment; *thou shalt pay for that which thou shalt receive of thy brother.*

> 55 And if thou obtainest more than that which would be for thy support, thou shalt give it into my storehouse, that all things may be done according to that which I have said.
>
> ....
>
> 62 Thou shalt *ask,* and it shall be *revealed* unto you in mine own due time *where the New Jerusalem shall be built.*
>
> 63 And behold, it shall come to pass that my servants shall be sent forth to the east and to the west, to the north and to the south.
>
> 64 And even now, let him that goeth to the east *teach them that shall be converted to flee to the west,* and this in consequence of that which is coming on the earth, and of secret combinations.
>
> ....
>
> 70 The priests and teachers shall have their stewardships, even as the members.
>
> 71 And the elders or high priests who are appointed to assist the bishop as counselors in all things, are to have their families supported out of the property which is consecrated to the bishop, for the good of the poor, and for other purposes, as before mentioned;
>
> 72 Or they are to receive a *just remuneration for all their services,* either a stewardship or otherwise, as may be thought best or decided by the counselors and bishop.
>
> 73 And the *bishop,* also, shall receive his *support, or a just remuneration* for all his services in the church.[4]

The meaning of the word consecration as used in section 42 is discussed in detail in chapter 17. Here, we will confine our examination to the section's contribution to the administrative mechanisms of the gathering. We should note that verses 30-35 put some resources into the bishop's hands to enable him to care for the poor. Verses 70-77 describe the provisions made for the administrators of the Kirtland welfare program.

It is important to note that the bishop's counselors and the bishop were the only ones of the "non-poor" to receive any income from the donations to the church. If these men spent full time on church business, they were to receive a regular wage or its equivalent. If their full time was not required, they were to be paid for their "church" time while they used their extra time in some other profitable pursuit. The "just remuneration" rule makes them much like employees paid at an hourly rate rather than putting them in the position of having the "right" to be kept regardless of their economic contribution, as in a priestcraft situation.[5]

For our purposes here, the meaning of verse 70, with its use of the word "stewardship," is simply that neither the priests and teachers nor the members were to get any of their living from the church's resources (unless they are considered "poor"). They are to take care of themselves in the usual way, using property and skills they have acquired as anyone else would.[6] The extra or unusual element is that because of Kirtland's special role as a staging area for the gathering of the saints, the bishop was involved to some extent as an advisor and administrator in the process of finding space for settling newcomers, and this might cause some temporary crowding and extra sharing.

The Kirtland members were asked to donate land to the cause. If they did not wish to donate, then the land was often purchased from them by the westbound saints. Or they could simply refuse to help in any way. Some obnoxious cases involving fraud and deception were tried for their fellowship (but not membership) over their behavior.[7] Land was also purchased from non-members for use in settling the saints temporarily.

In this early time there were many kinds and levels of organization created as the need arose. Section 44, given in late February 1831, speaks of a conference ("the elders should be called ... together") held on June 3-6, 1831, in Kirtland, at which the church is to be organized "according to the laws of man." The church was originally organized in New York. It is likely that new formal organizing steps needed to be taken in the State of Ohio.

This new organization may have given the church temporal powers such as the right to hold real estate or other property in the church's name. This would be a necessary step in building chapels and temples and in setting up a system of storehouses, etc., to care for the poor. However, the large-scale operations of the united order would be outside that essentially ecclesiastical organizational entity. The full text of section 44 is presented here:

> 1 Behold, thus saith the Lord unto you my servants, it is expedient in me that the elders of my church should be called together, from the east and from the west, and from the north and from the south, by letter or some other way.
>
> 2 And it shall come to pass, that inasmuch as they are faithful, and exercise faith in me, I will pour out my spirit upon them in the day that they assemble themselves together.
>
> 3 And it shall come to pass that they shall go forth into the regions round about, and preach repentance unto the people.
>
> 4 And *many shall be converted,* insomuch that ye shall obtain *power to organize yourselves according to the laws of man;*
>
> 5 That your enemies may not have power over you; that you may be preserved in all things; that you may be enabled to keep my laws; that every bond may be broken wherewith the enemy seeketh to destroy my people.
>
> 6 Behold, I say unto you, that ye must visit the poor and the needy and administer to their relief, that they may be kept until all things may be done according to my law which ye have received. Amen.[8]

Verse 4 of section 44 links conversions to the power to organize and may be related to a need to have a certain number of believers among local citizens before a church could be organized, like the New York requirement of a minimum of six members. Perhaps a local membership base of state citizens was required, and transients such as migrating saints would not meet the requirements. In a similar vein, section 52 mentions the need to organize in Missouri, and when the saints arrived in Nauvoo, they also organized under an Illinois law. These organizational steps will be discussed at greater length hereafter.

The law mentioned in verse 6 is section 42, and notice that it is here interpreted to be a directive to care for the poor; no mention is made of any more stringent economic requirement. The phrase "that they may be kept until all things may be done according to my law which ye have received" most probably means they are to be assisted until they can acquire or be given
permanent lands in Missouri so they may support themselves.

Let us next examine section 48 which begins to provide instructions on the large number of land transactions needed to effectuate the migration plans:

>Upon inquiry how the brethren should act in regard to purchasing lands to settle upon,* and where they should finally make a permanent location, I received the following:
>
>Revelation, given at Kirtland, March, 1831.
>
>1 It is necessary that ye should remain for the present time in your places of abode, as it shall be suitable to your circumstances.
>
>2 And inasmuch as ye have lands, ye shall impart to the eastern brethren;
>
>3 And inasmuch as ye have not lands, let them *buy for the present time in those regions round about,* as seemeth them good, for it must needs be necessary that they have *places to live for the present time.*
>
>4 It must needs be necessary that ye *save all the money that ye can,* and that ye obtain all that ye can in righteousness, that in time ye may be enabled to *purchase land for an inheritance, even the city.*
>
>5 *The place is not yet to be revealed;* but after your brethren come from the east there are to be certain men appointed, and to them it shall be given to know the place, or to them it shall be revealed.
>
>6 And they shall be appointed to purchase the lands, and to make a commencement to lay the foundation of the city; and then shall ye begin to be gathered with your families, every man according to his family, according to his circumstances, and as is appointed to him by the presidency and the bishop of the

church, according to the laws and commandments which ye have received, and which ye shall hereafter receive. Even so. Amen.

[Footnote by editor of the History].
* This question was agitating the minds of the brethren in consequence of the expected arrival in the near future, of the saints from New York, who had been commanded to gather to Ohio, and *for whose reception it was necessary to make preparations.*[9]

The transactions described in section 48 included subdividing and sharing existing land where the owners were willing and able, and purchasing new land where holdings were insufficient. These instructions prepare for the temporary "bivouacking" of the saints in Kirtland, and relate to section 38 which tells the eastern saints to move to Kirtland, and also to section 42 which sets up a general relief fund and mechanism for the saints already in Kirtland and those to come. Section 48 also foretells the selection of men to handle the land and other transactions related to the move to Missouri.

The prophecy contained in verses 5 and 6 makes reference to the men and administrative functions that were needed to launch the gathering process and which foreshadowed and matured into the united order organization defined in section 82. After a goodly number of settlers have moved as far as Kirtland and are poised ready to move even further west (v. 5), and money is available to purchase new lands (v. 4), then men are to be appointed to purchase those lands (v. 6) and will be told the place to make the purchases (v. 5).

Section 48 was given in March 1831. By section 52, given June 7, 1831, Edward Partridge and others were sent to Missouri to make preparations for what was expected to be a permanent settlement of the saints, and the location of the land purchases for the new city was revealed in section 57, given July 1831. Nine months later on April 26, 1832, the united order was organized as directed in section 82.

Notice that secrecy was to be maintained right up to the last moment before the land transactions could be made. That secrecy was necessary to prevent anyone from trying to make a quick profit by purchasing the land first and inflating the price to the saints. This would have been very disruptive to the planned migration and would have required more resources than the saints could raise.

Apparently to save money (D&C 48:2, 4) for the later move to Missouri, rather than sink it into possibly unsalable land, the saints were not to buy any more new land in Kirtland than was absolutely necessary. (We should remember that some of the land in New York had to be left unsold, D&C 38:37, thus limiting the amount of cash available for land purchases in Missouri.) Instead, the land already held by the saints in Kirtland was to be given or sold to incoming members to the extent the Kirtland members felt they could do so. This very practical short-term requirement should not be taken to be related to any permanent doctrinal requirement.

Again, this pooling of land resources to keep money resources liquid was necessary to make possible the large block purchases of land to be made in Missouri. This pooling did not imply a long-term socialistic system. It was merely a short-term, one-time plan for carrying out the migration to Missouri.

The Kirtland saints who were asked to give some of their land to incoming saints did not necessarily need to expect that they would never get anything in return. The monies saved by their gifts and reserved to purchase cheap Missouri land would make it possible for all participating saints to make a beneficial move to Missouri. (The land in Missouri, at $1.25 an acre, was probably one-tenth or less of the price of land in Kirtland and the eastern cities). By "paying their dues" the Kirtland saints could expect to receive help in their own move to Missouri. The pooling operation had a leap-frog effect for many. Help at one point could be repaid by help at another point.

The saints were to move to Missouri as soon as possible, many that same year. It was expected that Kirtland would be a gathering place for only about five years. (D&C 64:21; 51:16). In line with this plan, in 1838 the saints remaining in Kirtland were told to move to Missouri. (D&C 117).

Arrival of the Eastern Saints in Kirtland

Section 51, May 1831, concerns the saints from New York who were told in section 38 to organize themselves for the migration west to Kirtland. They began to arrive in Kirtland, and the section 48 interim land use rules needed to be applied to them:

> ... The saints from the State of New York began to come on, and it seemed necessary to settle them; therefore at the solicitation of Bishop Partridge, I inquired and received the following:
>
> 1 Hearken unto me, saith the Lord your God, and I will speak unto my servant Edward Partridge, and give unto him directions; for it must needs be that he receive directions how to organize this people.
>
> 2 For it must needs be that they be organized according to my laws; if otherwise, they will be cut off.
>
> 3 Wherefore, let my servant Edward Partridge, and those whom he has chosen, in whom I am well pleased, appoint unto this people their portions, every man equal according to his family, according to his circumstances and his wants and needs.
>
> 4 And let my servant Edward Partridge, when he shall appoint a man his portion, *give unto him a writing that shall secure unto him his portion,* that he shall hold it, even this right and this inheritance in the church, until he transgresses and is not counted worthy by the voice of the

church, according to the laws and covenants of the church, to belong to the church.

5 And if he shall transgress and is not counted worthy to belong to the church, he shall not have power to claim that portion which he has consecrated unto the bishop for the poor and needy of my church; therefore, he shall not retain the gift, but shall only have claim on that portion that is deeded unto him.

6 *And thus all things shall be made sure, according to the laws of the land.*

7 *And let that which belongs to this people* [branch] *be appointed unto this people* [branch].

8 And the money which is left unto this people - let there be an agent appointed unto this people, to take the money to provide food and raiment, according to the wants of this people.

9 And let every man deal honestly, and be alike among this people, and receive alike, that ye may be one, even as I have commanded you.

10 *And let that which belongeth to this people not be taken and given unto that of another church.*

11 *Wherefore, if another church [branch] would receive money of this church, let them pay unto this church again according as they shall agree;*

12 And this shall be done through the bishop or the agent, which shall be appointed by the voice of the church.

13 And again, *let the bishop appoint a storehouse unto this church* [branch] and let all things both in money and in meat, which are more than is needful for the wants of this people, be kept in the hands of the bishop.

14 And let him also reserve unto himself for his own wants, and for the wants for his family, as he shall be employed in doing this business.

15 And thus I grant unto this people a privilege of organizing themselves according to my laws.

16 And *I consecrate unto them this land for a little season, until I, the Lord, shall provide for them otherwise, and command them to go hence;*

17 And the hour and the day is not given to them, wherefore let them act upon this land as for years, and this shall turn unto them for their good.

18 Behold, this shall be an example unto my servant Edward Partridge, in other places, in all churches.[10]

The focus of section 51 is to find a place for newcomers. It was not for the purpose of reorganizing the existing Kirtland settlers into some new utopian society. In considering each practical and doctrinal question, it must be remembered that relatively short-term, high turnover quartering of migrating saints in Kirtland was expected.

It seems that the word "organize" as used in verses 1 and 2 is often taken to imply something complex and specific such as a socialistic, economic system and associated charters and rules. However, all that is intended by D&C 51:1-2 is the orderly assigning of a temporary (Ohio) or more permanent (Missouri) dwelling area through consultation and negotiation between newcomers and the local real estate agent, the bishop. The normal use of the word "organize" by Joseph Smith implied only a simple arrangement or location of people or things.[11]

Another possible connotation of the word "organize" as used in verse 2 relates to the modicum of discipline required to carry out a migration in an orderly fashion. There was a tendency for the saints to become irreverent in this spiritually motivated migration, and to jostle and compete with one another for size and location of plots of land, some striving to seek advantage over others or to speculate, thus raising the overall costs and generating hard feelings (see chapter 5 for examples). These were more than sufficient reasons to remind the saints of the rules of the gathering. There is no reason to interpret the references to "laws" as meaning some more complex requirement. Golden Rule behavior was sufficient to meet that request for order.

Something more might be said about the economics of the migration effort. The laws of nature, including physics and economics, are rather strict, impersonal, and unchangeable. It requires a certain amount of energy or resources to accomplish a given change in status or location. A failure to conduct the migration in harmony with those laws would make it difficult or impossible to reach the desired goal; some would be "cut off" because they had not the means to complete the move. Frugality, cooperation, and consideration for other's needs were all necessary to success.

The reference in verse 3 to wants and needs relates to the expected short-term stay of the single pioneer company of New York saints, "this people." Because of the need to conserve cash, it was expected that many would be cramped for space in Kirtland while they made arrangements to move to Missouri and more commodious circumstances.

Verses 4 and 5 are further efforts at maintaining order and avoiding controversy. If land is transferred to a man under the auspices of the church resettlement system, he gets a clear and uncontestable statement ("a writing") of his rights of use or ownership.[12] The other side of the coin is that land which is transferred from someone to another cannot later be reclaimed on some whim, to the damage of the one residing there ("he shall not have power to claim that portion.") "And thus all things shall be made sure, according to the laws of the land."

There was no particular reason for the bishop to hold title to all lands involved in transfers, although, of course, he would hold title to lands that would be set aside for general church use. His role was to look out for the church's interest in real estate transactions, and to see that all parties received the proper documents from the proper source. If that could be accomplished without his direct intervention, all the better. No purpose would be served in generating and registering a multiplicity of land transactions when a smaller number would do.

As an example of a land transaction, assume a Kirtland member held 10 acres and wished to donate 5 acres to the use of the migrating saints. That person might deed over the five acres directly to incoming saints or to the bishop, as seemed most convenient. The donating party would then receive through normal legal channels a new deed describing his remaining 5 acres.

There is nothing mystical or complex about the suggestion that the members of the traveling branch be made equal according to wants, needs and circumstances (v. 3). As a traveling company, making a temporary stopover (v. 16), they might reasonably be expected to accept equivalent lodging arrangements, regardless of their actual economic status before the migration journey began, and their expected status after it ended in Missouri.

In verses 7, 10, and 11, the words "people" and "church" should all be mentally equated with the word "branch."[13] Those verses ensure that all the properties of the traveling branch will be kept and controlled by that single branch. They are not to be required to subsidize any other group. They might choose to make a loan or otherwise assist others, but that is their free choice, based on their own judgement as to needs and conditions.

Verse 8 suggests that the group appoint a quartermaster or agent to acquire the supplies they need. During their temporary status as a pioneer company, their affairs could be handled most inexpensively and efficiently if they were to operate somewhat like an army on maneuvers. Bulk purchases are normally less expensive and more convenient for such a traveling group. The wants he is to supply are the practical needs of the short-term stay. He is not a commander or commune leader.

Verse 12 provides that if they do choose to help other groups through loan arrangements, the bishop is to act as the magistrate and coordinator to see that financial commitments are kept. Normal civil administrative mechanisms would either not be available at all, or would be inappropriate because they would bring in non-church, possibly hostile, administrators or judges to settle legal problems between church members.

One example of a loan made enroute to Missouri is the one made by the Tippetts group to Joseph Smith. The Tippetts group had to have the money to complete their journey and make their land purchases. The loan was made with the understanding that it would be repaid in time for that group to continue its journey to Missouri after a stopover in Ohio for the winter.[14]

There are two possible interpretations of verse 13, both of which may be correct. If we assume that the phrase "this church" means a specific branch as it does elsewhere in the revelation, then verse 13 would make the bishop the banker and warehouseman of excess "things both in money and in meat" for the poor of that specific traveling group. Verses 7, 10, and 11 could be read to assure that the ownership of the "excess" stays with that traveling group. But the bishop could help with efficient storage and transfer of money and goods according to the wishes and decisions of the branch concerning its own people.

Another way to express it would be to say that since the "storehouse" was related just to this single branch, "this church," or "this people," perhaps we can say that the branch had a welfare account for its own members, with the bishop acting as administrator. That would allow the branch to care for its own, without the concern that its resources would be drained off for the use of others and perhaps make it impossible for the branch to complete its migration to Missouri.

Verse 13 might only (or also) refer to donations made for the benefit of groups outside the donor's branch. Of course, if some desired to make contributions to the poor or other worthy causes outside of their branch, including the sustenance of the bishop himself, the bishop would gladly receive them and administer them in accordance with section 42 (verse 34 and others). The individual saints were to decide just how much was "more than is needful" for their wants. The bishop had no authority to do more than suggest what level of contribution was appropriate in the circumstances. Since each branch was already to have an agent to see to its needs (v. 8), that may indicate that this second interpretation is more accurate.

The saints arriving in Kirtland were told (v. 16) that they would only be there a short time, but verse 17 counsels the pioneer company of saints from New York to take a long term view of things and to "act upon this land as for years" since the time to move on was unknown. Improving the land with buildings and agricultural labors makes good economic sense. It would help the immediate owner and make the plots of land more usable to the next occupants. Presumably the owner would be reimbursed for his labors through the sale price of the land, regardless of whether his stay (and his labors) were long or short, much or little. Some saints stayed for years, some stayed for months such as those who stayed through the winter before moving on, and some stayed only for a few weeks. As mentioned before, one of the earliest examples was the Colesville branch which arrived in Ohio during May 1831, and left for Missouri during June 1831.[15]

This policy of improving the land for others' use is somewhat akin to the cooperative efforts of the pioneers traveling to Utah under Brigham Young's direction. Some prepared land and planted crops and moved on. Others tended and harvested the crops. Those who first planted might well expect to benefit from this effort by sharing in the harvested grain transported west by succeeding companies of pioneers. One significant difference is that it was not necessary to gain title to the prairie land used by Brigham Young's group because of the even more transient nature of its use than that of the Ohio land. The saints received permission from Indian tribes to use their lands temporarily in return for teaching the Indians farming skills and rendering other assistance.[16]

Verse 18 states that the rules given in preceding verses are to be generally applicable to all aspects of the administrative processes of the gathering. One of the main principles is that there is to be no forced or required pooling of money or other property (verses 6-7, 10-11). It is all voluntary, and then is normally done using standard business practices such as loans, etc.

As mentioned in verse 18, the procedures for settling Missouri would be similar to those described in section 51. For example, in section 57 (v. 7) Bishop Partridge is told to "divide unto the saints their inheritances" just as he was told to do in D&C 51:3. However, there would be the rather significant difference that in Missouri the settlements were intended to be permanent, and much more land was available for each family to own and use.

In these "appoint ... portions" or "divide ... inheritances" instructions, no mention of money is made but it was assumed without tedious or nagging repetition that one did not get something for nothing. (See D&C 42:54). The saints were to purchase their lands in Missouri and Ohio. Generous contributions were appreciated (D&C 42:55) but nothing was taken against the owner's wishes (D&C 51:7, 10, 11). Although it is not repeated in every verse concerning the gathering, in nearly all transactions involving transfers of property or goods, it is assumed that it is an exchange transaction, that is, people pay for what they get.

Moving On to Missouri

Section 52, given June 7, 1831, states that the next conference is to be held in Missouri, presumably as a further step in organizing the church in all the many ways necessary to support the gathering there:

1 Behold, thus saith the Lord unto the elders whom he hath called and chosen in these last days, by the voice of his Spirit -

2 Saying: I, the Lord, will make known unto you what I will that ye shall do from this time until the *next conference,* which shall be held in Missouri, *upon the land which I will consecrate unto my people,* which are a remnant of Jacob, and those who are heirs according to the covenant.

3 Wherefore, verily I say unto you, let my servants Joseph Smith, Jun., and Sidney Rigdon take their journey as soon as preparations can be made to leave their homes, and journey to the land of Missouri.

4 And inasmuch as they are faithful unto me, it shall be made known unto them what they shall do;

5 And it shall also, inasmuch as they are faithful, be made known unto them the land of your inheritance.

....

39 Let the residue of the elders watch over the *churches,* and declare the word in the regions round about them; and let them labor with their own hands that there be no idolatry nor wickedness practised.

40 And remember in all things the poor and the needy, the sick and the afflicted, for he that doeth not these things, the same is not my disciple.

41 And again, let my servants Joseph Smith, Jun., and Sidney Rigdon and Edward Partridge take with them *a recommend* from the church. And let there be one obtained for my servant Oliver Cowdery also.

42 And thus, even as I have said, if ye are faithful ye shall assemble yourselves together to rejoice upon the land of Missouri, which is the land of your inheritance, which is now the land of your enemies.[17]

The conference announced in section 52 was probably similar to the one held in Kirtland as directed in section 44, discussed earlier. This organizational step would allow the church to be legally operating in Missouri as well as Ohio, and give it rights and powers that it would not have had without those formalities.

Note that Joseph Smith, Sidney Rigdon, Edward Partridge and Oliver Cowdery are mentioned (V. 3, 41) as attending the conference. These were four of the initial nine men to be organized into the united order. These men and others added later were stepped through the elements of the migration process so that they could advise and assist the saints in the main movement. All were later involved in the more formal version of the united order.

Oliver Cowdery had assisted in the original organization of the LDS church and the translation of the Book of Mormon. Sidney Rigdon had been the religious leader of a group of people in Kirtland area before he joined the LDS church. Edward Partridge had been one of his followers.

The brethren attending the conference were told (52:41) to take a recommend with them as a means of identification and proof of standing in the church. This security measure became even more important later on as a means of helping the bishop in Missouri determine who should be allowed to acquire land with the saints under the church land purchase and migration program. Many non-members would surely have liked to enjoy the benefits provided by that program. Apparently, the recommend, together with other documents, also helped to determine the price they should pay for the land, based on prior service and contributions to the church. It may seem strange that a recommend from their branch was required of these leading brethren, but it would serve as a training experience and an example to others, just as the presiding brethren today carry recommends.

Section 54, received in early June 1831, deals with the branch at Thompson, Ohio, many of whose members had moved there from Colesville, New York, and were settled in Ohio according to the instructions in section 51. Apparently

(D&C 54:4) there was some dispute related to their plan to continue westward in accordance with the general commandment. This may be somewhat like section 39 where James Coville first agreed to accept a commandment to migrate to Ohio (D&C 39:14), and then failed to carry it out (D&C 40). Some of the Thompson branch had moved as far as Ohio on their way to Missouri, and then had second thoughts.

At least some of the Thompson saints were still willing to go ahead, and they were told (D&C 54:7-8) to elect a leader to help administer the move to Missouri. As to their fate when they arrived in Missouri, they were told that "after you have done journeying, behold, I say unto you, seek a living like unto men, until I prepare a place for you" (v. 9). This indicates that the organization was merely that necessary to make the difficult journey, and that no long-term economic entwining or entanglement of the group members was contemplated. The group did not have to wait long for more specific instructions because section 57, given the next month, July, named the gathering place.

According to the headnote to section 54 in the 1981 edition, apparently there were other planned land transactions that fell through and interfered with the migration. One who had agreed to donate land, or otherwise make it available for the use of newcomers, had changed his mind.[18] This episode shows another reason for the need for the irrevocable deed of gift on land to be used as a gathering place. A last-minute change of mind could leave large groups of people with no place to go, or cause them to have to pay high prices for any land they might be able to find in their vulnerable situation.

The events of the conference in Missouri scheduled in section 52 and the location of the land to be purchased are described in section 57, dated July 21, 1831:

> 1 Hearken, O ye elders of my church, saith the Lord your God, who have assembled yourselves together,

according to my commandments, in this land, which is the land of Missouri, which is the land which I have appointed and consecrated for the gathering of the saints.

2 Wherefore, this is *the land of promise,* and the place for the city of Zion.

3 And thus saith the Lord your God, if you will receive wisdom here is wisdom. Behold, the place which is now called *Independence is the center place;* and a spot for the temple is lying westward, upon a lot which is not far from the court-house.

4 Wherefore, it is wisdom that the land should be purchased by the saints, and also every tract lying westward, even unto the line running directly between Jew and Gentile;

5 And also every tract bordering by the prairies, inasmuch as my disciples are enabled to buy lands. Behold, this is wisdom, that they may obtain it for an everlasting inheritance.

6 And let my servant *Sidney Gilbert* stand in the office to which I have appointed him, to receive moneys, to be an *agent* unto the church, *to buy land* in all the regions round about, inasmuch as can be done in righteousness, and as wisdom shall direct.

7 And let my servant *Edward Partridge* stand in the office to which I have appointed him, and *divide unto the saints their inheritance,* even as I have commanded; and also those whom he has appointed to assist him.

8 And again, verily I say unto you, let my servant *Sidney Gilbert* plant himself in this place, and *establish a store,* that he may sell goods without fraud, that he may *obtain money to buy lands* for the good of the saints, and that he may obtain whatsoever things the disciples may need to plant them in their inheritance.

9 And also let my servant *Sidney Gilbert obtain a license* - behold here is wisdom, and whoso readeth let him understand - that he may *send goods also unto the people,* even by whom he will as *clerks* employed in his service;

10 And thus provide for my saints, that my gospel may be preached unto those who sit in darkness and in the region and shadow of death.

11 And again, verily I say unto you, let my servant *William W. Phelps* be planted in this place, and be established as a *printer* unto the church.

12 And lo, if the world receive his writings - behold here is wisdom - let him obtain whatsoever he can obtain in righteousness, for the good of the saints.

13 And let my servant *Oliver Cowdery assist him,* even as I have commanded, in whatsoever place I shall appoint unto him, to copy, and to correct, and select, that all things may be right before me, as it shall be proved by the Spirit through him.

14 And thus let those of whom I have spoken be planted in the land of Zion, as speedily as can be, with their families, to do those things even as I have spoken.

15 And now concerning the *gathering* - let the bishop and the agent make preparations for those families which have been commanded to come to this land, as soon as possible, and plant them in their inheritance.

16 And unto the residue of both elders and members further directions shall be given hereafter. Even so. Amen.[19]

Here certain men are told the place of the gathering and assigned responsibilities as foretold in D&C 48:5, 6. Again, all the men specifically mentioned here later became part of the united order. Sidney Gilbert is added to that list as first intimated in D&C 53. W. W. Phelps is also added.

(Algernon) Sidney Gilbert was the senior partner of the successful Kirtland merchandising firm of Gilbert and Whitney. His junior partner was Newel K. Whitney. Before coming to Kirtland, William Wine Phelps had lived in the state of New York where he was a newspaper editor and was active in state politics.

The concept of a supplies agent, mentioned earlier in D&C 51:8, to act on behalf of a single branch, is reiterated and made one step more general and formal by the appointment in D&C 57:9 of Sidney Gilbert to furnish supplies in Missouri. Sidney is told in 57:9 to send goods to this people, but again there was no expectation of something for nothing. Brother Gilbert was to sell the goods (D&C

57:8) and the saints were the ones to purchase them. In fact, Brother Gilbert was expected to make a profit which would be applied to other church projects such as purchase of land, printing and care of the poor. This was before formalizing his merchandizing operations as part of the united order firm. Apparently he later had some problems carrying out his prime mission of supplying goods, probably because the saints either couldn't or wouldn't pay him for goods received on credit.[20]

The business arrangements made in section 57 are very similar to and foreshadowed those made under the auspices of the later united order. An agent was appointed to buy large tracts of land (v. 6), a bishop was appointed to sell the land to the saints or otherwise manage it (v. 7), a merchandising operation was set up to provide needed supplies (v. 8-10), and a printing function was begun (v. 11-13). These same men later continued these same functions within the more mutually supportive framework called the united order.

In section 58 the Missouri administrators are given further instructions, and Martin Harris, who had earlier assisted Joseph Smith financially in translating and publishing the Book of Mormon, is given a specific assignment and thus added to the pool of future united order members:[21]

> Revelation given through Joseph Smith the Prophet, in Zion, Jackson County, Missouri, August 1, 1831. On the first Sabbath after the arrival of the Prophet and party in Jackson County, Missouri, a religious service was held and two members were received by baptism. During that week, members of the Colesville branch and others arrived.
>
> 1 Hearken, O ye elders of my church, and give ear to my word, and learn of me what I will concerning you, and also concerning this land unto which I have sent you.
> ....

14 Yea, for this cause I have sent you hither, and have selected my servant Edward Partridge, and have appointed unto him his mission in this land.

....

17 And whoso standeth in this mission is appointed to be a judge in Israel, like as it was in ancient days, to divide the lands of the heritage of God unto his children;

....

21 Let no man break the laws of the land, for he that keepeth the laws of God hath no need to break the laws of the land.

....

24 And now, as I spoke concerning my servant Edward Partridge, this land is the land of his residence, and those whom he has appointed for his counselors; and also the land of the residence of him whom I have appointed to keep my storehouse;

25 Wherefore, let them bring their families to this land, as they shall counsel between themselves and me.

....

35 It is wisdom in me that my servant *Martin Harris* should be an example unto the church, in laying his moneys before the bishop of the church.

36 And also, this is a law unto every man that cometh unto this land to receive an inheritance; and he shall do with his moneys according as the law directs.

37 And it is wisdom also that there should be lands purchased in Independence, for the place of the storehouse, and also for the house of the printing.

38 And other directions concerning my servant Martin Harris shall be given him of the Spirit, that he may receive his inheritance as seemeth him good;

....

40 And also let my servant William W. Phelps stand in the office to which I have appointed him, and receive his inheritance in the land;

....

49 And let there be an agent appointed by the voice of the church, unto the church in Ohio, to receive moneys to purchase lands in Zion.

> 50 And I give unto my servant *Sidney Rigdon* a commandment, that he shall write a description of the land of Zion, and a statement of the will of God, as it shall be made known by the Spirit unto him;
>
> 51 And an epistle and subscription, to be presented unto all the churches to obtain moneys, to be put into the hands of the bishop, of himself or the agent, as seemeth him good or as he shall direct, to purchase lands for an inheritance for the children of God.
>
> ....
>
> 57 And let my servant Sidney Rigdon consecrate and dedicate this land, and the spot for the temple unto the Lord.[22]

Section 58 gives some instructions to new participants in the Missouri gathering and makes some adjustments to the administrative assignments of various men as first set out one month earlier in section 57. Martin Harris (D&C 58:35-37) is to set the example for the Missouri move by giving money to the bishop to be used to purchase land for himself, for Church business purposes, and perhaps for other individuals. Sidney Gilbert had been appointed to buy land (D&C 57:6) as well as operate a store (D&C 57:8-9). In section 58 his name is not mentioned, but an agent (whether a second one or a replacement is not clear) is to be appointed (v. 49) to handle land sales, that is, to receive money from the eastern saints to be used in buying land for those same eastern saints and others as excess funds allowed. This may have left Gilbert free to better mind the store. Sidney Rigdon (v. 50) was to do the advertising needed to help the saints prepare to come to Missouri. Monies were to be collected by "epistle and subscription" (v. 51) to purchase lands.

During the period of January 1831 to August 1831 the gathering process began and built up momentum as various groups of saints such as those in the Fayette and Colesville branches traveled west to Kirtland and continued on to Missouri, buying land and caring for their poor as necessary. Specific opportunities to be of assistance were identified as those saints reached each stage of their migration, and qualified individuals were assigned to offer that assistance. Within a few months, all the administrative requirements of a workable migration program were experienced and understood. To those involved it must have become apparent that a somewhat more formal organization was needed at the church-wide level to efficiently meet the needs of the many saints who would be traveling. In such a large migration, it would be inefficient to require every new group of travelers to re-discover or re-invent all procedures and preparations necessary for a successful relocation to Missouri. As discussed in the next chapter, section 78 paved the way for this more comprehensive organization.

Chapter 3 Notes

1. D&C 38:16-37. HC 1:140. Jan. 2, 1831.

2. There seems to have been a division of responsibility among three kinds of administrative bodies in the early church. The bishop was to care for the poor, the united order was to handle the large economic transactions needed to support the gathering, and the high council dealt with spiritual matters. That same general segregation of duties exists in the church today.

If a man held a position in more than one of these organizations, he kept his activities in each separate from his activities in the others. An example is Bishop Partridge who functioned both as a bishop and as a member of the united order. In the one case, he was an official of an organized church and cared for its poor. In the other case he was a partner in a business firm which engaged in real estate development to accomplish the migration of the saints. HC 1:362-364.

3. For example, see D&C 39:14; 54:7-8; 58:35-52.

4. D&C 42:30-42, 53-55, 62-64, 70-73.

5. Alma 1:3; 2 Nephi 10:5; 26:29-30.

6. HC 2:295-296. October 30, 1835. Kirtland. "... every man enjoys his own property ...." See also HC 6:37-38. September 24, 1843. Nauvoo. "In Nauvoo everyone is steward over his own."

7. HC 2:445-446. June 1836.

8. D&C 44.

9. HC 1:166-167; D&C 48. March 1831.

10. HC 1:173-174; D&C 51.

11. In conjunction with the events surrounding the solemn assembly in the Kirtland temple in January 1836, the use of the word "organize" and its synonyms referred merely to the seating arrangements for formal meetings. This may seem a small matter, but the Twelve's reaction to the seating arrangements at one meeting, and the possible implications for their position within the governing bodies of the kingdom, was treated as a major concern. HC 2:372.
The words and phrases "organized" or "organizing" (HC 2:368, 382, 385, 386), "placed" (HC 2:372, 374), "arrange" or "arranged" (HC 2:374, 376, 389), "seated" (HC 2:370), "set ... quorums in order" (HC 2:388), and "seated ... in ... order" (HC 2:377), in their contexts, all signify merely assigning to a certain location. In one case (HC 2:368), there is a recognition that a minimum of order requires that one be appointed to preside, but that again only applies to formal meetings of a large group who wish to maintain reverence. See chapter 11.

12. Apparently the saints usually gave to the bishop the money they would otherwise have used to purchase land from some other person. They got land provided by the saints in Kirtland, and the bishop got the money. The money

of course would be used to purchase land in Missouri. Verse 5 indicates that the incoming saints made a "consecration" or contribution to the church and received land in return, much as though they had purchased it from the bishop. Verse 8 indicates that the bishop didn't take all their money, but only what he thought was an appropriate amount. Again, that money could be used by the bishop for the benefit (in Missouri) of both incoming saints who supplied the cash, and the resident saints who supplied the land. Verses 10 and 11 indicate that except for this special land deal, all other economic relationships were to remain normal - no other poolings or centralizations. The branch would continue to function much like a pioneer company for a time, sharing some resources and responsibilities among themselves for the duration of the journey, somewhat like an army unit.

This same maneuver might be made to work many times with the same land as different groups moved in and out. Land transactions might have been analogous to the loan transactions of the Tippitts family from Essex, New York: purchase and sale of land would be much like short term investment and withdrawal of funds. HC 2:172, 253. See chapter 7 for a description of the Tippitts transaction.

13. See D&C 52:39 for use of the word "churches" to designate various branches.

14. HC 2:172, 253.

15. D&C 51, 54. HC 1:173, 181. See index to vol. 1, entry for "Colesville branch."

16. CHC 3:143.

17. D&C 52.

18. Leman Copley, HC 1:180, 167.

19. D&C 57.

20. HC 1:365.

21. It appears that only Newel K. Whitney and John Whitmer had not yet been given revealed assignments.

22. D&C 58.

CHAPTER 4

Organizing the First United Order Firm or Partnership to Assist in the Gathering

The pioneering and colonizing feats of Brigham Young in the West are well known to almost everyone. Not so well known is the feat Joseph Smith performed in gathering together thousands from many parts of the globe. Brigham began with a large and seasoned group. Joseph began with only a few friends.

Part of the reason that Joseph's accomplishments are so little known is probably that the gathering was accomplished through individuals and small groups of people finding their way on their own to the designated locations of Kirtland and Independence. The traveling bodies were usually no larger than a portion of a branch of the Church. For example, there were about sixty souls in the branch moving to Missouri from Colesville, New York.[1] Following a similar course, the branch from Essex County, New York, led by members of the Tippitts family, appears to have had about eight adults.[2] Even Joseph's travels with Zion's Camp of one hundred and thirty men[3] can hardly compare with the large-scale western movements of saints under Brigham's direction.

In the beginning, the travelers took care of themselves completely, beginning with the initial sale of their eastern lands to acquire funds, continuing on through the westward journey itself, and finally ending with the purchase of land in the appointed places. Later, agents were appointed at various times to simplify the migration process by purchasing blocks of land in advance and providing for the shipping of needed supplies.

As the migration went on, it must have become evident that a more permanent planning, coordinating, and funding body would be even more effective in accomplishing the commandment to gather the saints together. Meeting the needs of these travelers did require some foresight and capital, but did not require a large military-like command and control system such as that employed by Brigham Young.

When section 78 was received in March 1832, at Hiram, Ohio, the migration had been under way for more than a year, and much experience had been accumulated. That section directs three men who had been involved in the gathering process from the beginning, Joseph Smith, Sidney Rigdon, and Newel K. Whitney, to meet with the saints in Zion (v. 9), to organize a firm or "order" (v. 3, 4, 8) for conducting the business of the gathering:

> 1 The Lord spake unto Enoch [Joseph Smith, Jun.], saying: Hearken unto me, saith the Lord your God, who are ordained unto the high priesthood of my church, who have assembled yourselves together;
> 2 And listen to the counsel of him who has ordained you from on high, who shall speak in your ears the words of wisdom, that salvation may be unto you in that thing which you have presented before me, saith the Lord God.
> 3 For verily I say unto you, the time has come, and is now at hand; and behold, and lo, it must needs be that there be an organization of my people, in regulating and establishing the affairs of the storehouse for the poor of my people, both in this place and in the land of Zion --
> 4 Or in other words, the city of Enoch [Joseph], for a permanent and everlasting establishment and order unto my church, to advance the cause, which ye have espoused, to the salvation of man, and to the glory of your Father who is in heaven;

5 That you may be equal in the bonds of heavenly things, yea, and earthly things also, for the obtaining of heavenly things.

6 For if ye are not equal in earthly things ye cannot be equal in obtaining heavenly things;

7 For if you will that I give unto you a place in the celestial world, you must prepare yourselves by doing the things which I have commanded you and required of you.

8 And now, verily thus saith the Lord, it is expedient that all things be done unto my glory, by you who are joined together in this order;

9 Or, in other words, let my servant Ahashdah [Newel K. Whitney] and my servant Gazelam, or Enoch [Joseph Smith, Jun.] and my servant Pelagoram [Sidney Rigdon], sit in council with the Saints which are in Zion;

10 Otherwise Satan seeketh to turn their hearts away from the truth, that they become blinded and understand not the things which are prepared for them.

11 Wherefore, a commandment I give unto you, to prepare and organize yourselves by a bond or everlasting covenant that cannot be broken.

12 And he who breaketh it shall lose his office and standing in the church, and shall be delivered over to the buffetings of Satan until the day of redemption.

13 Behold, this is the preparation wherewith I prepare you, and the foundation, and the ensample which I give unto you, whereby you may accomplish the commandments which are given you;

14 That through my providence, notwithstanding the tribulation which shall descend upon you, that the church may stand independent above all other creatures beneath the celestial world;

....

17 Verily, verily, I say unto you, ye are little children, and ye have not as yet understood how great blessings the Father hath in his own hands and prepared for you;

18 And ye cannot bear all things now; nevertheless, be of good cheer, for I will lead you along. The kingdom is yours and the blessings thereof are yours, and the riches of eternity are yours.[4]

One might wonder whether a new organization of some sort was actually formed at the time of Section 78, consisting of the three men named in verse 9, or whether section 78 simply paved the way for a later event. Based on later comments and events, it is much more likely that it merely paved the way and that no actual organization occurred until a meeting was held in Missouri as directed by verse 9, and the revelation now known as section 82 was given at the moment needed to guide those proceedings.

Most, if not all, of the men expected to be at the meeting in Zion (Missouri) were already heavily engaged by individual assignments in the work to be done by the new organization. Some had been involved for over a year in the same or related activities. Another layer of sophistication was to be added to existing arrangements by joining these men together for mutual support. The action to be taken at the Missouri meeting was part of an incremental increase, a natural growth pattern or sequence of events, and not a sudden eruption of a new organization. This step was part of the "line upon line, precept upon precept" pattern of revelation and change.

In verse 2 the Lord speaks of "that thing which you have presented before me." Apparently, Joseph Smith had felt a need for a more substantial organization for assisting the gathering of the saints. Joseph most likely presented the problem to the Lord as he saw it and perhaps suggested a solution. Most, if not all, of the revelations received by Joseph were at his request. He presumably had learned the lesson well to "study it out in your mind (D&C 9:8)", before requesting aid and confirmation.

The new organization was to regulate "the storehouse for the poor of my people" (v. 78:3), both in Kirtland and Zion, and "advance the cause" (v. 78:4), that cause being the gathering process. Notice that the poor were to be helped in the context of the gathering. There is no intimation of any socialistic economic entanglements.

Verse 4 states that the new organization was to be "a permanent and everlasting establishment and order unto my church" (see D&C 82:20).⁵ The united order was the first example of a formal business unit to hold title to property and administer central church affairs. A temple committee had been formed earlier, but it had a much more local and limited purpose. Some legal forms have been changed since the time of the united order, but the function has continued without interruption and is much the same today as it was then. The Corporation of the President is the successor to that united order organization.

Verses 5 and 6 speak of being equal. In theory and in practical application, this meant only that those who were very poor should be assisted so that they could live much like others who were more fortunate. In this particular setting, it meant mostly that those who did not have means to acquire land should be helped by those who did have funds. Any equalization was to be done through the gifts or alms of the rich to the poor. No forced leveling process is implied here.

Verse 11 mentions the need for a "bond or ... covenant that cannot be broken." This is similar to the "deed that cannot be broken" language of D&C 42:30. Both mean the same thing, that is, the actions taken and commitments made must be done in a legally enforceable way. This would eliminate any uncertainty as to ownership and responsibility in any situation.

Of some interest here is a subtle difference between the headnote for section 78 in the 1968 edition of the Doctrine and Covenants, and the headnote in the 1981 edition. The older edition contains the phrase:

> The Order given of the Lord to Enoch [Joseph Smith, Jun.] for the purpose of establishing the poor.

In the new edition, the corresponding phrase reads:

> The order given of the Lord to Joseph Smith for the purpose of establishing a storehouse for the poor.

One difference is that the word "order" is capitalized in the older edition, and not capitalized in the new, indicating a less formal interpretation of the word. Another difference to be noted is that between "establishing the poor" and "establishing a storehouse for the poor." "Establishing the poor" sounds more like a broad social experiment was in the wind, while "establishing a storehouse for the poor" sounds like the simpler step of giving aid to the poor was intended. These two differences both imply that a simple solution for a simple problem was all that was to be implemented,
rather than some sweeping doctrinal and sociological revolution.

In his history, Joseph describes the fulfillment of the directive to organize the order outlined in section 78:

> April first (1832), I started for Missouri, in company with Newel K. Whitney, Peter Whitmer, and Jesse Gause, to fulfill the revelation.... We ... were joined by Elder Rigdon ... [and] by stage arrived at Independence, Missouri, on the twenty-fourth of April....
>
> On the 26th, I called a general council of the church, and was acknowledged as President of the High Priesthood, according to a previous ordination at a conference of High Priests, Elders, and members, held at Amherst, Ohio, on the 25th of January, 1832. The right hand of fellowship was given to me by the Bishop, Edward Partridge, on behalf of the church. The scene was solemn, impressive and delightful. During the intermission, a difficulty or hardness which had existed between Bishop Partridge and Elder Rigdon, was amicably settled, and when we came together in the afternoon, all hearts seemed to rejoice and I received the following:
>
> [Section 82 appears at this point in the history].[6]

In his comment quoted above that he was going to Missouri "to fulfill the revelation," Joseph Smith was of course speaking of Section 78 which had directed the men to go to Missouri for the formal organizing of a church-related business firm. As noted above, during the organizational meeting for the united order firm, April 26, 1832, at Jackson County, Section 82 was revealed. Portions of that section are reproduced here:

> 8 And again, I say unto you, I give unto you a new commandment, that you may understand my will concerning you;
> 9 Or, in other words, I give unto you directions how you may act before me, that it may turn to you for your salvation.
> ....
> 11 Therefore, verily I say unto you, that it is expedient for my servants Alam and Ahashdah [Newel K. Whitney], Mahalaleel and Pelagoram [Sidney Rigdon], and my servant Gazelam [Joseph Smith], and Horah and Olihah [Oliver Cowdery], and Shalemanasseh and Mahemson [Martin Harris], to be bound together by a bond and covenant that cannot be broken by transgression, except judgement shall immediately follow, in your several stewardships --
> 12 To manage the affairs of the poor, and all things pertaining to the bishopric both in the land of Zion and in the land of Shinehah [Kirtland];
> 13 For I have consecrated the land of Shinehah [Kirtland] in mine own due time for the benefit of the saints of the Most High, and for a stake to Zion.
> ....
> 15 Therefore, I give unto you this commandment, that ye bind yourselves by this covenant, and it shall be done according to the laws of the Lord.
> 16 Behold, here is wisdom also in me for your good.
> 17 And you are to be equal, or in other words, you are to have equal claims on the properties, for the benefit of managing the concerns of your stewardships, every man according to his wants and his needs, inasmuch as his wants are just --
> 18 And all this for the benefit of the church of the living God, that every man may improve upon his talent, that every man may gain other talents, yea, even an hundred fold, to be cast into the Lord's storehouse, to become the common property of the whole church --

> 19 Every man seeking the interest of his neighbor, and doing all things with an eye single to the glory of God.
> 20 This order I have appointed to be an everlasting order unto you, and unto your successors, inasmuch as you sin not.
> 21 And the soul that sins against this covenant, and hardeneth his heart against it, shall be dealt with according to the laws of my church, and shall be delivered over to the buffetings of Satan until the day of redemption.
> 22 And now, verily I say unto you, and this is wisdom, make unto yourselves friends with the mammon of unrighteousness, and they will not destroy you.[7]

This pivotal section will be discussed in detail beginning with the headnote and continuing through many individual verses. As with the headnotes of section 78, the differences between the headnote of Section 82 in the 1968 edition of the D&C and the headnote in the new 1981 edition are of interest here. In the older edition it is asserted that the revelation shows:

> the order given to Enoch, and the church in his day.

The later edition drops that statement and says nothing about events in Enoch's day. A likely reason is that on a review of pertinent documents from the Joseph Smith period, the scholars preparing the 1981 edition found no evidence to support the statement. According to the title page of the 1968 edition, the headnotes to chapters or sections were added in the 1921 edition, and may have been influenced by the definitions coming from the Brigham Young period.[8]

Section 78 uses the code names of both Gazelam and Enoch to refer to Joseph Smith, while section 82 uses only Gazelam. The appearance of the word Enoch in the early editions without the clarifying note that this referred to Joseph Smith, may have caused some ambiguity and confusion which was not corrected until later.

The men listed by code name in verse 11 have now all been identified by their real names. The five men identified in pre-1981 editions of the D&C are Newel K. Whitney, Sidney Rigdon, Joseph Smith, Oliver Cowdery, and Martin Harris. These were the men who resided in Kirtland. The other four men have recently been identified as follows: Alam (Edward Partridge), Shalemanasseh (William W. Phelps), Mahalaleel (Sidney Gilbert), and Horah (John Whitmer).[9] These were the men who were living in Missouri and who continued to labor there after this organizational meeting. For reasons to be discussed later, it was probably more important to keep the names of the Missouri brethren more secret and for longer than those in Ohio.

The nine men in attendance at the meeting were already deeply involved in the business of gathering the saints to Kirtland and Missouri. These same men were now to be organized (v. 11) into a business unit that could more efficiently administer that process. The secret names given for these men served a protection purpose and are of some importance in understanding the whole matter, but a detailed discussion of that point will be delayed until later. These nine men were the only members of the order. There is no indication that any other church members were also to be order members.

The men of the order were "to manage the affairs of the poor, and all things pertaining to the Bishopric both in the land of Zion and in the land of Shinehah [Kirtland]." (v. 12). Notice again here as in section 78:3-4, that the unit was not assigned to manage every aspect of the Saints' lives, but only the affairs of the poor and of specific central church interests.

The section says very little about how the church is to get the means to "manage the affairs of the poor." D&C 83:6 helps somewhat by explaining that "consecration," meaning contributions, are to be the means of assisting the poor. But the united order's responsibilities went far beyond direct assistance to the poor, and included large real estate and other transactions. Verse 22, which mentions "the mammon of unrighteousness," meaning the riches and rich men of the world,[10] lets it be known that many functions are to be accomplished using borrowed money, as a business unit would normally do. This use of borrowed money as a means of gaining access to capital is in contrast to the means many people would imagine would be used by a communal organization - some kind of comprehensive pooling of members' property.

Using a code name for Kirtland in verse 13 also served a protection purpose by keeping secret the place where the united order was to carry on some of its land development operations. If one knows the place, one can discover the people operating there.

Verse 17 begins a discussion of the operation of the business unit. The men were to "have equal claims on the properties, for the benefit of managing the concerns of your stewardships." This is a simple but accurate description of how a normal business partnership operates. "To have equal claims on the properties" is the normal mode of operation for a partnership. In normal business law, unless otherwise agreed, all partners are to have equal claims on the resources of the firm. A general partner has the power to commit all or any part of the assets of the firm, unless otherwise determined and proper notice is given to all affected parties. This allows one man to be the agent of all the others in a business deal. At the same time, it is assumed unless otherwise agreed, that all partners will share equally in any profits that are declared. In this situation where many or even all the brethren involved spent their entire efforts in church business, there needed to be an arrangement for their support.

In a partnership, the law assumes that each partner is equally qualified and empowered to act as an agent of all the others and to commit the full assets of the firm. At the same time, for purposes of paying debts, the assets of the firm also includes any personal assets of all the partners. So in a very real sense, each would have "equal claims on the properties."

For example, giving title to a house to a partner is not really a loss of assets to the firm. It can still get to that house if need be to pay debts, or rather the creditors can.

All of the men who joined together in the firm had been individually carrying economic burdens of various types and sizes for the benefit of the church. There was an unfairness in expecting these uneven burdens to be borne for years on end. These burdens, great and small, were to be made more equal through the partnership mechanism. It gave the individuals a formal means of sharing the work, risks, and financial liabilities of their various activities. This sharing gave the individuals the encouragement and means to expand even further the scope of their operations. Thus the equality spoken of deals with a business arrangement among named men. It was not addressed to everyone in the church, and does not indicate a need for a leveling of all church members' economic status.

In this context, the term stewardship relates to the specific business assignments each man had within the partnership structure. The stewardship idea will be further developed later with specific examples of business assignments.

One reason for choosing a partnership as the vehicle for central church administration is the simplicity of forming it. Under the law a partnership can be formed at will, without any need for legislative authorization, and begin operations at once. Here, the united order partnership was formed in part of one day, and immediately began functioning and transacting business, and continued to do so through four days of meetings. A corporation would have taken a great deal of time and preparation to create. At that time, with no general enabling law for corporations, a separate and special act of the state legislature would have been required. That was a long and difficult process, and the likelihood that a charter would be granted was very low.[11] Enterprises such as a railroad or a canal were the more usual subjects of legislative corporate charters.

The various points of law and business practice concerning partnerships in general and the united order firm in particular will be confirmed and expanded as we consider other historical materials.

As verse 18 explains, the united order was to be operated "all ... for the benefit of the church of the living God." All the money collected from any source was to be "cast into the Lord's storehouse, to become the common property of the whole church." These statements again emphasize that the purpose of the business unit was to manage the affairs of the church for the good of the whole church. There was no time to deal with too many local details. As we shall see, after the order had made the large scale general preparations for the gathering process, much of the detailed administration in assisting the poor was turned over to the bishops, just as is done today.

Verse 18 also hints at the normal method used in partnerships for collecting and distributing income. All funds from all sources are collected in one account. "All" benefits from transactions, not just "surplus" over personal needs, goes into the firm's coffers. This also indicates that it is a business organization. In a normal partnership, all income normally goes into a common pool. Profits, if any, must then be specifically declared and disbursed, if the partners are to receive any income. Any distributions are made pro rata unless unless otherwise specified. Any undistributed remainder may be used to expand the holdings or operation of the partnership. This same technique was to apply to the united order firm or partnership.

The phrase "becomes the common property of the whole church" makes it clear that this is a central church operation. It would have been altogether impractical to consider placing all economic aspects of all church members under one umbrella as would be necessary for fairness if all income were to be pooled. This was never intended or attempted; the united order's purpose was specific and limited only to the gathering the saints and other central church matters. Contrast this pooling of central church funds with the earlier directive in D&C 42 to the effect that a church or branch's property, to the extent it was temporarily pooled during migration operations, remains that branch's property and is not to be siphoned off to any other. That directive was said to apply to all future situations and was not repealed by section 82.

It is always advantageous for neighbors to cooperate, as mentioned in verse 19, but in a partnership relationship it is a must, since each man holds the legal power to destroy economically not only himself but also all his associates.

Verse 20, again as in D&C 78:4, reiterates the everlasting nature of the new unit. The church was restored for the last time during this dispensation, never to be taken again from the earth until the second coming of Christ. In order to fulfill its mission during this long period, the church requires a central administrative body. A single small-scale, ward-level economic unit of a few men, subject to splits and recombinations based on demographic changes in local church population, would not likely receive the level of concern shown in the scriptures for the unit known as the united order.

The term "successors" appearing in verse 20 is a legal and business term relating to ownership and liabilities in a business organization. In contrast, the term "children" or "posterity" is used when personally owned property or "inheritances" are discussed. See D&C 38:19-20 for a contrasting reference to children. This contrast indicates the nature of the "united order was that of a business organization.

Those charged with central church business bear a heavy responsibility. Verse 21 contains a strong warning requiring fidelity of the partners to the firm and to the church it is to serve. With the authority they held the partners could bring many troubles to the saints by their errors; thus the strong warning.

The reference in verse 22 to the "mammon of unrighteousness" is an indication that they should establish ties with organizations able to make large loans for the future real estate development and merchandising operations of the church as the migration got under way. Local banks plus those in New York, Boston, and elsewhere were tapped for funds at various times.[12]

There are many topics contained in or implied by the two sections, 78 and 82. Other chapters deal with a number of these topics and should help in gaining a grasp of what these two sections really mean. At this point we will examine other historical materials related to the organizational meetings held in Missouri. Joseph Smith continues his narration of those meetings:

> On the 27th [of April 1832] we transacted considerable business for the salvation of the saints, who were settling among a ferocious set of mobbers, like lambs among wolves. It was my endeavor to so organize the church, that the brethren might eventually be independent of every encumbrance beneath the celestial kingdom, by bonds and covenants of mutual friendship, and mutual love....
>
> On the 30th, I returned to Independence, and again sat in council with the brethren, and received the following:
> [Section 83].
>
> 1 Verily, thus sayeth the Lord, in addition to the laws of the church concerning women and children, those who belong to the church, who have lost their husbands or fathers:
> 2 Women have claim on their husbands for their maintenance, until their husbands are taken; and if they are

not found transgressors they shall have fellowship in the church.

3 And if they are not faithful they shall not have fellowship in the church; yet they may remain upon their inheritances according to the laws of the land.

4 All children have claim on their parents for their maintenance until they are of age.

5 And after that, they have claim upon the church, or in other words upon the Lord's storehouse, if their parents have not wherewith to give them inheritances.

6 And the storehouse shall be kept by the consecrations of the church; and widows and orphans shall be provided for, as also the poor. Amen.[13]

The final council meeting associated with the organizing of the united order was held on May 1, 1832:

> Our council was continued on the 1st of May, when it was ordered that three thousand copies of the Book of Commandments be printed in the first edition; that William W. Phelps, Oliver Cowdery, and John Whitmer, be appointed to review and prepare such revelations for the press as shall be deemed proper for publication, and print them as soon as possible at Independence, Missouri; the announcement to be made that they are "published by W. W. Phelps & Co." It was also ordered that W. W. Phelps correct and print the hymns which had been selected by Emma Smith in fulfilment of the revelation.
>
> Arrangements were also made for supplying the saints with stores in Missouri and Ohio, which action, with a few exceptions, was hailed with joy by the brethren.*

[The following footnote was inserted by B. H. Roberts, editor of the Joseph Smith history]

*The arrangements here referred to for the establishment of stores in Missouri and Ohio, as disclosed by the minutes of these council meetings of the 26th, 27th, 30th of April, and the 1st of May, were that the brethren in mercantile pursuits in Kirtland and Zion be united in one firm; and the establishments in Kirtland and Zion respectively were regarded merely as branches of the one firm. Still it was resolved that each of these branches should have a separate company name. The name of the branch in Zion was to be "Gilbert, Whitney & Company," and the one in Kirtland "Newel K. Whitney & Company." W. W. Phelps and A. S. Gilbert were appointed to draft the bond for the united firm. A. S. Gilbert and Newel K. Whitney were appointed to be the agents of the new firm. It was also resolved that whenever any special business should arise it would be the duty of the united firm by its branches at Jackson county, Missouri, and Geauga county, Ohio, to regulate the same by special agency. It was also resolved that the united firm negotiate a loan of fifteen thousand dollars at six per centum. The firm of Newel K. Whitney & Co. was appointed to transact the business.[14]

The circumstances of the organization of the united order and its first transactions should give us many clues concerning the real nature of the new administrative body. First of all, one might guess that they were primarily a business organization for dealing with central church matters because that is all they discussed for the four days they were meeting in council. Even the fact that they met in council for that length of time and conducted much business shows that they really were a small group, consisting of only nine men, and primarily concerned with specific business matters. If an entire community of saints were involved, no such proceedings would have been possible.

They considered church-wide policy concerning aid to the poor and asked for direction, as evidenced by Section 83 dealing with women and children without husbands or fathers; they provided for the printing of the *Book of Commandments;* they arranged for supplying the saints with stores in Missouri and Ohio; they resolved to procure a loan to assist with operating expenses. In general terms they "transacted considerable business for the salvation of the saints, who were settling among a ferocious set of mobbers,"[15] showing that their main concern was to assist the international gathering process in any way they could.

There is no mention at all of any of the trivial and individual matters that would surely come up in a meeting of a local communal group, such as how many cows a man could have before some were considered "excess." Joseph never attempted to set forth any such rulings.[16] He did make requests for donations and heartily appreciated any contributions, but he never tried to override a man's conscience as to what donations, if any, should be made.

In the May 1 meeting, three of the men, W. W. Phelps, Oliver Cowdery, and John Whitmer, who are partners in the united order, are given the business assignment or "stewardship" of presenting themselves to the world as the firm of W. W. Phelps and Co., known elsewhere in the history as the literary firm. This subset of the partners is not really a separate firm, but is merely a "doing business as" manifestation of the larger firm. As mentioned in the main text of the history and expanded in the editor's footnote, other "doing business as" subsets of the united firm partners were formed to handle merchandising operations in Kirtland and Missouri under the names of Newel K. Whitney and Company, and Gilbert, Whitney and Co.[17]

B. H. Roberts himself seems to have been taken in by the organizational sleight of hand and to have missed part of the point of all these arrangements. He refers only to the joinder of certain merchandising people into a united firm with two branches. The literary firm, real estate transactions, and other operations were also part of this group's activities. Again, regardless of the number of business names used, there was still really only one firm, with the partners holding various assignments. The appearance to the world was intended to be different than the actual underlying structure. Notice that W. W. Phelps was part of the "literary firm" section of the united firm rather than the merchandising section, but as mentioned in the editor's note, nonetheless he was the one who drafted the necessary papers for the loan being sought. The editor assumes that the loan was only for the merchandising division of the firm, but the $15,000 loan was to be for the use of all partners or divisions of the partnership, with the "Newel K. Whitney & Co." section of the firm appointed to procure the loan under its adopted business name. As shown later in this chapter, the merchandising operations were required to use their profits and other resources to support the literary firm, showing the interdependence of the segments of the firm.

As we will see later, these subsets of the main firm were themselves called orders, so that we have orders within orders. The word "order" simply means any kind of business arrangement or organization to accomplish some purpose. See chapter 15 on tithing for another use of the word "order" in this same way.[18]

The editor's note also mentions the special agencies or powers of attorney to be used in conducting special business. That special business would probably be only those circumstances where the already organized subsets of the main firm were not suitable or sufficient to be used to handle a certain transaction. Agency law and partnership law go hand in hand, and this comment recognized that fact. Again the editor seems to miss the point that any and every kind of central church business handled by the partnership might employ the special agency procedure, not just the merchandising operation.

It should be emphasized again that this business unit that conducted business related to merchandising, care of the poor, purchasing of land, printing, borrowing money, etc., did so right after its organization under the terms of Section 82. We should therefore conclude that the organization formed and the other business steps taken were those intended by section 82.

Section 83, received during the first meetings of the church partnership, is an obvious extension of the previous directives on care of the poor, such as appear in Sections 42, 78, and 82. It was not the care of all people that was being discussed, but only the poor. Care of the poor was one of the major responsibilities of the new church partnership. Presumably this revelation was delivered in response to the specific questions it answers, the proper treatment of worthy widows and fatherless children. This shows one aspect of what the men in the meeting were concerned about, and their questions to the Lord. The responsibilities of families to provide for each other are stated to be essentially as they are today. Husbands and fathers are to provide a maintenance for their families. They are to assist their children to become self-supporting. Only if the father is unable to do so does the church have any responsibility.

The Lord's storehouse represents the welfare program of the church. It does not represent some all-inclusive communal economic system. It is for exceptions only, not the main-stream economic activity. Verse 3 of section 83 makes it clear that assistance by the welfare system depends on worthiness, but at the same time, church standing has no effect on property ownership. That was in every case handled according to the laws of the land, the only unusual feature being the large-scale movement of saints, coordinated and assisted by the united firm. Once the land was procured in the new location, the church had no further economic control over its ownership or use, or the use of its products.

There are a number of other events and transactions which contain information bearing directly on the personnel and the structure of the united order. Sections 92 and 96 are important because they reveal that two other men were later added to the nine named in Section 82, bringing the partnership total to eleven. The care with which these men were prepared and chosen indicates that this was no mass organization of all members, but a small group with a special mission. First let's look at Section 92, dated March 15, 1833:

> 1 Verily, thus sayeth the Lord, I give unto the united order, organized agreeable to the commandment previously given, a revelation and commandment concerning my servant Shederlaomach [Frederick G. Williams], that ye shall receive him into the order. What I say unto one I say unto all.
>
> 2 And again, I say unto you my servant Shederlaomach [Frederick G. Williams], you shall be a lively member in this order; and inasmuch as you are faithful in keeping all former commandments you shall be blessed forever. Amen.[19]

The new member of the order is Frederick G. Williams, a physician and land owner in the Kirtland area when converted to the gospel in 1830. In verse one, the phrase "organized agreeable to the commandment previously given" refers to the commandment given in section 82, and also implies approval by the Lord of the actions taken.

Notice that Frederick G. Williams was given a calling as a counselor to Joseph Smith in D&C 81:1, dated March 1832. Similarly, in D&C 90:6-7, dated March 8, 1833, Frederick G. Williams and Sidney Rigdon are made counselors to Joseph Smith and ordained. Revelations were received for both the special callings of Frederick G. Williams as counselor to the president (D&C 81; 90) and as partner in the firm (D&C 92), making it appear that those two positions were of equal importance, both being significant callings and not something which came to everyone. These revelations and events also indicate that being appointed to a spiritual calling did not automatically make him a member of the order, a "temporal" calling. Notice that although already serving as a counselor, Frederick G. Williams was not placed into the original Section 82 group. If he only needed to be a good member to join the united order, he would probably have been included. This strengthens the idea that only those with the right experience and attitude could be called to the heavy "temporal" responsibilities of the united order which had so much effect on the success of the gathering of the saints, and thus on spiritual matters.

Section 96, dated June 4, 1833, added John Johnson to the church partnership:

> 2 Therefore, let my servant Ahashdah [Newel K. Whitney] take charge of the place which is named among you, upon which I design to build mine holy house.
> 3 And again, let it be divided into lots, according to wisdom, for the benefit of those who seek inheritances, as it shall be determined in council among you.
> 4 Therefore, take heed that ye see to this matter, and that portion that is necessary to benefit mine order, for the purpose of bringing forth my word to the children of men.
> ....
> 6 And again, verily I say unto you, it is wisdom and expedient in me, that my servant Zombre [John Johnson] whose offering I have accepted, and whose prayers I have heard,
> ....
> 8 Verily I say unto you, it is expedient in me that he should become a member of the order, that he may assist in bringing forth my word unto the children of men.
> 9 Therefore ye shall ordain him unto this blessing, and he shall seek diligently to take away incumbrances that are upon the house named among you, that he may dwell therein. Even so. Amen.[20]

Table 4-1. Membership of the united order firm

Normal Name	Secret Name	Authorizing Revelation	First or Main Assignment, if known
Joseph Smith	Gazelam	D&C 82 Apr 26, 1832	
Oliver Cowdery	Olihah	"	
Martin Harris	Mahemson	"	literary firm
Sidney Rigdon	Pelagoram	"	
Newel K. Whitney	Ahashdah	"	merchandising
Edward Partridge	Alam	"	land transactions
William W. Phelps	Shalemanasseh	"	literary firm
John Whitmer	Horah	"	literary firm
A. S. Gilbert	Mahalaleel	"	merchandising
F. G. Williams	Shederlaomach	D&C 92 Mar 15, 1833	literary firm
John Johnson	Zombre	D&C 96 Jun 4, 1833	

The term "inheritances" used in verse 3 had no legal effect on the way one acquired or used land.[21] Land transactions were perfectly normal. However, the term did emphasize a general spiritual principle which was to support the gathering of the saints. Apparently, John Johnson's business assignment or "stewardship" in the church partnership would have to do with printing church materials (see verse 8). In verse 9, he is also to raise funds through some process to pay for the house he was to use.

John Johnson, of Hiram, Ohio, was baptized by Joseph Smith about 1831 at the age of 52. He was known to the Prophet as Father Johnson and had housed Joseph and his family while he translated a portion of the Bible. Father Johnson apparently owned a large plot of farm land.

All the participants in the united order have now been discussed. A summary of the firm's membership is contained in Table 4-1.

An entry dated June 26, 1833, at Kirtland, Ohio, gives several items of information relating to the structure and transactions of the united firm:

> ... we wrote to Brother W. W. Phelps, and others in Zion from Kirtland, as follows: [Sidney Rigdon actually penned the letter]
>
> Brethren: -
> .... With regard to the copies of the Book of Mormon, which are in the hands of Brother Burkett, we say to you, get them from Brother Burkett, and give him a receipt for them in the name of the literary firm.
> .... Concerning Bishops, we recommend the following:
> Let Brother Isaac Morley be ordained second Bishop in Zion, and let Brother John Corrill be ordained third.

> Let Brother Edward Partridge choose as counselors in their place, Brother Parley P. Pratt and Brother Titus Billings, ordaining Brother Billings to the High Priesthood.
>
> .... Zombre [John Johnson] has been received as a member of the firm, by commandment, and has just come to Kirtland to live; as soon as we get a power of attorney signed agreeably to law, for Alam [Edward Partridge] we will forward it to him, and will immediately expect one from that part of the firm to Ahashdah [Newel K. Whitney], signed in the same manner. We would again say to Alam [Edward Partridge], be sure to get a form according to law for securing a gift. We have found by examining the law, that a gift cannot be retained without this.
>
> ..... You will remember that the power of agency must be signed by the wives as well as the husbands, and the wives must be examined in the matter separate and apart from the husbands, the same as signing a deed, and a specification to that effect inserted at the bottom, by the justice before whom such acknowledgement is made, otherwise the power of attorney will be of none effect.[22]

The literary firm mentioned in the beginning of the June 25 letter is presumably the same as that organized at the May 1, 1832 meeting of the united order, and consisted of W. W. Phelps, Oliver Cowdery, and John Whitmer. As was made clear in that meeting, the men were not really a firm separate from the united firm, but only gave that appearance to the world. Here the "literary firm" is acknowledging receipt of books, and presumably accepting the obligation to pay for them. In this case, the Kirtland branch instructed its agents in the Missouri branch as to which subunit name to use. This shows that the true underlying organization was kept as much a secret from the church members as it was from any other creditors.[23] This begins to explain the use of secret names in revelations, letters, and other church documents. These church members could raise as much havoc with the economic arrangements of the united firm as could any distant creditors, if they realized that technically they could collect from any of several "firms" or manifestations of the church partnership, and not just the single one with which they transacted business. And of course if any of the members knew, then it would not be long until the more distant creditors heard of it.[24]

The apparent secrecy from everyone outside the firm, including all church members, would argue very strongly that the order was in fact a small and elite business unit rather than a "consumer level" economic/social organization. If no ordinary person in the church even knew about it, it would be rather hard for such people to ever attempt to use it or live it.

That contemporary secrecy even from church members may also account for part of the misunderstanding of the "united order" issue today. Joseph did not put his history together until after the saints had made the great move to Missouri and the secrecy requirements were past. It is therefore very possible that no one in his generation had a correct view of what had transpired, except the very few involved, and they may have agreed to never talk about it. That would have helped protect the involved brethren from creditors in and out of the church, as when in the early Nauvoo period, church partnership debts were disavowed. (See chapter 10 for more on old debts.)

These multiple manifestations of the single firm served the useful purpose of increasing the borrowing power of the church partnership. Multiple loans could be procured under different names, each group apparently having only one loan to repay. This would make their "credit rating" look better to bankers than one firm with many large loans.

However, there was no deception involved. The men who signed for the loan were in fact the ones responsible for its repayment, although they might receive help from their colleagues. The main advantage of such an arrangement was that money lenders would look only to those few men for repayment and would not bother the others in their separate activities. If a creditor knew of the underlying arrangement, he could look to any of the various "firms" for payment of his claim.

The partners could still rely on each other for assistance in time of need, but by keeping that knowledge of the true structure a secret from creditors, the total borrowing power was maximized. This is similar to families of corporations today where the corporate device provides both the overall stability and the explicit liability control that the united firm legally accomplished by a different mechanism.

The paragraph discussing John Johnson is full of interesting and useful information. Here John was "received as a member of the firm, by commandment." This letter is dated only three weeks after the revelation of Section 96. The word "commandment" must refer to Section 96, and the word "firm" must refer to "the order" mentioned in that section. Just a few lines later, Joseph discussed getting a document "from that part of the firm," the branch in Missouri. These references make it clear that the central church partnership or firm, having branches in Missouri and Ohio, and the united order spoken of in various sections, were one and the same thing.[25]

The identification of Alam as Edward Partridge is also valuable. Somehow that identification has not made its way into the list of names in section 82. Knowing that Bishop Partridge was one of the four previously unidentified partners makes it likely that the remaining secret names were those of his counselors or close associates. One might have guessed anyway because Newel K. Whitney, a firm member, was the Bishop in the Kirtland area, making it likely that the Bishop in the Missouri area was also a member. Incidentally, Newel K. Whitney's prior experience as an Indian trader in Michigan made him a good choice to handle temporal affairs including merchandising.

W. W. Phelps and John Whitmer were at the organization meeting and became members of the "literary firm" division of the united firm. That made them rather likely candidates for two of the three remaining code names. The last name was Algernon Sidney Gilbert, who had been a successful merchant in Painesville, Ohio, and was obviously a good man for the merchandising operation. John Corrill and Isaac Morley, counselors to Bishop Partridge, almost certainly had close associations with the firm.

It is also worth noting that the five men whose real names are given in section 82 were all living in the Kirtland area at the time, and presumably were the entire Kirtland branch of the firm. It may well have been necessary to protect the identity of the men in Missouri for a longer time than those in Kirtland, and that is why their names do not appear in a de-coded form in any place. The mobbers of Missouri would surely have been even more threatening to those men assisting the gathering if they knew of their association with the firm. There may have been other reasons as well.

The power of attorney document is of interest here. Adding a new partner to a firm technically amounts to a kind of reorganization. Apparently on the occasion of the addition of John Johnson to the firm, each branch of the firm completely re-executed a delegation of authority or power of attorney, and sent it to the other branch, ensuring that, by the law of the land, each branch could represent the other in any business matter that came up. The slow communications would probably often require that one branch act for the other without time for consultation or transmission of documents.

The next paragraph also relates the law of agency and partnerships to the church firm, on the topic of a wife's potential interest in her husband's land transactions. The usual rule is that general partners have unlimited personal liability in their business dealings. When a man is married there is always the question as to what property he owns that may be used as security or sold for debts. The question is especially important in real estate transactions because of the concept of dower whereby a wife may often claim an interest in any land her husband may have had title to at any time. Unless that dower interest is clearly removed, the title to the land is clouded and any transactions with the land are inhibited because of the fear of a later claim by the wife to a portion of the land. Presumably this is the concern behind the careful instructions to the Missouri brethren to make sure all the procedures are adhered to as far a securing a good release by the wives of any interests in any land that may be temporarily held by any of the partners.

The admonition "we would say again to Alam, be sure to get a form according to law for securing a gift," is also significant. The Kirtland brethren stress it "again," as the Lord does in the scriptures,[26] for a very practical reason. Gifts, that is property which is donated (or "consecrated" which means the same thing), require proper documentation to avoid the bad effects of any later "second thoughts" on the part of the donor. Attempts to repossess property could disrupt the administration of land and other property held by the church, and cripple the gathering process.

There is also another interesting item in this letter. Edward Partridge (Alam) is addressed both in his public, spiritual capacity as Bishop, and in his secretive and temporal capacity as a member of the united order firm. As Bishop, and using his normal name, he is directed to ordain other Bishops and select new counselors, and in the next quotation below, he and the other Bishops are to "see to the poor, according to the laws of the church." As Alam, his code name, he is directed to perform certain business functions concerning powers of attorney and deeds of gift, that are not part of his role as bishop, but relate to his partnership affiliation.

In this letter, the church roles of the various brethren, e.g. Edward Partridge, are "in the clear", but the business roles are discussed in code.[27] This argues that the "order" was not intended to be part of the main body of the church but was only a small part. The whole body could not function in code: it would be too clumsy. Note that secret names are used only in connection with the "firm."

This shows that the secret names were related only to special functions of a small group and there was no need for secrecy in the normal ecclesiastical activities carried on concurrently. Using secrecy makes sense in the limited business context described so far, but would be unworkable and pointless if the united order idea was supposed to mean that whole communities of saints were secretly involved in some socialist system.

Another letter written at the same time adds further to our understanding of the nature of the united order:

> Items of Instruction Concerning
> the Consecration of Property
>
> Brother Edward Partridge:
> ....ANSWERS TO QUERIES TO BROTHER PHELP'S LETTER OF JUNE 4TH.
>
> First, in relation to the poor: when the bishops are appointed according to our recommendation, it will devolve upon them to see to the poor, according to the laws of the church.
>
> .... As to Shederloamach [F. G. Williams], all members of the united firm are considered one. The order of the literary firm is a matter of stewardship, which is of the greatest importance; and the mercantile God commanded to be devoted to the support thereof, and God will bring every transgression unto judgement.[28]

The first paragraph of the quotation relates to the instructions to bishops in the preceeding quotation. Here we can see that the "law of the church" or "law of the Lord" had a welfare clause, but not a socialism clause. The poor are to be cared for, but no other economic requirements are laid down for the bishops to administer.

The second paragraph is of greatest interest here. Joseph makes it clear that regardless of a man's assignment or "stewardship" in the united firm, they are all partners on the same level, or "one," as he says. The subsets of partners such as the literary division or group (doing business as W. W. Phelps and Co.), and the mercantile division or group (doing business under two different names) hold those positions by assignment and are to support each other. In this case, the mercantile groups and their profits are to provide funding for the efforts of the printing group. This confirms the idea that the "oneness" language that appears in the scriptures concerning the united firm or united order, is directed at a business group which would fail miserably in its goals without that oneness of purpose and sharing of resources.

From the phrase "the order of the literary firm is a matter of stewardship" we learn that there is such a thing as an order within an order, the literary firm within the united firm. If we can learn about the part, the order within an order, we will probably learn much about the whole. The limited, business nature of the literary firm is fairly easy to see and understand. By adding several of these smaller "orders" together, we get the larger "order." Some of the other parts were the mercantile establishment, the real estate development section, the temple building section, etc. Each has a fairly narrow, business nature, related to the needs and activities of the central church.

Other organizational concepts are shown by the following meeting minutes:

> September 11 [1833]. - The following members, residing in Kirtland, viz.: F. G. Williams, Sidney Rigdon, N. K. Whitney, with myself, and

Oliver Cowdery, delegate to represent the residue of the members in Independence, Missouri, met in council, to consider the expediency of establishing a printing press in Kirtland, when it was:

> Resolved, unanimously, that a press be established, and conducted under the firm name of F. G. Williams & Co.
> Resolved, that the above firm publish a paper, as soon as arrangements can be made, entitled the *Latter-day Saints' Messenger and Advocate.*
> Resolved, also, that the *Evening and Morning Star,* formerly published in Jackson county, Missouri, by the firm of F. G. Williams & Co., to be conducted by Oliver Cowdery, one of the members of the firm, until it is transferred to its former location.[29]

This is an account of a united order firm meeting consisting of five of the Kirtland members, with Oliver Cowdery also assigned to act as a delegate on behalf of the four or five members in Missouri. Oliver Cowdery probably had just returned from a trip to Missouri. At this point there were eleven members of the firm. A partnership is essentially a group of people who have agreed to give and accept powers of agency among themselves. Here Oliver Cowdery is acting in the role of agent or delegate for the Missouri brethren.

F. G. Williams and Company was to be the "doing business as" name for this particular manifestation of the united order firm; it was to publish the new paper called the *Latter-day Saints' Messenger and Advocate.* F. G. Williams & Company was also the name used in Missouri for publishing another paper, the *Evening and Morning Star.* The *Star* was transferred temporarily to Oliver Cowdery's care. Since both firms called F. G. Williams & Co., and both papers, were really under a single ownership and management, the united order firm, it was a simple matter to transfer a portion to Oliver Cowdery, one of the general partners in the firm. There was no real change in ownership, merely a change in partnership assignment or "stewardship."

The following entry shows the close interplay between the needs of the church and the actions of the united order firm, as well as some of the organizational niceties employed in those actions.

> [To pay for the prosecution of law suits associated with the Saints' first losses from the actions of Missouri mobs,] Brothers Phelps and Partridge gave their note of one thousand dollars, endorsed by Gilbert & Whitney.[30]

In this transaction, Phelps and Partridge, as leading residents of Jackson County, probably appeared to the mobbers to be signing the notes in their individual capacities. To make the note seem more reliable, redeemable, and negotiable, the extra signature of a recognized economic unit, Gilbert and Whitney, was added. Of course, unknown to the mobbers, the fact was that all the signers were part of the united order firm, and it was because of that role that they were involved at all.

Who actually signed for Gilbert and Whitney is not clear. For the best public relations results, it should have been signed by a third person, Sidney Gilbert. But technically it could have been signed by either Phelps or Partridge, acting as general partners of the firm. It would be assumed merely that Gilbert and Whitney had agreed in this instance to act as guarantors of the note, possibly for a fee.

This chapter has mapped out some of the basic elements of the united order structure. The next chapter will focus on the transactions of the united order firm.

Chapter 4 Notes

1. HC 1:196n.

2. HC 2:174.

3. HC 2:64.

4. D&C 78.

5. Many, if not most, business organizations specify the intended term of existence. In this case, it is to be perpetual.

6. HC 1:266-7.

7. D&C 82.

8. See HC 1:365 where a footnote by the editor uses the term "order of Enoch." The history and its footnotes are the product of B. H. Robert's editorial labors in the early 1900's.

9. David J. Whittaker, "Substituted Names in the Published Revelations of Joseph Smith," *BYU Studies* 23 (Winter 1983):103-112. Sidney Gilbert's full name was Algernon Sidney Gilbert, but his first name, Algernon, was rarely used.

10. See footnote 12.

11. See chapter 1 footnote 2 and related text concerning corporations.

12. See D&C 104:81 and H.C. 2:492 for other references to these financial institutions. One might wonder why the Lord would choose to use a derogatory term in referring to the banking and lending industry when the capital they could supply was apparently so important to the success of the migration plans. Perhaps an explanation can be taken from D&C 64:28 where the Lord had earlier told the brethren that they should not fear negotiating for loans because they were on the Lord's errand and he could "take when he please, and pay as seemeth him good." This planned exploitation of money interests might be easier to justify and accept if the lenders are labeled as sinners, their punishment being to assist the gathering with their means. See also Luke 16:9, 11, 13; Matthew 6:24; Bible Dictionary "mammon."

13. HC 1:269-70. D&C 83. April 30, 1832. Independence, Mo.

14. HC 1:270. April 26, 1832. Independence, Mo.

15. HC 1:269. April 27, 1832.

16. For example, see JD 2:298, where Brigham Young quotes Joseph Smith as saying "I don't want a dime of their money," concerning the 1838 "excess property" clause of section 119.

17. Supplies such as nails, seed, plows, axes, shovels, food, etc., were needed until production started. The migrating saints could not bring it all with them in just the right quantities. A transportation and trading group was needed to supply them. They were to pay for it of course, but

they needed a service provided by friends who would not try to take advantage of them in their weakness. D&C 57:8.

This merchandising operation was somewhat like the later Zion's Cooperative Mercantile Institution (ZCMI), organized in Utah in 1869, in the sense that it was created to serve the saints and protect them from risks and costs of doing business with their enemies. However, it was operated as a normal business and had none of the many layers of doctrinal and political overtones, including required economic cohesiveness, that were presented to support the later ZCMI project. *Building the City of God,* p. 91.

18. See HC 5:327-333, April 6, 1843, and comments in chapter 15 where an "order" was to be created to collect tithing.

19. D&C 92. March 15, 1833. Kirtland, Ohio.

20. D&C 96:2-5, 6, 8-9. June 4, 1833. Kirtland, Ohio. Verses 2 through 4 of section 96 speak of a parcel of land in Kirtland which was to be used for the temple site and a printing shop, with the remainder to be used or sold as residential lots. Some of this property was probably that distributed to firm members as directed in section 104. In the comment at HC 2:295-296, Joseph was presumably selling one of these very lots.

21. See 1 Ne. 13:15 where it is foretold that the gentiles will get inheritances (be permanently established) on the American continent. The word as used there has a long-term spiritual significance, but does not imply any particular economic doctrines.

22. HC 1:362-364. June 26, 1833. Joseph Smith. Kirtland, Ohio.

23. Even Brigham Young probably did not know of it until it had ceased to operate. Note the later Missouri acceptance of the "literary firm." HC 2:482-483, April 1837. This indicates that they still may not have known of the subsidiary nature of that organization.

24. It should be noted that today's church business structure is probably much like that of Joseph Smith's united order in that there is a parent organization (Corporation of the President) with many subsidiaries and "doing business as" manifestations to the world. Joseph Smith's united order was concerned with such things as publishing, real estate, and retail operations, and the same is true today. Bonneville International, ZCMI, *Deseret News,* Beneficial Life, Zion's Bank, Deseret Industries, Beehive Clothing Mills, Deseret Book, and Brigham Young University are a few of the "doing business as" names for past or present church associated business units. There are surely many other operating entities with similar ties with the church. It may be that the effectiveness of some would be diminished if church involvement were widely publicized.

There are many other complicated organizations in existence today that are somewhat analogous to the church's business organization. One type is the international conglomerate which may control widely dissimilar operating units such as life insurance, bakery, and telephone component firms.

The church finance and business structure today has some of the same incentives to limit the flow of confidential information to outsiders as did the united order firm of Joseph Smith's day. Popular magazines and scholarly books have commented on that tendency to secrecy. There is no intention to deceive or defraud anyone, but merely a desire to avoid giving the church's enemies the power to weaken the church's efforts that detailed financial information might provide.

The church is certainly not unique in this. It is common for most business and governmental units to maintain some level of confidentiality or secrecy to protect themselves from competitors and enemies. There are also many laws in existence concerning and affecting secrets. They may serve to either protect, require, discourage, or control various kinds of secrets and their use. Trade secret laws, official or government secrets laws, freedom of information laws, and stock market insider trading laws are examples of these.

25. The phrase "received as a member of the firm, by commandment," ties together the term "order," used in the commandment, D&C 96:8, with the term "the firm," by which the "united order" (D&C 92:1; 104:1, 47, 48, 53) or "order" (D&C 78:4; 82:20; 92:1, 2; 96:8; 104:1, 21, 36, 53) was known to the eleven or twelve men involved.

Note that sometimes it is "a" united order or "an" order (D&C 78:4; 82:20; 104:1, 47, 53), and sometimes "the" united order or order (D&C 92:1; 96:8; 104:1, 21, 36, 48).

26. See D&C 42:30, 32; 51:5-6.

27. See also D&C 84:112, where N. K. Whitney's name is used "in the clear," in referencing a non-order function - care of the poor. Compare with D&C 96:2 where Whitney's code name is used in reference to a land deal, an "order" function. D&C 82:11 is the location of the original use of Whitney's code name.

Some recently published sources offer some further insights. In a letter from Joseph Smith, dated March 30, 1834, at Kirtland, "To Edward [Edward Partridge], Williams [William W. Phelps] and others of the firm," a number of interesting transactions and relationships are mentioned. The "firm," of course, is the united order. A New York debt is mentioned related to Zion; the Missouri brethren have placed their reliance on the Kirtland brethren for money; the sale of firm owned lands to members is recommended to obtain money for a law suit; a clarification is made that a press in Missouri is "ours" not "yours." Only first names are used throughout, perhaps as an attempt at maintaining secrecy, and mention is made that many things cannot be communicated by letter. Dean C Jessee, ed., *The Personal Writings of Joseph Smith* (Deseret Book: SLC, Utah. 1984) p. 314.

An earlier letter dated December 10, 1833, was addressed to "Beloved brethren; E. Partridge, W. W. Phelps, J. Whitmer, A. S. Gilbert, J. Carrel, I. Morley, and all the saints whom it may concern." Thus the letter was essentially to the same men, and was also directed in a public way to all the saints in Missouri. In it, the full names are used, and no mention is made of the firm. However, the brethren are counseled that "it is better that you should die in the eyes of God, than that you should give up the Land of Zion, the inheritances which you have purchased with your monies," and that "I would advise to give deeds as far as the brethren have legal and just claims for them and then let every man answer to God for the disposal of them." This makes it clear that there was nothing unusual about the purchase and sale of land and the related handling of deeds.

Joseph also said that although the Lord did express displeasure with some behavior of the Saints, the Lord refused to say why the Saints were ejected from Missouri or when they would be able to return. There was no hint that a failure to observe some communal mechanism was any part of the reason for the saints being forced to leave. *Personal Writings,* p. 308-309.

Pres. J. Reuben Clark, Jr., has stated flatly that the single deed often mentioned as an example of communal transactions, was not in accordance with gospel principles. See October 3, 1942 address quoted in note 1 of chapter 1. President Clark also made other strong statements that support the thesis of this book. See note 1 of chapter 1 for quotations from later article "The United Order ....," especially the following: "The Church never was, and under existing commandments never will be, a communal society, under the directions thus far given by the Lord. The United Order was not communal nor communistic. It was completely and intensely individualistic ...."

Apparently, President Clark studied united order history sufficiently to satisfy himself on related questions, but devoted only a small amount of time to developing an historical argument to buttress his doctrinal conclusions. A more full treatment of the subject by such a qualified person would have been most interesting.

A legacy from the Brigham Young period is the tendency to assign the cause of the expulsion from Missouri to a failure to
"live the united order." It assumes a definition of the united order and its history from the Brigham Young period which bears little relation to the practices or beliefs of Joseph Smith's day. There is a possibility that a general lack of righteousness kept the Lord from unsheathing his sword on behalf of the Saints, but that is a far different thing than punishing them for failure to live a specific commandment.

There is indeed an apparent inconsistency between the teachings and practices of Brigham Young and those of Joseph Smith. Rather than ignore the difference or try to reconcile the irreconcilable (at the level of first impression), it is more fruitful to admit the inconsistency and go to another level to
seek resolution.

28. HC 1:364-365. June 25, 1833.

29. HC 1:409. September 11, 1833.

30. HC 1:425. October 1833.

CHAPTER 5

Transactions of the First United Order Firm.

The term "united order" is closely connected in the minds of many with the term "consecration." Historical materials from the Joseph Smith era do in fact show that the two concepts are associated, and that a large portion of the united order transactions involved an aspect of "consecration." However, the meanings and interrelationships of the two terms as used during Joseph Smith's life are substantially different than commonly accepted today. In order to understand what the term consecration meant during Joseph Smith's time and its link with the united order, we must examine several items from the history and scriptures, and synthesize a definition.

An early comment on the Missouri "consecration" land transactions appears in a letter from Joseph Smith to W. W. Phelps, dated November 27, 1832 at Kirtland, a portion of which was canonized as section 85:

> ... While I dictate this letter, I fancy to myself that you are saying or thinking something similar to these words:
> -- "My God, great and mighty art Thou, therefore show unto Thy servant what shall become of those who are essaying to come up unto Zion, in order to keep the commandments of God, and yet receive not their inheritance by consecrations, by order of deed from the Bishop, the man that God has appointed in a legal way, agreeably to the law given to organize and regulate the Church, and all the affairs of the same."

Brother William, in the love of God, having the most implicit confidence in you as a man of God, having obtained this confidence by a vision of heaven, therefore I will proceed to unfold to you some of the feelings of my heart, and to answer the question.

Firstly, it is the duty ....." [and here follows section 85].

1 It is the duty of the Lord's clerk, whom he has appointed, to keep a history, and a general church record of all things that transpire in Zion, and of all those who consecrate properties, and receive inheritances legally from the bishop;

2 And also their manner of life, their faith, and works; and also of the apostates who apostatize after receiving their inheritances.

3 It is contrary to the will and commandment of God that those who receive not their inheritance by consecration, agreeable to his law, which he has given, that he may tithe his people, to prepare them against the day of vengeance and burning, should have their names enrolled with the people of God.

4 Neither is their genealogy to be kept, or to be had where it may be found on any of the records or history of the Church.

....

7 And it shall come to pass that I, the Lord God, will send one mighty and strong, ... to set in order the house of God, and to arrange by lot the inheritances of the saints whose names are found ... enrolled in the book of the law of God.

8 While that man, who was called of God and appointed, that putteth forth his hand to steady the ark of God, shall fall by the shaft of death, like as a tree that is smitten by the vivid shaft of lightning.

9 And all they who are not found written in the book of remembrance shall find none inheritance in that day.

....

11 And they who are of the High Priesthood, whose names are not found written in the book of the law, or that are found to have apostatized, or to have been cut off from the church, as well as the lesser priesthood, or the members, in that day shall not find an inheritance among the saints of the Most High;[1]

The next item is a letter dated June 25, 1833, from Joseph Smith to Edward Partridge:

> Items of instruction concerning the consecration of property.
>
> Brother Edward Partridge:
> Sir: I proceed to answer your questions, concerning the consecration of property: -
> First, it is not right to condescend to very great particulars in taking inventories. The fact is this, a man is bound by the law of the Church, to consecrate to the Bishop, before he can be considered a legal heir to the kingdom of Zion; and this, too, without constraint; and unless he does this, he cannot be acknowledged before the Lord on the Church Book. Therefore, to condescend to particulars, I will tell you that every man must be his own judge how much he should receive and how much he should suffer to remain in the hands of the Bishop. I speak of those who consecrate more than they need for the support of themselves and their families.
> The matter of consecration must be done by the mutual consent of both parties; for to give the Bishop power to say how much every man shall have, and he be obliged to comply with the Bishop's judgement, is giving to the Bishop more power than a king has; and upon the other hand, to let every man say how much he needs, and the Bishop be obliged to comply with his judgement, is to throw Zion into confusion, and make a slave of the Bishop. The fact is, there must be a balance or equilibrium of power, between the Bishop and the people, and thus harmony and good will may be preserved among you.
> Therefore, those persons consecrating property to the Bishop in Zion, and then receiving an inheritance back, must reasonably show to the bishop that they need as much as they claim. But in case the two parties cannot come to a mutual agreement, the Bishop is to have nothing to do about receiving such consecrations; and the case must be laid before a council of twelve High Priests, the Bishop not being one of the council, but he is to lay the case before them.
> Say to Brother Gilbert that we have no means in our power to assist him in a pecuniary way, as we know not the hour when we shall be sued for debts which we have contracted ourselves in New York. Say to him that he must exert himself to the utmost to obtain means himself, to replenish his store, for it must be replenished, and it is his duty to attend to it.[2]

A little later, in July 1833, a letter or circular came from the brethren in Missouri, "The Elders Stationed in Zion," back to the brethren in the east, instructing them on how to prepare for a trip to Missouri and the procurement of land:

.... Members of the Church have, or will have, "deeds" [to their lands] in their own name.

One Bates, from New London, Ohio, -- who subscribed fifty dollars for the purpose of purchasing lands, and the necessaries for the saints -- after his arrival here, sued (Bishop) Edward Partridge, and obtained a judgement for the same. Bates shortly after denied the faith, and ran away on Sunday, leaving debts unpaid. ... No man that has consecrated property to the Lord, for the benefit of the poor and needy, by a deed of gift according to the laws of the land, has thought of suing for it, any more than the men of the world, who give, or donate to build meeting houses, and colleges; or send missionaries to India or the Cape of Good Hope....

One object in writing this epistle is, to give some instructions to those who come up to the land of Zion. Through a mistaken idea many of the brethren abroad, that had property, have given some away, and sacrificed some, they hardly knew how. This is not right nor according to the commandments. We would advise in the first place, that every disciple, if in his power, pay his just debts so as to owe no man, and then if he has any property left, let him be careful of it; and he can help the poor, by consecrating some for their inheritances; for as yet, there has not been enough consecrated to plant the poor in inheritances, according to the regulation of the Church and the desire of the faithful.

This might have been done, had such as had property been prudent. It seems as though a notion was prevalent in Babylon, that the Church of Christ was a common stock concern. This ought not so to be, for it is not the case. When a disciple comes to Zion for an inheritance, it is his duty, if he has anything to consecrate to the Lord for the benefit of the poor and needy, or to purchase lands, to consecrate it according to the law of the Lord, and also according to the law of the land, ...

Again, while in the world, it is not the duty of a disciple to exhaust all his means in bringing the poor to Zion; and this because if all should do so, there would be nothing to put in the storehouse in Zion for the purpose which the Lord has commanded.

Do not think, brethren, by this, that we would advise or direct that the poor be neglected in the least; ....

The welfare of the poor has always a place in our hearts; .... To see numbers of disciples come to this land, destitute of means to procure an inheritance, and much less the necessaries of life, awakens a sympathy in our bosoms of no ordinary feeling.... For the disciples to suppose that they can come to this land without ought to eat, or to drink, or to wear, or anything to purchase these necessaries with, is a vain thought.

... To suppose we can take possession of this country without making regular purchases of the same, according to the laws of our nation, would be reproaching this great republic....

...All the tithes cannot be gathered into the storehouse of the Lord, that the windows of heaven may be opened, and a blessing be poured that there is not room enough to contain it, if all the means of the saints are exhausted, before they reach the place where they can have the privilege of so doing....

The disciples of Christ, blessed with immediate revelations from Him, should be wise and not take the way of the world, nor build air castles, but consider that when they have been gathered to Zion, means will be needed to purchase their inheritances, and means will be needed to purchase food and raiment for at least one year; or at any rate, food; and where disciples, or churches, are blessed with means to do as much as this, they would be better off in Zion than in the world ....

The Lord says, "And now, verily I say unto you, that as every Elder in this part of the vineyard, (the East) must give an account of his stewardship unto the Bishop in this part of the vineyard, a certificate from the judge or Bishop in this part of the vineyard, unto the Bishop in Zion, rendereth every man acceptable, and answereth all things for an inheritance, and to be received as a wise steward, and as a faithful laborer; otherwise he shall not be accepted of the Bishop in Zion....

We hope brethren, that you will be particular to teach the disciples abroad prudence and economy in all things. Teach them in plainness, that without regular recommends, they cannot be received in fellowship with the Church in Zion, until they have proven themselves worthy by their godly walk. And those who are recommended by you, we expect will be such as are personally known to you to be disciples indeed, and worthy of the confidence of all saints.

Viewing the quotation relative to your obtaining a certificate from the Bishop in the East concerning your worthiness, you cannot blame us brethren if we are strict on this point. It may be understood, therefore, by our brethren, the Elders, who come from the East and do not bring a regular certificate showing that their labors have been accepted there, that they cannot be accepted in Zion....

Our brethren who labor in the churches a distance to the west of the residence of the Bishop in the East, who do not render their accounts to him, should be particular to bring recommends from the churches in which they do labor, and present them with the accounts of their labors to the Bishop immediately after their arrival here. And those Elders who labor continually in preaching the Gospel to the world, should also be particular to render their account of the same, that they may show themselves approved in all things, and be known to be worthy of the high office in which they stand in the Church of Christ.[3]

With these three documents before us, perhaps we can begin to piece together what was in the minds of those sending and receiving the messages concerning land transactions. The third item, the circular letter from the Missouri brethren, is the most plain and practical in its approach. Starting there and working back to the more vague and general earlier documents should allow us to understand all three. Materials in other chapters will confirm and expand the definitions assembled here.

Let us start with an overview so perhaps we can understand what was happening without getting tangled up in insignificant details or lost in obscure reasoning. The Lord stated several times,[4] and Joseph repeated,[5] that the saints as a group controlled enough of the world's land, goods and moneys to enable all of them to complete the migration to Missouri. The purpose of the sharing that was suggested was to allow those with more to help those with less complete the move. It was not to create a series of small, static, inward-turning communities such as the Hutterites,[6] Mennonites, or other such groups, but rather to get the big job done of moving thousands of people to a frontier location with the minimum of trouble and suffering.

That is the theme of this letter. The lamentation that "for as yet, there has not been enough consecrated to plant the poor in inheritances," would not have been true "had such as had property been prudent."

More specifically, this letter makes it perfectly clear that there is no magic about the migration process, however one might be lifted above the mundane by the motivating and inspiring language of the scriptures. One is expected to bring enough money to buy land and other provisions for himself and his family - "means will be needed to purchase their inheritances, and means will be needed to purchase food and raiment for at least one year." He should donate to assist others in doing the same, where possible. He is not to waste his land or money in hopes that another will provide for him there. The comment "he can help the poor, by consecrating some for their inheritances," refers to a donation for the benefit of the poor. The poor should not to come until the rich have prepared the way for them. To "procure an inheritance" means to buy some land to live on. Deeds were to be given for the lands so purchased. One cannot pay tithing in Missouri to be used to help others, if one has no money when he reaches Zion. One cannot purchase land from the government or private owners if one has no money.

Here is a clear case where the general language of the scriptures is tied to the specific, common sense processes really intended. Probably the most verbose example is the following sentence from the letter just quoted:

> When a disciple comes to Zion for an inheritance, it is his duty, if he has anything to consecrate to the Lord for the benefit of the poor and needy, or to purchase lands, to consecrate it according

to the law of the Lord, and also according to the law of the land.

This sentence is "scriptureze" for saying simply that every man should pay for the land he gets, and that he will in turn receive the title for the land in the normal way and with the normal rights of ownership. Other similar euphemisms appear throughout, but the context makes clear the real meaning intended. The term "consecration" in this context simply means to use your money to further the gathering by buying land and provisions for yourself and perhaps helping someone else, if possible. The land is consecrated or dedicated to the Lord in the sense that it is to be used by the owning individuals to further His programs, in this case, the gathering.

Another important and very practical topic covered is that of recommends.[7] A recommend seems to have served several purposes. It was a mechanism used as a security measure to keep nonmembers and apostates from taking advantage of the preparations of the saints. Cheap land and a planned development effort would appeal to many people besides the saints. Even if such people paid cash they would be absorbing administrative efforts and land space intended to be reserved for the saints, and might cause trouble later if allowed to slip in among the faithful. After buying up land in the midst of the saints at low prices, they might wait a short time until land values had gone up significantly through the saints' labors in cultivating the place, and then sell to other outsiders at a substantial profit. The brethren did not want land speculation to interfere with the gathering.

The recommend probably also served the purpose of a statement showing the past contributions, both financial and spiritual, which would entitle the member to certain credit or consideration in his negotiations with the Bishop for land. And last but not least, it probably served as a membership record showing what priesthood one might hold and positions in which one might be qualified to serve. There was no temple at the time in either Kirtland or Missouri, so it could not have served the purpose of a temple recommend.

The Bates episode illustrates several things. Apparently he donated money in Kirtland to be used in Missouri, and then upon arrival in Missouri changed his mind. His action to recover his money shows the need for the "deed of gift" to make such contributions nonrefundable. If the money had already been spent on lands (and could not be reclaimed from the government), the bishop might be financially embarrassed by a law suit such as this. If this practice became common it could be a great blow to any attempt at planning and budgeting for the whole migration operation.[8]

It is interesting that the word "deeds" is enclosed in quotes in the first line of text quoted from the July 1833 letter. Without seeing the original document itself, it cannot be known for certain, but it is quite possible that the editor of the history placed those quotes there, just as the bracketed phrase "[to their lands]" was presumably inserted by him, for the purpose of indicating, consistent with the editor's theory, that the deeds were not in fact ordinary deeds, but some unique church-invented document. However, there is little to support such a theory. Joseph Smith specifically directed that ordinary deeds be given, and later events show that such deeds were given.[9]

Having examined the third document, we can now move back to the second document, the letter from Joseph Smith to Bishop Partridge. The consecration transactions discussed in that document were simply the same land purchase transactions discussed in the third document, with the price and amount of land set to some extent by the resources and needs of the buyer. In the June 25 letter, if in most cases the word "much" were followed by the word "land," then the meaning would be clearer, and would reflect the real intent of the instructions. For example, "those persons consecrating property to the Bishop in Zion, and then receiving an inheritance back, must reasonably show to the bishop that they need as much [land] as they claim." Other phrases would read similarly: "say how much [land] every man shall have;" "say how much [land] he needs." These excerpts show that there was a bargain made very much in the normal way - so much money or goods in return for so much land, something (hopefully) from the member in return for land from the Bishop. The real question was how to balance the "sale" based on all the factors - the need for others for land, the means that the member had, etc.

The purpose of the inventory was not to allow exercise of extensive economic control over individuals and communities, but merely to establish one's ability to pay for land. For that purpose, only a rough idea of a person's wealth and possessions was necessary for the administrative procedure. The real issue here, and Joseph's concern, is how much land individuals were to get in Missouri. The bishop was really combating the freeloaders - the people who wished to get land for free, or for an unfairly low price. The worst case would be non-member free-loaders. The requirement to "consecrate" meant mostly that the people who got land should pay for it if at all possible. That was the reason for the inventory and the recommends - to see if people were good church members, and if they had anything to pay for the land they received. Missionary work or other service might also qualify one to receive land, and this could be indicated in recommends.

The phrase "he cannot be acknowledged before the Lord on the Church Book," appearing in paragraph one, refers, presumably, to section 85. Perhaps Joseph Smith is saying this is like baptism, an important ordinance, but one which is at the beginning of the journey to salvation, and should not be taken to represent the end of perfection and thus very difficult to attain. It is a minimum level requirement and should not be used to keep good people out.

Paragraph three refers to "those persons consecrating property to the Bishop in Zion, and then receiving an inheritance back." Notice that the property being consecrated was not land but rather money. These people had moved to Zion to get land, and were to have brought money with them. They obviously could not have brought any land with them. And few could have brought enough personal property to be of significance. Almost any personal property they brought with them would be just what they would need to survive in that wilderness - horses, wagon, plow, etc. In other words, the only transaction possible was the purchase of land for money.

The major concerns of the bishop were (1) for each family to have enough land to live reasonably well, (2) to not have them get more land than they could use, and either waste it or try to resell it at a profit, either to members, or, worse, to non-members, and (3) to collect enough money from those coming to pay for the land they individually got and perhaps collect a bit more to make up for the lack of money of some who were arriving. Thus the inventory information was only to help the Bishop know if people were making a fair contribution to the cause. He would also know who needed help and how much, and who might be willing and able to donate to help them. The phrase in paragraph one that "every man must be his own judge how much he should receive, and how much he should suffer to remain in the hands of the bishop" (how much he should contribute) was much the same rule as we have today concerning contributions. No one today "tells" us how much to contribute, and neither did they then.

There was a complicated balancing computation going on here. The bishop had to estimate how much money people would have to spend on land so he could buy or contract for the proper amount of land from the government or other sellers. And then he had to determine the proper parcel size to be sold or assigned to each member arriving.[10]

All the economic information he could get was barely enough to meet his needs.

The last paragraph of the letter deals with a topic related to another aspect of the gathering process, making sure the saints had the supplies they needed. Joseph answers Brother Gilbert's request for funds for his store (part of the united order activities) by saying that the Kirtland brethren could not help because of their already large and burdensome debts.[11]

Sidney Gilbert had previously done extensive trading with the western Indians, and probably had the contacts to get credit in his own name.[12] This last paragraph also indicates again the close working relationship between the various businesses or parts of the order. Without that close relationship, Gilbert would not have reason to be requesting assistance.

Finally we come on our backward route to the first document, section 85. That section is filled with emotion-laden words, but, if viewed out of its historical context, gives us little information about the migration and "consecration" process. Rather than any immediate consequence, the penalty for not using the established procedure was delayed until a time far in the future, "in that day," (v. 9) during a millennial or judgement-day time. This reflects the fact that the brethren had no economic power whatsoever over the migrating saints. Only the willingness of the individual saints to obey the council of the prophet could cause them to follow the procedure. The saints were being asked to pay tithing (v. 3), that is, use their personal resources for a gospel purpose, by getting themselves moved to Missouri, and providing funds for others to do so as well. They were paying in the present for blessings in the future. They were not to "steady the ark" (v. 8) by inventing their own procedures and presuming to act on their own.

Behind the mysterious words in section 85 on the topic of "consecration" is the simple economic fact that the bishop had to charge some members more than the cost of the land, so that he could charge other poorer folk less than the cost of the land, and thus fulfill his duty to see that the poor also had adequate inheritances in Zion. The problem was that the people who had the extra money would prefer to pay a lower price for the land by purchasing it directly from the government themselves, rather than purchasing through the bishop. There was also the problem that the individuals with money often wished to purchase much more land than they could use directly themselves, hoping to make a profit on its sale later. This was in direct conflict and competition with the bishop's goals which were to accumulate all the gains possible through differential pricing of the land, and use that extra money to further the gathering process in many ways, but especially by providing land for the worthy poor. The bishop would have tried to limit the size of the land purchases of the more wealthy, and requested some of those persons' remaining funds as donations or as extra price for the land.

The people with extra money who tried to circumvent the established procedure, and have dealings with the outsiders[13] instead of the bishop, caused many problems. The saints had enough property to carry out the commandment to gather if wisdom, judgement, and coordination were used, but otherwise it could not be done. When people made their own land arrangements, the bishop lost some of his control over the migration, and was unable to plan how much land he should buy. He would not wish to repeat some of the experiences in Kirtland where Joseph bought tracts of land expecting to resell it to migrating members, and then was left with land for which he was unable to pay.[14] There was much talk of speculation in land and other property at all stages of the gathering process, and the damage it did to that process by raising the overall cost.

There *were* two ways of getting an inheritance (a place for permanent settlement), the "legal" way through the bishop (consecration), and the "illegal" way through others (non-consecration). It apparently seemed easier to some members to be "illegal" than to be "legal," making it a sacrifice to be "legal." Either way they acquired a legal title, as to the laws of the land. The mechanics of getting land were much the same, whether through the bishop or otherwise: money was traded for land. But there were important religious and practical differences. For those using the "illegal" way, the doctrine of the gathering was given small importance, and their behavior made the way harder for those who did honor the gathering principle.

This examination of three documents should be helpful in the process of understanding the economics and doctrines involved in the Missouri migration process. This basic discussion has an important relationship to many topics throughout the book.

Let us leave the Missouri land transaction topic for a time and examine other activities of the united order firm. Because of their many large responsibilities and their dependence upon the Lord for success in their far-flung efforts, the brethren of the united order firm often met together in prayer as they were counseled to do:[15]

> On the evening of the 11th of January [1834], Joseph Smith, Jun., Frederick G. Williams, Newel K. Whitney, John Johnson, Oliver Cowdery, and Orson Hyde united in prayer, and asked the Lord to grant the following petitions:
>
> 1. - That the Lord would grant that our lives might be precious in His sight; that he would watch over our persons, and give His angels charge concerning us and our families, that no evil or unseen hand might be permitted to harm us.
>
> 2. - That the Lord would also hold the lives of all the United Order as sacred, and not suffer that any of them should be taken.

....

4. - That the Lord in the order of His providence, would provide the Bishop of this Church [at Kirtland] with means sufficient to discharge every debt, in due season, that the Order owes, that the Church may not be brought into disrepute, and the Saints be afflicted by the hands of their enemies.

5. - That the Lord would protect our printing press from the hands of evil men, and give us means to send forth His record, even His Gospel, that the ears of all may hear it; and also that we may print His scriptures; and also that He would give those who were appointed to conduct the press, wisdom sufficient that the cause may not be hindered, but that men's eyes may thereby be opened to see the truth.

6. - That the Lord would deliver Zion, and gather in his scattered people to possess it in peace; and also, while in their dispersion, that He would provide for them that they perish not from hunger or cold; and finally, that God, in the name of Jesus, would gather His elect speedily, and unveil His face, that His Saints might behold His glory, and dwell with Him. Amen.[16]

This was a meeting of the Kirtland branch of the united order firm in which they prayed for themselves and their fellows in the firm (v. 1, 2). The five men first listed were clearly members of the firm; we can speculate a little about the sixth man, Orson Hyde. The last person to become a member of the united order firm by recorded revelation was John Johnson, in D&C 96, dated June 4, 1833. Because of Orson Hyde's associations with the firm, it is quite possible that he later became a member of it also, but no verification of it appears in the history.

The most important single purpose of the united order was to borrow large amounts of money to finance the land acquisition program needed for the gathering of the saints, and that, of course, meant large debts (v. 4). That financing operation should certainly be considered a central church function, operating above and separate from the activities of the individual branches. It would be a strange thing for an "order " of the collectivist community type often envisioned by church members, to be so heavily involved in large scale interstate real estate development.[17] There is nothing really communalistic at all about that. Most of the transactions were those of purchase and sale, with a few involving donations of land. There is no evidence of any positive leveling mechanism. The brethren repeatedly denied any such activity and their recorded actions are consistent with their words.

Paragraphs 5 and 6 show the firm's preoccupation with the gathering, and the importance of printing the scriptures, directions, and exhortations needed to spur and guide the movement. Notice in paragraph 4, where the worrisome debts are mentioned, that there is a differentiation between the order and the church, showing that the order is separate from the church and the saints.

On another occasion, some of the united order brethren met to pray for assistance in their task of acquiring land through donation or purchase:

> On the evening of the 28th of January [1834], Brothers Oliver Cowdery, Frederick G. Williams, and myself, being agreed, bowed before the Lord and united in prayer ... that God would soften the hearts of Eden Smith, --- Jones, --- Lowd, --- Lyman, and also Mr. Bardsley, that they might obey the Gospel; or if they would not repent, that the Lord would send faithful Saints to purchase their farms, that this stake may be strengthened and its borders enlarged.[18]

The basic process in "building up Kirtland" was to acquire land by donation or purchase for use in settling migrating saints in a semi-permanent location subject to the five year plan mentioned in D&C 64:21. Apparently, the five brethren were not willing to donate portions of their land. The alternatives were to either have individual members purchase all or portions of the land for their own use and possibly sell or donate portions to other saints, or to have the united order (central church business unit) purchase the land for sale or donation.

The aftermath of the ejection of the Saints from Jackson County, Missouri, gives us some indication of the promises the saints made who were allowed to purchase land in Missouri as part of the "consecration" process. The saints were forced to leave their land behind when they were driven from Missouri, and this comment from that time period gives us a clue to what the original land transactions entailed:

> They also said that none of their lands were sold into the hands of our enemies, except a piece of thirty acres owned by Brother William E. McLellin, which he sold into the hands of the enemy, and seven acres more which he would have sold to the enemy if a brother had not come forward and purchased it and paid him his money.[19]

From this we can see that one of the many different meanings of "consecration" used by the saints of Joseph Smith's time, was that the purchase of land in Zion implied a promise to never sell that land, even if loss of the land with no compensation was the alternative. In no other place did the Saints make that particular commitment. It was a willingness to lose or "donate to the Lord" so that the Saints might have the right to claim the land at some distant future, perhaps millennial, time.

Here is another example of a meeting of some of the united order brethren (plus Heber C. Kimball), held to deal with the usual topics of personal safety and need for financial assistance:

> April 7. (1834) - Bishop Whitney, Elder Frederick G. Williams, Oliver Cowdery, Heber C. Kimball, and myself, met in the council room, and bowed down before the Lord, and prayed that He would furnish the means to deliver the Firm from debt, that they might be set at liberty; also, that I might prevail against that wicked man, Hurlburt, and that he might be put to shame.
>
> The presidency wrote Elder Orson Hyde, who yet remained in the State of New York, as follows:
>
> Kirtland, April 7, 1834
>
> Dear Brother Orson: - We received yours of the 31st ultimo in due course of mail, and were much grieved on learning that you were not likely to succeed according to our expectations. Myself, Brothers Newel, Frederick, and Oliver, retired to the translating room, where prayer was wont to be made, and unbosomed our feelings before God; and cannot but exercise faith yet that you, in the miraculous providences of God, will succeed in obtaining help. The fact is, unless we can obtain help, I myself cannot go to Zion, and if I do not go, it will be impossible to get my brethren in Kirtland, any of them, to go; and if we do not go, it is in vain for our eastern brethren to think of going up to better themselves by obtaining so goodly a land, (which now can be obtained for one dollar and one quarter per acre,) and stand against that wicked mob; for unless they do the will of God, God will not help them; and if God does not help them, all is vain....
>
> Now, Brother Orson, if this church, which is essaying to be the Church of Christ will not help us, when they can do it without sacrifice, with those blessings which God has bestowed upon them, I prophesy - I speak the truth, I lie not - God shall take away their talent, and give it to those who have no talent, and shall prevent them from ever obtaining a place of refuge, or an inheritance upon the land of Zion; therefore, they may tarry, for they might as well be overtaken where they are, as to incur the displeasure of God, and fall under His wrath by the way side, as to fall into the hands of a merciless mob, where there is no God to deliver, as salt that has lost its savor, and is thenceforth good for nothing, but to be trodden under foot of men.

> We therefore adjure you to beseech them, in the name of the Lord, by the Son of God, to lend us a helping hand; and if this will not soften their hearts to administer to our necessity for Zion's sake, turn your back upon them, and return speedily to Kirtland; and the blood of Zion be upon their heads, ...
> Your brethren in the New Covenant,
> Joseph Smith, Jun.,
> Frederick G. Williams,
> Oliver Cowdery.[20]

This quotation begins with another prayer to deliver the firm from debt. Apparently, until the debts for land, printing expenses, etc., in Kirtland were discharged, Joseph's duty to his creditors made it improper for him to leave the Kirtland area. Land sales to members might reduce some of the debts gradually, but other expenses, such as for printing, would probably require donations. In any event, Joseph clearly felt that the gathering process was being retarded by the lack of available funds. After paying off Kirtland debts, there was still the financial problem of acquiring even more lands in Missouri.

The brethren regularly sought contributions from church members to help the cause as Orson Hyde was doing. Another example is a conference held a few weeks earlier in Avon, New York, on March 17, 1834, to get money to purchase land in Zion and convince members to go there and settle it.[21]

The Missouri land was selling for $1.25 an acre. This compares rather favorably with the $10 to $30 price for land in Kirtland, and presumably even higher prices in the East. Thus, it was easily feasible ("can do it without sacrifice") for the saints to sell their existing properties or otherwise acquire funds to be sent to the brethren to buy enough land for themselves and for those who had little money.

From these limited glimpses of the united order's activities, we can see that they were heavily oriented toward sponsoring and promoting the gathering in as many ways as possible.

Chapter 5 Notes

1. HC 1:298, Nov. 27, 1832, Kirtland. D&C 85.

2. HC 1:364-365. June 25, 1833.

3. HC 1:381, 382, 383, 386, 387. July 1833.

4. D&C 101:73-75. See also D&C 104:15-18; 45:65; 42:39, 67; 38:16-19, 34-39; 124:31; 1 Ne 3:7; Matt 14:28-30.

5. HC 2:48-49.

6. Victor Peters, *All Things Common: The Hutterian Way of Life,* (New York: Harper & Row, 1965).

7. Wilford Woodruff recorded in his journal his priesthood licenses as a teacher and as a priest, and his recommend as a member of the Church. They were signed in New York by Zerah Pulsipher, in Clay County by John Whitmer, and in Liberty, Clay County, Missouri, by Lyman Wight, respectively. The last mentions his service in Zion's Camp and his general worthiness. Scott G. Kenney, *Wilford Woodruff's Journal* (Midvale, Utah: Signature Books, 1983), vol. 1, pp. 6, 14, 17.

8. From other sources it appears that Ezra Thayre was another person who considered deviating from the standard program. In D&C 52:22, June 7, 1831, he was directed to go to Missouri. In D&C 56:5, 8-11, also June 1831, he is rebuked. The language in verse 9 stating that "there shall be no divisions made upon the land," probably indicates that he wished to have the money he contributed used to buy a large tract of land to be deeded to him. He could then lease it or resell it at a profit. In D&C 56:8, reference is made to a commandment given him (not recorded in the history of the

church) concerning his Kirtland property. This commandment probably concerned his allowing migrating saints to use, purchase, or be given his land. Thayre is also mentioned in D&C 33.

9. Directive to give deeds: *Personal Writings,* p. 308. See Chapter 4 note 24. Evidence that deeds were given: HC 2:39. February 24, 1834. Joseph Smith at Kirtland. See main text associated with note 17. See JD 13:80; 17:59.

President J. Reuben Clark, Jr, has stated flatly concerning the single deed of Titus Billings (HC 1:365n-367n), often mentioned as an example of communal transactions, that "this instrument is not in accordance with the principle laid down in the revelations touching upon the United Order." See note 1 in chapter 1 for reference.

A possible explanation for the existence of this deed follows: Titus Billings was baptized in Kirtland in 1830 (HC 1:266), probably indicating that he had been a resident there for a time, and probably had some useful knowledge of the area. That might have made him a good candidate for being a real estate agent. Titus Billings is first mentioned in conjunction with the administration of real estate in Kirtland in the 1831 revelation directing him to travel to Missouri:

> 38 Wherefore, let my disciples in Kirtland arrange their temporal concerns, who dwell upon this farm.
> 39 Let my servant Titus Billings, who has the care thereof, dispose of the land, that he may be prepared in the coming spring to take his journey up unto the land of Zion, with those that dwell upon the face thereof, excepting those whom I shall reserve unto myself, that shall not go until I shall command them.
> 40 And let all the moneys which can be spared, it mattereth not unto me whether it be little or much, be sent up unto the land of Zion, unto them whom I have appointed to receive. (D&C 63:38-40)

We may fairly assume that since Titus Billings had the care of a farm on which many lived, and the land was held in a single title, it is likely that most of those people were there on either a free guest or rental or lease basis, the lease basis being more likely since some might expect to remain for an extended time. If leases were used in Kirtland and administered by Billings, it is quite possible that upon his move to Missouri he might propose a similar system for use there, especially since he would be dealing with the same group of people whom he dealt with on the farm in Kirtland. As counselor to Bishop Partridge (HC 1:366), he was charged with similar real estate responsibilities in the new location. It would be tempting to use a lease system in Missouri because it would avoid the administrative burdens of getting land deeds for everyone, and would be a way of enforcing the counsel that individuals should not sell their land to non-members -- what they did not own they could not sell. It would also make it easier to expel people who may have occupied land under false pretenses or who later left the Church.

If made, this lease proposal was not accepted, and according to Joseph Smith's instructions, deeds were given in most cases. In some cases, lands were signed over to mobbers at gunpoint, showing that the mobbers assumed that the "mormons" held title to their property and could transfer it to others.

Wilford Woodruff records the following in his journal (his spelling used throughout):

> I Consecrated and Dedicated Myself, Properties, and Effects unto the Lord before the Bishop in Zion on the 31st Dec. 1834. .... This that I may be a lawful heir to the Celestial Kingdom of God." (*Journal,* p. 34. See note 7 above.)

The more full account is as follows:

Believeing it to be the duty of the latter day Saints to consecrate and dedicate all their properties with themselves unto God in order to become lawful heirs to the Celestial Kingdom of God It was under such a view of the subject that I consecrated before the Bishop of the Church of the latter day Saints in Clay County Dec 31st 1834. The following is a copy of the Consecration:

Clay Co Missouri Dec 31st 1834

Be it known that I Willford Woodruff do freely covenant with my God that I freely consecrate and dedicate myself together with all my properties and affects unto the Lord for the purpose of assisting in building up his kingdom even Zion on the earth that I may keep his law and lay all things before the bishop of his Church that I may be a lawful heir to the Kingdom of God even the Celestial Kingdom.

The following is an inventory of my Property:

	$ cts
One Due Bill payable in one year	20.00
One trunk and its contents principly Books	18.00
Hat boots and clothing	23.00
One valiece	2.50
One english watch	8.00
One rifle and equipments	9.00
One sword	5.00
One pistol	1.50
Also Sundry articles	3.00
And Notes which are doubtful and uncertain	150.00
Total	$240.00

(*Journal,* vol. 1, p. 16.)

Wilford Woodruff had traveled to Missouri with Zion's Camp beginning May 8, 1834, and remained in Missouri for the rest of the year. He lived at Lyman Wight's place in Clay County and assisted him in making bricks and building a house for another.

Shortly after the consecration event, on January 13, 1835, he left on a mission to Tennessee and Kentucky, after which he returned to Kirtland, on November 25, 1836.

(*Journal,* p. 106). On April 13, 1837, (*Journal,* pp. 140, 216) he married Phebe W. Carter in Kirtland.

This consecration transaction appears to have had no more temporal effect than the symbolic ordinance of baptism. There is no specific statement as to whether he retained the property or transferred it to the Church, but it seems highly likely that he did retain possession, and that the document was merely an inventory and served no other purpose. The property listed was minimal, and with the possible exception of the rifle and sword, would be suitable equipment for a missionary. The transaction occurred just before leaving on his mission, and it may have been similar to receiving a patriarchal blessing or attending the temple to make covenants and receive blessings before going on a mission.

The fact that he was single while in Missouri, was living with Lyman Wight, and left on a two-year mission and did not return directly to Missouri, would indicate that he probably owned no property in Missouri. This increases the likelihood that the "consecration" transaction was a symbolic one only. It may have had a practical purpose in giving the Bishop in Zion some statistical information on the members there so that requests could be make for assistance if necessary.

10. The old settlers were scornful and worried about the small size of the plots the brethren were being given - about 30 acres apiece. See Joseph A. Geddes, *The United Order Among the Mormons (Missouri Phase)* (Salt Lake City, Utah: Deseret News Press, 1924), p. 49. G. A. Smith, JD 13:79, estimated plot size to be "from 40 acres to a section of land." The poverty of most of the Saints would keep most plots very small. See Geddes, p. 111.

Whatever the actual sizes were, to the old settlers they were too small. Perhaps to them it was like building high rise apartments or densely packed town houses right in the middle of an exclusive "no less than two acres" subdivision. It hurt the quality of their land, and threatened them with "slums." It would probably be hard to raise any number of cattle on such a small plot after building a house, preparing a garden, and planting wheat or other crops. The real objection, of course, was probably the fact that the old settlers would quickly be outnumbered by the "closely packed" newcomers and would lose political control.

The old settlers probably had been using free grazing and farming rights on U.S. land. They would lose that free benefit when the land was sold to the immigrants. It may have been a situation like that in Texas and other western places where the "squatters" were resisted because of their threat to interfere with the economic interests of the ranchers. The ranchers had been the first there, had enjoyed the economic advantages of free unfenced grazing land, and did not wish to see the land denied to them by fencing, plowing, etc.

11. Compare reference to New York debts with D&C 104:81; 82:22; HC 2:492.

12. See HC 1:145.

13. HC 1:299. The example of someone dealing with outsiders was the Israelite who "took a wife of the daughters of Barzillai the Gileadite." Ezra 2:61, 62

14. Essentially the same rules for land transactions were observed in Kirtland, Missouri, and Nauvoo. See HC 2:478-480 for a directive to the Kirtland saints to use the proper procedure for land transactions. Those instructions are similar to those given the Missouri saints contained in section 85. The same instructions were given to the saints in Nauvoo. HC 5:35, 272.

15. For example, see D&C 104:80.

16. HC 2:2-3.

17. It would be most unlikely that conservative banking concerns would be willing to risk large loans to communal organizations whose willingness and ability to make repayment would be suspect. The fact that such loans were acquired is itself strong evidence that the united order operated on normal and recognized business principles.

18. HC 2:24. Jan. 28, 1834. Joseph Smith at Kirtland.

19. HC 2:39. Feb. 24, 1834. Joseph Smith at Kirtland.

20. HC 2:48-49. April 7, 1834. Kirtland.

21. HC 2:44. March 17, 1834. See also many other cites in D&C and the history to "get money" or "contribute money."

CHAPTER 6

The United Order Firm Becomes Two Firms

The united order, organized as directed in section 82, operated for two years as a single firm having two branches, one in Ohio and one in Missouri. The firm began when there were fewer saints in Missouri than there were in Kirtland. During that two-year period a large number of saints had moved to the western area. Apparently, the higher concentration of saints, the resulting increase in firm business activity, and the slow communications made it advisable to allow the western branch to become an independent firm.

A journal entry dated April 10, 1834 at Kirtland shows that some reorganization was being contemplated:

> On the 10th, had a council of the United Order, in which it was agreed that the order should be dissolved, and each one have his stewardship set off to him.[1]

During another Kirtland meeting of the united order held later that month, section 104 was given to guide the reorganization:

> April 23. - Assembled in Council with Elders Sidney Rigdon, Frederick G. Williams, Newel K. Whitney, John Johnson, and Oliver Cowdery; and united in asking the Lord to give Elder Zebedee Coltrin influence over Brother Jacob Myres, to obtain the money which he

has gone to borrow for us, or cause him to come to this place and bring it himself. I also received the following: [Section 104].[2]

The brethren in the united order firm met often in council,[3] and the matters they discussed always related to financing various activities related to land transactions, printing, merchandising, etc. As recommended in D&C 104:80 and as shown in the above quotation, they usually engaged in prayer to seek divine assistance for the order. Note here that Elder Coltrin was acting as agent for the united order. Apparently the order used agents who were not actually members of the order. They were more like employees or voluntary assistants.

The pertinent parts of section 104, including its headnotes, are reproduced here with comments interspersed:

> Headnote - (1968 edition)
> Revelation given to Enoch [Joseph Smith the prophet] April 23, 1834, concerning the United Order, or the Order of the Church for the benefit of the poor.

The use of the name Enoch to designate Joseph Smith may have caused confusion. There is no indication in the history that the Enoch referred to is the Enoch of ancient times, or that the ancient Enoch received a similar directive. Note that the 1981 edition makes no reference to Enoch.

> Headnote (1981 edition)
> Revelation given to Joseph Smith the Prophet, April 23, 1834, concerning the United Order, or the Order of the Church for the benefit of the poor. HC 2:54-60. The occasion was that of a council meeting of the First Presidency[4] and other high priests, in which the pressing temporal needs of the people had been given consideration. The United Order at Kirtland was to be temporarily dissolved and reorganized, and the properties as stewardships were to be divided among members of the order.

When one partner dies or leaves a partnership, the partnership is legally and technically "dissolved." Normally, however, the partnership is really just reorganized and goes on, especially when it has large holdings as did this one. Here the reorganization was comprised of a division into two separate partnerships and the distribution of what was probably a small portion of the firm's property. Some of the distributions merely converted some "company housing" for a few firm members into individually owned housing, a benefit they had probably earned by their labors. The distribution of a few houses was a small incident. The really important action had to do with large-scale land deals and merchandising operations.

The united order probably had debts beyond those related to the property mentioned, and almost certainly held and sought to hold other properties beyond those mentioned. Prior to the split, large tracts of land in Missouri and Kirtland had been held for sale to migrating members.

Some of the larger properties that were "distributed" were probably still considered assets of the firm, to be managed or sold or pledged as the situation indicated. Because of the need for secrecy, the firm would have difficulty in many instances in holding real estate property in the firm's name. The literary and merchandising subgroups could hold appropriate land for their operations, but designating the owner as a large general real estate development firm would cause too much of a stir. A sensible solution would be to hold the property in the names of individuals who were members of the firm. Some of the property would truly be personally owned, but most would be held merely as a nominee of the firm. Because of the nature of a partnership, with its unlimited personal liability for all partners, even the "personally" held property might be taken or pledged for partnership debts.

It is likely that none of the united order property was ever held directly in the firm name, even the property here "distributed." Joseph Smith held much of the property in his own name, but it was really united order property, which often was funded by loans negotiated by others such as F.G. Williams & Co. Some of the "distributions" here were no more than just a release of a company claim on the property, unless extreme circumstances made recall necessary. The property was probably already in the individuals' names who "received" it. This adjustment of titles and liabilities may be somewhat similar in principle to the release of certain liabilities of two of the partners, W.W. Phelps and John Whitmer, on another occasion.[5]

We can now begin our analysis of the text of the section:

> 1 Verily I say unto you, my friends, I give unto you counsel, and a commandment, concerning all the properties which belong to the order which I commanded to be organized and established, to be a united order, and an everlasting order for the benefit of my church, and for the salvation of men until I come -

The title "friend of God" is not one lightly bestowed. Abraham was known as a friend of God because of his closeness and faithfulness to God.[6] The Jerusalem Twelve were called the friends of God.[7] The early leaders in this dispensation, especially the leaders involved in the united order, were essentially carrying out the duties of apostles, although the quorum of the twelve had not yet been formally organized.[8]

The "everlasting order" is for the benefit of all the church and all men, not just a small group for a short time. A central Church management group has been in existence since Joseph's time to handle the world-wide affairs of the Church including property for welfare and other purposes.

> 15 And it is my purpose to provide for my saints, for all things are mine.
>
> 16 But it must needs be done in mine own way; and behold this is the way that I, the Lord, have decreed to provide for my saints, that the poor shall be exalted, in that the rich are made low.

Since one of the main purposes of the order was to "provide for my Saints," as more people moved to Missouri, a larger and more independent organization was required in Missouri.

The verses dealing with the personal distributions are not included here in the quotes from section 104, but it should be noted that verses 24, 25, 33, 37, 40, and 42 mention that some portions of the stewardships are for the steward and his "seed." In other words, the property becomes individually owned, and might become an inheritance for his children if he retained it until his death. This is in contrast to the clearly firm-owned property. The word "successors" (DC 82:20) is used to apply to the transfer of firm property from one set of administrators to another. The exact property that was owned by the firm and the part that was transferred to the Missouri firm is not specified. Only the unusual and personal transactions are mentioned. The other matters were probably obvious to the parties involved and did not need to be spelled out in detail.

> 47 And now, a commandment I give unto you concerning Zion, that you shall no longer be bound as a united order to your brethren of Zion, only on this wise -
>
> 48 After you are organized, you shall be called the United Order of the Stake of Zion, the City of Shinehah [Kirtland]. And your brethren, after they are organized, shall be called the United Order of the City of Zion.

49 And they shall be organized in their own names, and in their own name; and they shall do their business in their own name, and in their own names;

50 And you shall do your business in your own name, and in your own names.

51 And this I have commanded to be done for your salvation, and also for their salvation, in consequence of their being driven out and that which is to come.

....

53 Therefore, you are dissolved as a united order with your brethren, that you are not bound only up to this hour unto them, only on this wise, as I said, by loan as shall be agreed by this order in council, as your circumstances will admit and the voice of the council direct.

The procedure to be followed for the reorganization was set out rather clearly. In verses 47 through 50, the one order becomes two orders, each with its own name. Each is to do business separately using sets of individual and "doing business as" names appropriate to each firm. Verse 53 allows for loans between the two firms, as the judgement of the partners of each order dictates. In light of verses 47 to 50, the word "dissolved" used in verse 53 clearly means "separated." The two firms are not to go out of existence, but rather are to go on at least as vigorously as before (v. 1, 15, 49, 50), but now acting independently of each other.

The phrase "this order in council" (v. 53) emphasizes the business administration role of the organization. The normal items of business were church-wide matters, not the local, personal items that a small communal order might consider. The term "council" is used often by Joseph Smith to refer to the united order.

> 54 And again, a commandment I give unto you concerning your stewardship which I have appointed unto you.
>
> 55 Behold, all these properties are mine, or else your faith is vain, and ye are found hypocrites, and the covenants which ye have made unto me are broken;
>
> 56 And if the properties are mine, then are ye stewards; otherwise ye are no stewards.
>
> 57 But, verily I say unto you, I have appointed unto you to be stewards over mine house, even stewards indeed.
>
> 58 And for this purpose I have commanded you to organize yourselves, even to shinelah [print] my words, the fulness of my scriptures, the revelations which I have given unto you, and which I shall, hereafter, from time to time give unto you-
>
> 59 For the purpose of building up my church and kingdom on the earth, and to prepare my people for the time when I shall dwell with them, which is nigh at hand.
>
> 60 And ye shall prepare for yourselves a place for a treasury, and consecrate it unto my name.
>
> 61 And ye shall appoint one among you to keep the treasury, and he shall be ordained unto this blessing.
>
> 62 And there shall be a seal upon the treasury, and all the sacred things shall be delivered into the treasury; and no man among you shall call it his own, or any part of it, for it shall belong to you all with one accord.

The phrase "all these properties are mine" (v. 55) is not further defined in the revelation, but surely included large properties in Kirtland and Missouri. It is not clear whether the few properties distributed (perhaps a better term would be "repositioned") earlier in the revelation are included in the total, but most probably are. Printing was an important activity of the order (v. 58).

Verse 62 is describing one of the standard features of a business partnership, the practice of placing all profits in a central fund ("treasury") from which they are distributed or applied to company purposes by the vote of the partners.

> 63 And I give it unto you from this very hour; and now see to it, that ye go to and make use of the stewardship which I

have appointed unto you, exclusive of the sacred things, for the purpose of shinelane [printing] these sacred things as I have said.

64 And the avails [proceeds] of the sacred things shall be had in the treasury, and a seal shall be upon it; and it shall not be used or taken out of the treasury by any one, neither shall the seal be loosed which shall be placed upon it, only by the voice of the order, or by commandment.

65 And thus shall ye preserve the avails of the sacred things in the treasury, for sacred and holy purposes.

66 And this shall be called the sacred treasury of the Lord; and a seal shall be kept upon it that it may be holy and consecrated unto the Lord.

67 And again, there shall be another treasury prepared, and a treasurer appointed to keep the treasury, and a seal shall be placed upon it;

68 And all moneys that you receive in your stewardships, by improving upon the properties which I have appointed unto you, in houses, or in lands, or in cattle, or in all things save it be the holy and sacred writings, which I have reserved unto myself for holy and sacred purposes, shall be cast into the treasury as fast as you receive moneys, by hundreds, or by fifties, or by twenties, or by tens, or by fives.

69 Or in other words, if any man among you obtain five talents [dollars] let him cast them into the treasury; or if he obtain ten, or twenty, or fifty, or an hundred, let him do likewise;

70 And let not any among you say that it is his own; for it shall not be called his, nor any part of it.

71 And there shall not any part of it be used, or taken out of the treasury, only by the voice and common consent of the order.

72 And this shall be the voice and common consent of the order - that any man among you say to the treasurer: I have need of this to help me in my stewardship -

73 If it be five talents [dollars], or if it be ten talents [dollars], or twenty, or fifty, or a hundred, the treasurer shall give unto him the sum which he requires to help him in his stewardship -

74 Until he be found a transgressor, and it is manifest before the council of the order plainly that he is an unfaithful and an unwise steward.

75 But so long as he is in full fellowship, and is faithful and wise in his stewardship, this shall be his token unto the treasurer that the treasurer shall not withhold.

76 But in case of transgression, the treasurer shall be subject unto the council and voice of the order.

77 And in case the treasurer is found an unfaithful and an unwise steward, he shall be subject to the council and the voice of the order, and shall be removed out of his place, and another shall be appointed in his stead.

Although couched in lofty language, the instructions just given in section 104 should be interpreted as applying to a practical business setting. Firm capital and income (v. 68-69) do not become individual property unless declared by the firm (v. 70-71). For business purposes, the partners have access to the firm's funds (v. 73-75). A disbursing officer is needed for the firm (v. 73). The partners and disbursing officer are held to account by the firm (v. 74, 77).

78 And again, verily I say unto you, concerning your debts - behold it is my will that you shall pay all your debts.

79 And it is my will that you shall humble yourselves before me, and obtain this blessing by your diligence and humility and the prayer of faith.

80. And inasmuch as you are diligent and humble, and exercise the prayer of faith, behold, I will soften the hearts of those to whom you are in debt, until I shall send means unto you for your deliverance.

81 Therefore write speedily to Cainhannoch [New York] and write according to that which shall be dictated by my Spirit; and I will soften the hearts of those to whom you are in debt, that it shall be taken away out of their minds to bring affliction upon you.

82 And inasmuch as ye are humble and faithful and call upon my name, behold, I will give you the victory.

83 I give unto you a promise, that you shall be delivered this once out of your bondage.

84 Inasmuch as you obtain a chance to loan money by hundreds, or thousands, even until you shall

loan enough to deliver yourself from bondage, it is your privilege.

85 And pledge the properties which I have put into your hands, this once, by giving your names by common consent or otherwise, as it shall seem good unto you.

86 I give unto you this privilege, this once; and behold, if you proceed to do the things which I have laid before you, according to my commandments, all these things are mine, and ye are my stewards, and the master will not suffer his house to be broken up. Even so. Amen.

Help is promised in dealing with the money lenders (v. 78-83). Verse 84 is puzzling in its use of the word "loan." The firm was normally borrowing money for certain purposes, rather than trying to act itself as a bank to loan money to others for the purpose of earning interest. It is likely that what is meant is that the firm is to borrow money, that is engage in loan transactions, the firm receiving the money.[9] The money would then be used to pay off other more pressing debts or those owned by unfriendly and impatient people. In other words, they were to "roll over" some of their loans to get some financial breathing space. This interpretation would fit with verse 85 where pledging of properties is mentioned. That is a common means of providing security to creditors for new loans.

The division of the firm into two parts was not attended with much fanfare.[10] As evidenced by the April 10, 1834, journal entry quoted at the beginning of this chapter, it is likely that many of the changes needed had already been decided upon, and section 104 was largely just a confirmation of an existing plan of action. There is a definite tendency toward a prudent gradualism of change throughout the united order firm's history.

Chapter 6 Notes

1. HC 2:49. April 10, 1834. Kirtland. Concerning the word "dissolved," see D&C 104:47, 53, this chapter, and HC 2:475, quoted in chapter 7, where the firm of Oliver Cowdery & Co. was "dissolved" and the property transferred to Joseph Smith and Sidney Rigdon.

2. HC 2:54. D&C 104. April 23, 1834. Kirtland.

3. Some examples of united order meetings are as follows: HC 1:268, 270, 409; 2:2-3, 24, 47-48, 49, 54, 234. See also HC 2:234 (united order members lead out in donations), 2:273 (literary firm appointees), and 2:291 (others are with united order members - praying for Missouri land).

4. It is interesting to note that at an earlier time, although Frederick G. Williams was a member of the First Presidency, he was not yet a member of the united order.

5. HC 2:434. April 2, 1836. Besides the release of liability item, the reference also includes a discussion of the firm's or company's assets and debts, and its goal to purchase Missouri land.

6. Jas. 2:23; 2 Chr. 20:7.

7. John 15:14, 15.

8. D&C 84:63, 77; 93:45, 51.

9. See chapter 7 for a discussion of the directives to the early brethren on the appropriate attitudes concerning loans during that period.

10. The rather casual way Joseph mentions the revelation, after mentioning a loan transaction in process, HC 2:54, tends to support this idea of "no surprises" gradualism, and makes it appear that the section 104 instructions were of much less practical significance than one might think on first reading.

CHAPTER 7

Transactions of the Kirtland United Order Firm

After the split of the original united order firm into two firms, the same kinds of transactions continued to be executed by largely the same people, the only difference being the probable lowered need for coordination and thus the increased freedom of action of the parties carrying out those transactions. As a practical matter, the Kirtland firm, containing the First Presidency of the Church, still continued to dominate the major planning and decision making, as evidenced by continuing conferences between the two firms. The Kirtland firm also received a boost in apparent importance because the history was largely prepared by Joseph Smith or under his direction, and most of the entries concerning the firm's activity naturally came from his more direct experience with events and people in Kirtland.

The first quotation for this chapter mentions a group that apparently had dealings with both of the united order firms -- one a loan transaction and the other a purchase transaction -- although the account largely deals with events in Kirtland:

> On the 24th [of August 1835] the High Council at Kirtland ... instructed ... that Joseph H. Tippits and J. W. Tippits go to Missouri this fall to

purchase land for the church in Essex, New York, according to previous appointment by the voice of said church.[1]

In November 1834, the Tippitts group had loaned money to the Kirtland united order,[2] and now was about to go to Missouri to buy land, probably from the Missouri united order. While waiting out the winter in Kirtland, these brethren lent some of their branch's funds to the united firm. Presumably they received it back in time to make their trip to actually purchase the land for the Essex Branch members.[3]

The original literary firm organized in Missouri consisted of W. W. Phelps and John Whitmer. Presumably they continued in that role for the Missouri firm, and others, mentioned in the following quote, were chosen to fulfill that function for the Kirtland firm:

> September 16 [1835]. -- The Presidency of the Church assembled and appointed David Whitmer and Samuel H. Smith a committee and general agents to act in the name of and for, the "Literary Firm."[4]

It is not clear whether the two men mentioned here, David Whitmer and Samuel H. Smith, were members of the order or just its agents. The "literary firm" was a "doing business as" name used by the order and would normally consist of a subset of the "partners" in the order. The last person appointed to the united order by published revelation was John Johnson (D&C 96, June 4, 1833), but others may have been added to the Missouri and Kirtland firms after the April 1834 division of the original firm. Whether agents or partners, it is possible that these men were acting on behalf of the Missouri "literary firm,' rather than as a separate firm themselves.

The next quotation shows one of the ways the united order acquired funds:

> Tuesday, 6 [October 1835]. - At home. Elder Stevens came to my house and loaned Frederick G. Williams and Co. six hundred dollars, which greatly relieved us of our present difficulties. May God bless and preserve his soul forever.[5]

Here the order ("us") was the real beneficiary of the loan to Frederick G. Williams & Co., a subset of the order partners. The name "Frederick G. Williams & Co." was a "doing business as" name, with some of the order in the role of silent partners and some as public or general partners. The money may have been needed for an installment payment on some land.

In the following excerpt, it appears that Joseph Smith is acting as agent for the united order in the sale of lands in Kirtland:

> Friday, 30 [October, 1835]. - At home. Mr. Frances Porter, from Jefferson County, New York, a member of the Methodist Church, called to make some inquiry about lands in this place (Kirtland), whether there were any valuable farms for sale, and whether a member of our church could move into this vicinity and purchase lands and enjoy his own possessions and property without making them common stock. He had been requested to make this inquiry by some brethren who live in the town of Leroy, New York. I replied that I had a valuable farm joining the Temple lot I would sell, and that there were other lands for sale in this place and that we had no common stock business among us; that every man enjoys his own property, or can, if he is disposed, consecrate liberally or illiberally to the support of the poor and needy, or the building up of Zion. He also inquired how many members there were in this church. I told him there were about five or six hundred who communed at our chapel, and perhaps a thousand in this vicinity.[6]

More loan transactions are described in the next entry:

> Friday, 4 [December 1835]. - In company with Vinson Knight, drew three hundred and fifty dollars out of

Painesville Bank, on three month's credit, for which we gave the names of Frederick G. Williams & Co., Newel K. Whitney, John Johnson and Vinson Knight. Settled with Brother Hyrum Smith and Vinson Knight, and paid Knight two hundred and forty-five dollars; also have it in my power to pay J. Lewis, for which blessing I feel heartily thankful to my heavenly Father, and ask him, in the name of Jesus Christ, to enable us to extricate ourselves from all embarrassments whatever, that we may not be brought into disrepute, that our enemies may not have any power over us.[7]

Here again, money was borrowed for the benefit of the united order, using the credit of a subset of the "partners" plus a "doing business as" name to get money for multiple united firm purposes. Hyrum Smith was paid off, Vinson Knight was paid off, and money was left over to pay another man, J. Lewis. Frederick G. Williams & Company did not appear to get any benefit at all from the transaction, only the liability to repay. Frederick G. Williams, Newel K. Whitney, and John Johnson were clearly members of the order. It is unclear whether Vinson Knight and Hyrum Smith were members of the firm. Knight did co-sign the loan along with F. G. Williams & Company and others, but he also participated in the immediate proceeds, making him look more like someone outside the firm. He may have been acting only as a surety and was not expected to actually repay any money.

Although the next item relates to the Kirtland Temple committee store rather than the united order, it shows that limited liability arrangements such as the use of "silent" or unknown partners were familiar to the Kirtland brethren:

Orson Hyde's Letter of Complaint.
December 15th, 1835

President Smith: Sir -
.... I ascertained that Elder William Smith [one of the twelve] could go to the [temple committee] store and

get whatever he pleased, and no one to say, why do ye so? until his account has amounted to seven hundred dollars, or thereabouts, and that he was a silent partner in the concern, but was not acknowledged as such, fearing that his creditors would make a haul upon the store....

I am, sir, with respect,
Your obedient servant,
Orson Hyde.[8]

As indicated here by the reference to creditors making "a haul upon the store", the partnership relationship is such that, at least in the eyes of the law, each partner agrees that all he possesses may be taken in payment of a debt contracted by another partner. In this case, the person contracting the debts was William Smith and the assets at risk were those of the store (operated by the temple committee).

The essence of the liability limiting arrangement was keeping from creditors the fact that there were others to whom they could look for payment. This is fair because the money or goods were loaned based on the credit of the "public" or "general" partners. Having access to the assets of the limited or silent partners would be an unexpected windfall to the creditors. The secret names used in Sections 78, 82, 92, 96, 104, etc., served the purpose well of keeping the "known" partners in any particular venture to a minimum and shielding the "silent" partners to use their personal credit as a "general" partner in some other venture.

William Smith was probably not a member of the united firm, although he was one of the Twelve and the Prophet's brother, and so may have had some knowledge of and association with its transactions.

Another meeting of the united order (referred to here and elsewhere as "the company" or "the firm" by its leadership group ("the council") is recorded on April 2, 1836:

Saturday, 2. - Transacted business of a temporal nature in the upper room in the printing office, in company with

Frederick G. Williams, Sidney Rigdon, Oliver Cowdery, William W. Phelps and John Whitmer, which was to have a bearing upon the redemption of Zion. After mature deliberation the council decided that Oliver Cowdery and myself should act as a board or committee to raise, in righteousness, all the money we could for a season, to send by, or to, certain wise men appointed to purchase lands in Zion in obedience to a revelation or commandment of the Lord, for the mutual benefit of the council.

Also, it was agreed by the council that Sidney Rigdon and Frederick G. Williams exert themselves in devising ways and means with the stock on hand, the available outstanding claims of the company, and such other means as they shall deem most proper, to discharge the company's debts. It was also agreed that W. W. Phelps, John Whitmer, and David Whitmer have five hundred books of Doctrine and Covenants, when bound, and five hundred Hymn Books, together with the subscription list for the *Messenger and Advocate* and *Northern Times,* now due in Clay County Missouri; and that *Messrs. Phelps and John Whitmer be released from the responsibility of claims on them, or either of them, as joint partners in the firm.* (emphasis supplied)

As soon as the above plans were settled, I started with President Cowdery on our mission, and our success was such in one half day as to give us pleasing anticipations that we were doing the will of God, and assurance that His work prospered in our hands.[9]

As usual, more efforts were to be made to raise money for purchasing land in Missouri to assist the gathering. Printing and sale of scriptures, hymn books and religious newspapers was another major aspect of the gathering and, therefore, part of the united order's business. The sale of the books and newspaper renewal subscriptions would help get the church message out and defray some of the printing expense. This example shows the level of support the printing effort received from all elements of the united order organization.

There are several interesting aspects to this meeting, including some puzzles. The men at the meeting were all members of the original united order firm organized in 1832 and consisting of two branches. The firm was split in 1834 into two firms, with W. W. Phelps and John Whitmer becoming members of the Missouri firm. In this meeting, those two men seem to be treated as members of the Kirtland firm rather than as delegates from the Missouri firm. Perhaps the explanation is that although technically there were two firms in existence, as a practical matter, the two groups continued to behave much of the time as though no formal split had ever occurred and there were still simply two branches of one firm. There are other events that tend to support this observation. Of course, the purpose of both firms was to aid the gathering to Zion, so it should not seem unusual that they would meet and make plans together.

At the same time they are treated as members of the council, they are also released from some unnamed liabilities or "responsibility" as "joint partners in the firm." The words just quoted are all aspects of the united order organization: all members of the united order were "joint partners" in a "firm" and had some legal "responsibility." The question here is, what liabilities were being released?

In 1837, a year after the April 1836 meeting just quoted, these two men were still carrying on real estate transactions in Missouri in the usual united order way. This, plus their active involvement in book sales, etc., indicates that these men were probably not breaking off all contact with the united order organizations.

A possible explanation of the release from liabilities is that the technicalities of the split of the two firms in 1834 were never really completed until the April 1836 meeting. It is also possible that some particular transaction or arrangement between these two men and the Kirtland firm was being terminated.

However, a more plausible explanation is this: The two men in question, W. W. Phelps and John Whitmer, comprised the first "literary firm" subunit of the united order at the time the first united order was organized in Missouri.

The fact that the April 1836 meeting considered issues relating to publication and distribution of church materials, and also mentions the release of responsibilities, may indicate that the original literary firm was being dissolved and reorganized, and that these two men were being released from further responsibilities for the literary firm. Perhaps because of the problems in Missouri, it became impractical to attempt any major publication effort there, and the Kirtland firm took on all those tasks. David Whitmer, mentioned as helping to distribute the scriptures and hymnals, was one of the two men chosen in Kirtland to act for the literary firm. His involvement in the transaction makes it a little more likely that where there may have previously been two separate literary firms, there was now only one, the Kirtland literary firm.

Whatever the explanation of all the questions raised, the April 2, 1836, meeting does provide more evidence that the united order was a business organization functioning according to the pattern described throughout this book.

The scriptures and history often mention the "wise men" of Zion who were placed there to purchase land, sell it to the saints, and do whatever else might be required to execute the gathering process. In the following quote, the wise men of Zion, or at least some of them, are named. These men, of course, were those who were members of the united order or were closely associated with it:

> Saturday, 9 [April 1836]. - Myself and the principal heads of the Church, accompanied the wise men of Zion, namely, Bishop Partridge and his counselors, Isaac Morley and John Corrill, and President W. W. Phelps, on their way home, as far as Chardon; and after staying with them all night, blessed them in the morning, and returned to Kirtland.[10]

The next item, dated June 16, 1836, gives some insight into the procedure used in requesting aid for the gathering process. It probably relates to the April 2, 1836 meeting mentioned earlier in this chapter where Joseph and Oliver assigned themselves to seek financial assistance:

> The High Council assembled in the Lord's house in Kirtland on the 16th of June, Presidents Sidney Rigdon, and Frederick G. Williams presiding, to investigate the charges of "A want of benevolence to the poor, and charity to the Church," which I had previously preferred against Brother Preserved Harris and Elder Isaac McWithy. After a full and lengthy investigation, the council decided that the charges were fully sustained against Preserved Harris, and that the hand of fellowship be withdrawn from him, until he shall see that the course he is pursuing is contrary to the Gospel of Jesus.
> In the pleas of the councilors, in the case of Elder McWithy, they decided that the charges had been fully sustained; after which, I spoke in my turn as accuser, and stated that I called on the accused, in company with President Oliver Cowdery, for money to send up to Zion, but could get none; afterwards saw him, and asked him if he would sell his farm. He at first seemed willing, and wished to build up Zion. He pleaded excuse in consequence of his liberality to the poor. We offered him three thousand dollars for his farm, would give him four or five hundred dollars to take him to Zion, and settle him there, and an obligation for the remainder, with good security and interest. He went and told Father Lyon that we demanded all his property, and so we lost four or five hundred dollars; because the accused told him [Lyon] such a story, [that] he calculated to keep it [the aforesaid four or five hundred dollars] himself.
> The accused, Elder McWithy, arose and said it was the first time he had been called upon to clear himself before a High Council. He complained of being called contrary to the rules of the gospel, before the council. The President decided that as the case was now before the Council, this plea could not now be urged, but should have been made in the beginning. Elder McWithy pleaded that he had relieved the

wants of the poor, and did so many good things that he was astonished that he should hear such things as he heard today, because he did not give all he had got to one man. If he had done wrong he asked forgiveness of God and the Church.[11]

There are no details concerning the actions of Preserved Harris leading to his being disfellowshipped, but presumably they were similar to the McWithy situation which involved not only lack of charity, but actual fraud or other dishonest behavior.

It appears that both men were considered out of touch with the needs of the church and so insensitive to the urgent need to support the migration, that they could properly be denied fellowship in the church. At that stage, just as at the end of the Nauvoo period, the doctrine of the gathering had great significance, and those unwilling to help would probably not be considered members in good standing. These people were like those who chose to stay behind when the saints went west. They essentially left the church for a time, at least active and useful membership in it. The plan suggested by Joseph Smith to McWithy included his own "gathering" to Zion. Apparently he did not wish to get that involved in the program and obey the direction to go to Zion.

A man would not necessarily be disfellowshipped for not paying any tithing or other contributions, but in that case, he has disfellowshipped himself by disassociating himself from active support of the church program. An evil or dishonest deed on top of that lack of involvement would justify being disfellowshipped.

The procedure followed by Joseph Smith with regard to Isaac McWithy is consistent with the highest regard for private property, and inconsistent with any church-required transfer of property. The cooperation of McWithy was certainly being sought, but it was not to become part of a life-long involvement in a static, confining "share the wealth" scheme (as most socialist communities were), but rather a short-term, hopefully one-time, large-scale relocation of the body of the saints, the involvement determined and limited by the practical needs of such a migration. There was no "double-deeding" expected here or any requirement to join some commune. Joseph Smith was merely exploring the various ways that members could help in the gathering process. This man was in a position to make a major contribution and he was asked to do so.

Joseph Smith first asked for a donation. He had no desire to force a donation and no means to do it. He later offered to buy the land at what was probably a fair price. The arrangement was essentially to give the man all the money he needed to relocate himself in Missouri including purchasing a large amount of land (the land in Missouri was probably priced at less than one-sixth the price of the Kirtland acreage), the rest to be paid him later, probably as his Kirtland plot was subdivided and sold to migrating members. The man could have refused and been left alone to enjoy his land as he chose, except that he decided to cheat Joseph Smith out of the $500 offered as a down payment.

Apparently he had provided some assistance to church members in the past and this may have helped him excuse his deception of Joseph Smith. It is possible that he rationalized that the $500 was merely a return to him of the gifts he had made before, perhaps with interest, he having mentally turned what were gifts when made into loans after the fact. This illustrates again the need for the deed of gift, and the problems it was intended to help avoid.

At this stage of the church's history, tithing and other contributions were as much a part of the program as they are today. However, circumstances made the regular collection of such donations difficult. Instead of the regular collection of small amounts, the procedure was more generally the collection of large sums on a spasmodic basis. A man's good standing in the church did not depend on paying a regular tithe, but only required that he be honest and contribute in some way to the church program.

In a sense the members retained the contributions themselves until some payment needed to be made on behalf of the church or some poor member. Instead of collecting money for years before a building was built, all collections were made at the very time that payment was to be made. It was better and more productive for the property to be held by the members and actively used until the moment of need. Otherwise, the assets would have lain idle. Who would manage them better than their original owners anyway?

The end of the account is ambiguous and does not make it clear whether or not McWithy was disfellowshipped. It may well be that he returned the money and was forgiven, although it seems unlikely that he would be willing to contribute any money or land directly, or be willing to part with his land without first receiving payment in full.

Note here that the High Council had ecclesiastical jurisdiction over a financial matter, but only in the limited sense that it affected a person's standing in the church. The High Council did not normally have any significant authority in the realm of finances. That authority had to rest somewhere, and that somewhere was the united order firm. In the next chapter there is an account of a dispute at Far West over the jurisdiction of the High Council in real estate and financial matters.

What follows is another account of a repositioning of church assets:

> On the first of February, 1837, the firm of Oliver Cowdery and Co. was dissolved by mutual consent, and the entire establishment was transferred to Joseph Smith, Jun., and Sidney Rigdon; and Warren A. Cowdery acted as their agent in the printing office and bookbindery, and editor of the *Messenger and Advocate*.[12]

This was a "form only" change since Oliver Cowdery and Company was just a "doing business as" name for the united firm. Originally held under the Oliver Cowdery and Company subunit of the order, the printing facility was here transferred to another subunit consisting of Joseph Smith and Sidney Rigdon, and placed under the management of Warren A. Cowdery. The agent was probably their employee rather than a member of the firm. The exact purpose of this change is not clear, but it may have related to a change of assignment for Oliver Cowdery or to a need to adjust apparent title and ownership to isolate and protect the important printing operation.

Three months later, in May 1837, the "ownership" was transferred to a new person, Marks, but Joseph Smith and Sidney Rigdon kept control by receiving a power of attorney:

> Some time this month, the *Messenger and Advocate* office and contents were transferred to William Marks, of Portage, Allegheny County, New York, and Joseph Smith and Sidney Rigdon continued the office, by power of attorney from said Marks.[13]

Putting the "ownership" in the hands of a party such as Marks (who probably had no significant debts), would keep it out of the pool of property which might be seized if other creditors of Joseph Smith and Sidney Rigdon wished to collect on land contracts, etc. This was probably a move to protect the very important printing operation from such interference.

The following item, dated April 6, 1837, probably does as much as any other to show the real nature of the united order, its aims and methods, and the practical aspects of the gathering process:

There are many causes of embarrassment, of a pecuniary nature now pressing on the heads of the Church. They began poor; were needy, destitute, and were truly afflicted by their enemies; yet the Lord commanded them to go forth and preach the Gospel, to sacrifice their time, their talents, their good name, and jeopardize their lives; and in addition to this, they were to build a house for the Lord, and prepare for the gathering of the Saints. Thus it is easy to see this must [have] involved them [in financial difficulties]. They had no temporal means in the beginning commensurate with such an undertaking; but this work must be done; this place [Kirtland] had to be built up. Large contracts have been entered into for land on all sides, where our enemies have signed away their rights. We are indebted to them, but our brethren from abroad have only to come with their money, take these contracts, relieve their brethren from the pecuniary embarrassments under which they now labor, and procure for themselves a peaceable place of rest among us. This place must and will be built up, and every brother that will take hold to help secure and discharge those contracts that have been made, shall be rich.

At 4 P.M. President Hyrum Smith addressed the assembly, principally in relation to the temporal affairs of the Church, and censured those who counseled such brethren as moved to this place, when they were not authorized to give advice. He also alluded, in terms of disapprobation, to the practice of some individuals, in getting money from brethren that come in, when it ought to be appropriated to the discharge of heavy debts that are now hanging over the heads of the Church, or for the payments of the land contracts which had been made for the benefit of the Saints in this place....

President Sidney Rigdon rose a little before 5 P.M., and after referring to the gathering, and the preaching of the gospel, as the first thing, alluded to the debt which had been contracted for building the Lord's house, and other purposes, and stated three principal items that constituted nearly the aggregate of debt that now remained unliquidated.

First a charge of six thousand dollars which was appropriated and expended in consequence of the brethren being driven by a lawless mob from their possessions in Jackson County. The second was the building of the Lord's House, the unliquidated debt of which was rising of thirteen thousand dollars. The third item of debt was for the purchase of land, that there might be a place of rest, a place of safety, a place that the

> saints might lawfully call their own. All this is to lay a foundation for the gathering of Israel, and when the Elders go abroad, they can speak understandingly, and urge the necessity and propriety of the gathering, from the fact that we have a place for them, and it is the will of God that they should come. Prey not upon one another, brethren, and for the time being say not, Pay me what thou owest; but contribute all in your power to discharge the great debts that now hang over the church.[14]

The united order was the unit that executed all or nearly all of the transactions mentioned in this excerpt from the history. The frank discussion of debts and "pecuniary embarrassments" is a natural consequence of the financial and administrative efforts of the order. The phrase in paragraph one, "and procure for themselves a peaceable place of rest," and the phrase in paragraph four, "the purchase of land, that there might be a place of rest, a place of safety, a place that the saints might lawfully call their own," are describing an "inheritance" as the gathering saints thought of it then. The same concerns and counsel concerning the acquisition of land was expressed in the Missouri and Nauvoo settings for the same reasons.[15]

As illustrated in the preceding quote and elsewhere, the large-scale financing of land and other property to support the gathering of the saints required large loans. Apparently there were a number of connections made during the 1830's with eastern money lenders to acquire such loans. One hint about these credit arrangements with eastern lenders appears in an entry dated June 11, 1837:

> ... President Brigham Young came into my house ... accompanied by Dr. Willard Richards, who had just returned from a special business mission to New York, Boston, and other eastern cities, on which he started with President Young on the 14th of March ....[16]

The establishment of such financial connections was recommended in 1832 in D&C 82:22:

> 22 And now, verily I say unto you, and this is wisdom, make unto yourselves friends with the mammon of unrighteousness, and they will not destroy you.

Section 82 was given to direct the actual organization of the united order firm, so it was perfectly logical that some comments on how to finance its activities would be part of that section. The united order is the embodiment of the instructions of the Lord to the brethren on how to successfully conduct church business in that setting, that is, how to arrange business liabilities and other matters to the best advantage of the saints.

A comment recorded June 25, 1833, a year after section 82 was given, shows that large debts had already been arranged with New York lenders:

> Say to Brother Gilbert that we have no means in our power to assist him in a pecuniary way, as we know not the hour when we shall be sued for debts which we have contracted ourselves in New York.[17]

In April 1834, in conjunction with the splitting of the firm (D&C 104), the brethren were instructed on how to deal with those New York interests. Help was promised on the writing of a letter and in the effect it would have on the recipients:

> 80 And inasmuch as you are diligent and humble, and exercise the prayer of faith, behold, I will soften the hearts of those to whom you are in debt, until I shall send means unto you for your deliverance.
> 81 Therefore write speedily to New York and write according to that which shall be dictated by my spirit; and I will soften the hearts of those to whom you are in debt, that it shall be taken away out of their minds to bring affliction upon you.[18]

This excerpt indicates that detailed instructions were given to help the firm in this large, new, and rather risky undertaking, including help in drafting letters. This close guidance in affairs of the world can be related to the detailed business instructions given in the case of the funding, construction, and operation of the Nauvoo house.[19] For a person with limited business experience, undertaking the very large transactions involved in the gathering and such new projects as building and operating a hotel, large amounts of specific help from the Lord would likely be appreciated.

In September 1831, at the beginning of the migration to Missouri, the Lord gave an interesting directive on the proper attitude toward such loans as these brethren were acquiring:

> 27 Behold, it is said in my laws, or forbidden, to get in debt to thine enemies;
> 28 But behold, it is not said at any time that the Lord should not take when he please, and pay as seemeth him good.
> 29 Wherefore, as ye are agents, ye are on the Lord's errand; and whatever ye do according to the will of the Lord is the Lord's business.[20]

To the brethren involved in these early movements, the Lord states his intention to "take when he pleases and pay as seemeth him good" through his agents. This comment on the borrowing, debt, and responsibilities to be associated with the gathering of the saints, was a precursor to the larger and more formalized united order firm organized for the same functions and purposes. Apparently the brethren were reluctant to arrange for loans, and they tried to use the Lord's prior counsel to avoid the task, but the Lord resisted and countered their logic. He had to overcome the natural hesitancy of cautious men to overextend themselves in executing such grand plans as the Lord had in mind for them.

The same theme stressing that resources would be made available as needed appears in the earliest revelations on the gathering where the Lord affirms that "the riches of the earth are mine to give."[21] In the Nephite setting, the Lord also indicated that the riches of the earth were obtainable by the saints for use in performing the Lord's work.[22]

Chapter 7 Notes

1. HC 2:253. August 24, 1835. Kirtland.

2. HC 2:172.

3. Many encouragements were given to groups of Saints to join forces and send agents to Missouri to purchase land on which to settle their group. The Tippitts brethren were some of those who were acting on such instructions. Early groups apparently arranged for their own land purchases, while later groups mostly repurchased land acquired by the united order.

There was a constant series of requests for saints to act on their own, and not be "commanded in all things". This decentralizing of administration and encouragement for individuals to act independently was characteristic of Joseph Smith's methods of operation. It was intended that those with means take care of themselves and buy their own land (from the bishop or with his counsel as to location), and that only those who had insufficient means rely on the bishop for ("free") land. The emphasis on independence minimized the planning and administrative burdens of the already hard-pressed central church brethren.

4. HC 2:273. September 16, 1835. Kirtland.

5. HC 2:287-288. October 6, 1835. Kirtland.

6. HC 2:295-296. October 30, 1835. Kirtland.

7. HC 2:324-325. December 4, 1835. Kirtland.

8. HC 2:335-336. December 15, 1835. Kirtland.

9. HC 2:433-434. April 2, 1836. Kirtland. For an example of the procedures used and the problems encountered as Joseph and Oliver went out to collect money, see the account of Harris and McWithy, this chapter.

10. HC 2:436. April 9, 1836. Kirtland.

11. HC 2:445-446. June 16, 1836. Kirtland.

12. HC 2:475. February 1, 1837. Kirtland. For the other uses of the term "dissolved," see HC 2:49 and D&C 104:53. HC 2:486 mentions another reorganization.

13. HC 2:486. May 1837. Kirtland. HC 2:475 is another case of dissolution and reorganization.

14. HC 2:478-480. Thursday, April 6, 1837.

15. See D&C 85 concerning Missouri, and HC 5:272 concerning Nauvoo.

16. HC 2:492. June 11, 1837. Kirtland.

17. HC 1:365. June 25, 1833. Kirtland.

18. D&C 104:80-81. April 23, 1834. Kirtland. The united order's reliance on large loans from outsiders is somewhat inconsistent with the usual idea of how one finances a communal body. The more usual conception is

that the people involved simply pool their resources to create the desired society. Often the very reason for establishing a communal society is to minimize or avoid contact with elements of the world outside the society. The usually poor economic record of such groups would not recommend them as good candidates for loans. What prudent businessman would be willing to invest a large amount of money in such an undertaking, unless he was also perfectly willing to lose it all? The usual outcome of such funding was exactly that - a total loss of all such funds, usually because of the inefficiency of such an organization, and because of the difficulty of holding individuals responsible for losses. There were many examples in the U.S. of such failures in spite of large amounts of funds from outside sources, such as French and British philanthropists. There was even one such example that occurred in Nauvoo after the saints left there.

The fact that the easterners were willing to lend money in large amounts indicates that the transactions of the united order were done in the normal business fashion with the usual risk or liability controlling contracts, etc. This argues against any "all in one pot" communal arrangement.

19. D&C 124:22-24, 60-82, 119, 121-122.

20. D&C 64:27-29.

21. D&C 38:39. Section 37 was revealed only a few days earlier than section 38. The headnote of section 37 indicates that section 37 was "the first commandment concerning a gathering in this dispensation."

22. Jacob 2:19.

CHAPTER 8

Transactions in Missouri by the United Order Firm and Other Units

Based on the number of saints who gathered to Missouri, there must have been a large number of transactions of many kinds conducted by the united order in Missouri, although few are recorded in Joseph Smith's history. As in the case of John Whitmer, some of those who did record the events took those records with them when they left the church. Joseph Smith spent very little time in Missouri, and so had little chance to record those events himself. Major events such as the expulsion of the saints are recorded, but the more common and everyday events are not. Still, there are a few items to give us some insight into economic events in Missouri.

The first quote below describes a decision regarding land sales at Far West:

> Minutes of the High Council at Far West
> Far West, Mo., April 7th [1837]
> At a meeting of the Presidency of the Church in Missouri, the High Council, Bishop and counselors, it was resolved that the city plat of Far West retain its present form; and that the alleys be opened by a majority of the owners of each square, or block, when they shall desire it; that the price and sale of the town lots be left to W. W. Phelps, John Whitmer, Edward Partridge, Isaac Morley, and John Corrill.[1]

This excerpt shows that real estate development went ahead very much as it would today, with lots identified, priced, and sold in an orderly and business-like way. Note that W. W. Phelps, John Whitmer, and Edward Partridge were all members of the united order, with the close association of the Bishop's counselors, Isaac Morley, and John Corrill, who may also have been united order members or associates by this time.

Some lengthy footnote materials in the history associated with this quote describe an organizational conflict that raged for a few days before the above decision was reached and recorded.[2] Apparently the two united order members, W. W. Phelps and John Whitmer, purchased the land from the government and held title to it. They started the process of selling lots in and around Far West and making other temporal plans without conferring with the local high council.

The local high council, bishopric, and resident apostles challenged the authority of W. W. Phelps and John Whitmer to handle the land sale transactions at Far West. There were claims made of fraudulent behavior as well, although none are detailed in the history. The two men had each pledged $1,000 from the proceeds of the land sales toward the building of the planned Far West temple. They may in fact have erred in some way, but the pledges make it appear that the brethren had not completely strayed from their united order real estate development duties. After several tense meetings and many suggested rearrangements,[3] affairs were returned to much the same condition as when the protests began.

It is tempting to speculate on the reasons for both the storm and the sudden calm after the storm. Perhaps the real issue was the jurisdiction of the high council and of the Quorum of the Twelve. The most vocal of the protestors was a member of the Quorum of the Twelve, David W. Patten. Both the united order and the Twelve had potentially world-wide jurisdiction, and it may be expected that these members might have reason to clash concerning a large scale operation such as the development of Far West. Although the united order won for the moment, as we will show later, this conflict was ultimately resolved by combining the functions of the united order with those of the Twelve. (See chapters 10 and 11 on this question.)

The local high council also had reason to claim general jurisdiction in Far West, perhaps following the example of the high council in Kirtland which had at times claimed nation-wide jurisdiction, even over the Twelve. It is possible that they too wished to participate in some of the expected profits. Having entered the scene after the initial land purchases, subdivision, and sales were under way, their claim to a right of participation would be weak and certainly no better than the two men they were challenging. After the April 7th meeting, it appears that the high council bowed out of the real estate development operation. It is also likely that the high council was ultimately restricted mainly to religious questions, as came to be true of the older Kirtland high council. The central church authorities, especially the united order (including Bishop Partridge), were recognized as being the proper people to conduct such business.

It is possible that the nature of the united order and the special callings of its members were explained to the brethren, and their objections were answered. At one point W. W. Phelps sought to hold a meeting with just the high council members. Perhaps he was planning to reveal to this smaller group the facts concerning the united order, hoping to keep the knowledge to as few as possible.

The question of the united order members possibly gaining some profit on the land transactions should not necessarily be considered as an evil thing. They were entitled to receive a living from their labors just as the bishop had the opportunity to do.[4] There are several indicators that the profit motive was purposely used by the Lord and his prophets to move the saints westward. For example, on April 6, 1837, just one day before the high council minutes quoted above, the brethren in Kirtland were encouraged by the statement that "every brother that will take hold to help secure and discharge those [Kirtland land] contracts that have been made, shall be rich."[5] At an earlier time, in a letter dated April 7, 1834, Joseph Smith recognized and employed the drawing power of the profit motive when he commented that if he and the brethren in Kirtland were unable to get the help they needed and go on to Missouri, it would be "in vain for our eastern brethren to think of going up [to Missouri] to *better themselves* by obtaining so goodly a land, (which now can be obtained for one dollar and one quarter per acre) ...."[6] (emphasis supplied). These statements may well have been based on an early scriptural promise of riches to the faithful who participated in the gathering.[7] Of course, the word "rich" has both material and spiritual meaning, but the focus of this book is the economic issues.

The following selection from the minutes of the High Council at Far West, May 22, 1837, shows a church court being used to serve the same function as a civil court - enforcing normal business contracts among members:

> Complaint Against J. M. Patten
>
> [four men] entered a complaint against John Patten, for not fulfilling his contracts, or covenants, in consequence of which they were materially injured....[8]

This example shows that business arrangements among members were much the same as in any other community, then or now.

A general meeting of all the church leaders at Far West gave its blessing to the business unit known as the literary firm:

> Resolved unanimously, that we sanction the literary firm, and give them our voice and prayers, to manage all the affairs of the same, as far as it concerns this place, according to the revelation in [section 70], given November, 1831 ....[9]

The literary firm was a subunit of the united order and its members were authorized to receive their support from their labors as in any other business.

The following excerpt deals mostly with non-land transactions by units other than the united order:

> ### Minutes of a High Council Meeting in Missouri
>
> At a meeting of the High Council, at the committee store, Far West, June 11, 1837, John Whitmer and W. W. Phelps presiding, Resolved by the Council and all present that the building committee be upheld in the mercantile business, by our prayers; that Lyman Wight, Simeon Carter and Elias Higbee by upheld in conducting a leather store; that John Corrill, Isaac Morley, and Calvin Beebee engage in the mercantile business if they choose; that the right of no man shall be infringed upon, to do as he choose according to the law of God and man; and that the above named men shall be upheld in purchasing goods as other men.
>
> It was reported that certain individuals, not of the Church, were desirous, or were about to establish themselves as grocers, retailers of spiritous liquors, and so forth, in Far West, whereupon it was resolved that we will not uphold any man or men to take a partner out of the Church to trade or traffic in this line of business, or sell for any man or men out of the Church, in his name, or on commission.
>
> David W. Patten requested that the Church pay his debts, and take him for security, that he might go forth and preach the Gospel.
>
> Resolved that Elder Pattens's request be granted, and that David W. Patten and Thomas B. Marsh, receive each a lot in the town of Far West, free of charge and that the Bishop, if he approve, give a title.
>
> John Corrill, Clerk.[10]

In paragraph 1, it is mentioned that various men are going to open stores or shops on their own. The brethren here are merely agreeing to patronize them. Any man was to have the right to employ his time as he saw fit or engage in any business. In paragraph 2 the brethren agree to close ranks to attempt to enforce a monopoly on local trade. This may have seemed necessary to keep out "enemies," but its anti-freedom aspect is disturbing and may well have backfired on them later.

The gift of a free city lot was a small enough repayment for work done by the two apostles. The lots were probably not more than an acre in size, and the land's original price was probably only $1.25 per acre. In contrast, land in Kirtland reached a peak of over $30 while the saints were there. Notice that Patten did not have his debt forgiven, but merely changed creditors, and had the debt postponed while he went on a mission.

On May 8, 1838, Joseph Smith recorded a comment relating to the procedure by which the saints acquired land and settled at Far West. He mentioned that he "spent the day with Elder Rigdon in visiting Elder Cahoon at the place he had selected for his residence."[11] It is a small point, but still worth noting that Elder Cahoon selected his residence; he was not assigned to it by some central authority. Most likely he paid a purchase price to the united order representatives which more than covered the cost of the land he chose.

The few fragments presented here of united order and other economic activities in Missouri seem sufficient to show that business transactions were carried on in fairly ordinary ways. There is evidence of natural cooperation, but not of any formal communalism.

Chapter 8 Notes

1. HC 2:481. April 7, 1837. Far West.

2. The following excerpt from the history gives the flavor of the meetings and some of the issues raised:

> Minutes of the High Council at Far West
>
> ....
>
> Resolved, that the Council request the Presidents W. W. Phelps and John Whitmer to give explanation of the following items:
> First - By what authority was this place [Far West] pointed out as a city and [a place for a] house of the Lord, and by whom?
> Second - By what authority was a committee appointed and ordained to superintend the building of the House of the Lord?
>
> ....
>
> Seventh - Should not the High Council and Bishop of Zion, who are appointed to do business for Zion, receive their inheritance in the care of that city in preference to one who is not particularly called to labor for Zion, or an unbeliever?
>
> ....
>
> Ninth - Are the two presidents entitled to the profits arising from the sale of land, on which the city is to be built in this place, independent of the authorities who have been appointed to labor with them for Zion and have suffered like tribulations with them?
>
> ....
>
> David W. Patten spoke against them with apparent indignation; stating that their proceedings had been iniquitous and fraudulent in the extreme, in unrighteously appropriating Church funds to their own enrichment, which had been plainly proven.
>
> ....
>
> The above named presidents agreed to give up the town plat of Far West with four eighties on the commons to be disposed of by the High Council, the Bishop and his counselors, and the said Apostles.

....
Also resolved that whereas W. W. Phelps and John Whitmer had subscribed $1,000 each to the House of the Lord to be built in this place - which they were before intending to pay out of the avails of the town plat - be considered exempt from paying that subscription. HC 2:483-484. April 3, 1837. Far West.

3. The first protests were entered on April 3, 1837. Two days later on the 5th, the high council agreed that after separating out the plat of Far West and transferring it to the bishop for resale, the two men plus the bishop could sell the remaining land.

After another two days, on the 7th, it was decided that Phelps, Whitmer, and the bishop and his counselors should participate in the sale of all lots. That put everything essentially back where it was before, but with the involvement of the bishop specifically mentioned.

Note, however, that on September 4, 1837 (HC 2:511), a revelation is recorded which may indicate that there was some substance to the charges against the two presidents. They had "done those things which are not pleasing in my sight, therefore if they repent not they shall be removed out of their places."

4. See D&C 42:73. See also D&C 70 where members of the literary firm had the opportunity to sustain themselves from their publishing activities.

5. HC 2:478-479. April 6, 1837. Kirtland.

6. HC 2:48-49. April 7, 1834. Kirtland. The economic setting in which the gathering took place is corroborated by a number of sources. The lure of cheap land or even free land drew many people westward. One description of a similar time and place, 1837 in Minnesota, will illustrate the economic incentives to pioneers:

> The farmer of Ohio does not expect to find better soil than he leaves; but his inducements are that he can sell his land at $40 or $50 an acre, and preempt as good in Minnesota for $1.25 an acre. This operation leaves him a surplus fund, and he becomes a more opulent man, with better means to adorn his farm and to educate his children. Christopher C. Andrews: Economic Advantages of the Frontier, *The Annals of America.* (Chicago: Encyclopedia Britannica, Inc., 1976), vol. 8, p. 379, 1857.
>
> A large number of articles dealing with early and mid 1800's frontier land issues appear in *The Annals* and provide some interesting background. A few articles are listed here:
> A Petition for Free use of Public Lands, vol. 5, p. 279, October 25, 1828. Gjert Hovland: Opportunities for Land and for Work, vol. 6, p. 115, April 22, 1835 (land for $1.25 an acre in Illinois). Public Lands and Squatters' Rights, vol. 7, p. 6, 1841; Gustaf Unonius: Problems of Frontier Land Ownership, vol. 7, p. 8, 1841; George Henry Evans: A New Homestead Policy, vol. 7, p. 208, November 30, 1844. Josiah Sutherland: Free Land and the Supply of Labor, vol. 8, p. 180, April 22, 1852.

7. D&C 38:18, 39.

8. HC 2:482. May 28, 1837.

9. HC 2:482-483. May 28, 1837. Far West.

10. HC 2:491. June 11, 1837. Far West.

11. HC 3:28. May 8, 1838. Far West.

CHAPTER 9

The United Order Firms Cease Operation.

All indications are that the united order organizations in Missouri and Kirtland ceased to operate sometime in the one year period preceding the summer of 1838. This chapter will explore the evidence that the united order firms ceased to operate, and consider some of the units which took their place.

An event of some importance occurred in January 1838: Joseph Smith was forced to flee Kirtland and move to Far West.[1] Joseph's flight was related to the apostasy of a significant number of the saints in Kirtland, numbering about two or three hundred, and constituting perhaps 10 to 15 percent of the total.[2] Even more serious than the loss of members was the change in leaders. "Between November 1837 and June 1838, ... almost one-third of the General Authorities were excommunicated, disfellowshipped, or removed from their Church callings."[3]

Brigham Young had fled even earlier on December 22, 1837, marking "the beginning of a mass exodus from Geauga County." More specifically, "between the end of December 1837 and the middle of July 1838, probably more than sixteen hundred members of the Kirtland branch migrated west ...."[4]

Joseph's forced change of residence and the surrounding events seems to constitute a watershed for several reasons. It signaled that the future center of church growth and leadership would be further in the west, and that Kirtland would decline in importance. The loss of members to the church through apostasy, and the loss of citizens to Kirtland through migration, were both significant changes. A change in the forms of organization used to accomplish the church's purposes might be an expected outcome of such a series of dislocations.

Joseph's arrival at Far West began a significant reorganization of the church. D&C 114:2, April 17, 1838, speaks of reorganizing the church to replace those leaders who have left. D&C 115, April 26, 1838, affects several administrative aspects of the church, including its temporal affairs. In verse 1, the president of the church and his counselors, the bishop and his counselors, and the high council of the church in Zion are recognized as the presiding authorities. The name of the church is made clear in verse 3. The gathering to Far West is recommended, verses 7 and 17, and a temple is commissioned, verse 8. Verse 13 directs that the leaders not incur personal debt to build the temple as before.

Sections 117, 118, 119, and 120 are all dated July 8, 1938, and direct another set of important organizational improvements. Section 117 is aimed at getting the bishops collected, reorganized, and reassigned. Section 118 addresses the personnel, functions and impending mission of the Quorum of the Twelve. Sections 119 and 120 accomplish a reorganization of the personnel and procedures for collecting and administering church funds.

Verse 13 of section 115 is worth a closer look. The need for individuals to act in their private capacities to finance and build up the church could only be a short-term and stop-gap method. Getting away from that procedure and moving toward a more corporate means of financing the church's large undertakings was the proper direction for creating a long-lasting institution. At the same time, that meant leaving behind the partnership form, the united order, which was the epitome of the personal liability that the brethren were now to avoid.

Sections 119 and 120 also require some special comment. In years previous, the saints were admonished to put their funds into the hands of members of the united order to buy land for themselves to accomplish their migration west. Where excess funds were available, the saints were requested to make donations for the benefit of others who had not the means to migrate. These excess funds were also administered by the united order personnel.

With the disintegration of the united order firms, and the other changes of circumstances associated with Joseph Smith's move to Far West, a different procedure was appropriate. Now an individual's major funds could be used to buy land directly from other entities such as the corporation of the city of Far West, and need not pass through any church organization. As to their excess funds, they were now directed by sections 119 and 120 to make their donations to the First Presidency and the other regularly established ecclesiastical bodies in Zion.

With these events in mind, let us review the standing of the united order at that point in history. Tracing each individual who made up the united order should give us some understanding as to the state of that institution.

The original united order firm organized in April 1832, D&C 82, consisted of nine men. Two men were added the next year, bringing the total membership to eleven. No others are specifically mentioned as becoming members of the firm.

As of June 1838, only four of the original eleven men were still in the church and holding leadership positions. Joseph Smith maintained his position as President of the Church, with Sidney Rigdon as one of his counselors. Edward Partridge and Newel K. Whitney continued in their ecclesiastical callings as bishops.[5] Three of the men were residing in Far West.[6] The fourth, Bishop Whitney, was in Kirtland.[7] Apparently Bishop Whitney did not make the move west to Nauvoo (previously known as Commerce) until spring 1839.[8]

The other seven men had passed out of the picture for one reason or another. Sidney Gilbert had died of cholera in June 1834.[9] Several of the others lost their standing as officers in the church when they were not sustained by the membership in meetings held September 3, 1837 in Kirtland,[10] and in Far West on November 7, 1837.[11] Although their partnership callings were technically separate from their ecclesiastical callings, it is hard to imagine one who is disfellowshipped or excommunicated continuing in a closely church related temporal calling.

Frederick G. Williams, Martin Harris, and John Johnson were in that group of disapproved officers. F. G. Williams was later excommunicated in 1839.[12] The history does not mention the time of excommunication of Martin Harris, but Joseph Smith refers to him as apostate, "too mean to mention," in a December 1838 letter.[13] John Johnson is simply not mentioned again in the history after the September 1837 meeting.[14] Oliver Cowdery was sustained as an assistant counselor to President Joseph Smith at the September meeting, but his need for repentance was made known.[15] He was excommunicated on April 12, 1838.[16]

The remaining two men, W. W. Phelps and John Whitmer, were on shaky grounds with the other brethren in Missouri during a series of meetings in Missouri in early April 1837.[17] Their need for repentance was confirmed in a revelation dated September 4, 1837.[18] They were removed from their positions as presidents in Missouri in February 1838,[19] and excommunicated in March 1838.[20] However, at least W. W. Phelps remained active in the temporal affairs and development of Far West, as indicated by his involvement in an application for Far West to be designated the county seat.[21]

With two-thirds of the membership of the united order gone, there was little left to constitute a significant temporal organization separate from the presidency and bishoprics of the church.

The specific business subunits of the order had ceased to function. The merchandising firms in Jackson County and Kirtland were no longer operating. The store in Jackson County had been lost to the mob,[22] and the store in Kirtland was closed by some time in 1838 or early 1839,[23] although the need for such a store had probably long since ended. The printing operation in Kirtland had been stopped by the church's enemies.[24]

The work of merchandising and land development which the united orders had carried on had still to be done in some way. But times had changed and other ways were available besides direct church sponsored units. In Far West there were a number of private merchandising concerns,[25] making a special church sponsored unit unnecessary. Similarly, there was no need to have a store associated with the planned temple construction. Instead, private enterprise was to supply any needed services.[26] The corporation of the city of Far West,[27] probably took over much of the real estate development functions that were needed.

It is unclear at this time just what was the main church business unit. The following excerpt from Joseph's historical entries, recorded Sunday, April 12, 1840, two years after the reorganizations discussed above, tends to indicate that the high council assumed some of the business functions previously performed by the united order:

> The High Council of Nauvoo met at my house, when I proposed that Brother Hyrum Smith go east with Oliver Granger to settle some business transactions of the Church which the council sanctioned; and voted, "That President Joseph Smith,

Jun., make the necessary credentials for Oliver Granger and Hyrum Smith."[28]

This use of the high council probably represents an interim step between the end of the partnerships and the transfer of control to the corporate church, with the Twelve (the traveling high council) and the First Presidency as the administrators. The jurisdiction of high councils had varied widely in the past, depending on who were members of the body, and what other organizations were available to accept responsibility.[29] But, of course, any council which contained the president of the church might also have all the authority that the church had on earth.

Having traced in general outline the ending of the united order and the establishment of its interim replacement, it may now be useful to go back and review some aspects of the united order and of church government in general that can be divined from its final transactions and death throes. The last chapter includes an example of what was probably a degenerate use of the authority of the united order. The united order was first created to supply a service not available through any other means, or available at too high a price. But as Far West was being developed, some of the united order members, W. W. Phelps and John Whitmer, seemed to other leaders to be using their positions too much for their own personal benefit. There was also an apparent attempt to exercise their authority to limit the entry of other firms into the area. This economic exclusiveness takes the united order beyond its original "shield" status of helping members with certain critical economic needs associated with the gathering, and tries to make it a "sword" to restrict all economic opportunities of church members. The normal consequence of such behavior is to limit the numbers of sellers and providers and so raise the price of goods and services to the bulk of the members. This is the opposite of the effect originally sought in setting up the united order.

The loss of many of the united order's members was an important aspect of its end. Associated with the April 1838 excommunication proceedings against Oliver Cowdery is an interesting insight into the nature of the temporal government of the church as he viewed it. As one of the original members of the united order,[30] his opinion should be significant. Among the nine charges that were originally made against him, numbers 4 and 5 are closely related and of greatest interest here:

> Fourth - For virtually denying the faith by declaring that he would not be governed by any ecclesiastical authority or revelations whatever, in his temporal affairs.
> Fifth - For selling his lands in Jackson county, contrary to the revelations.[31]

Taking the fifth charge first, and avoiding comment on the phrase "contrary to the revelations," he acknowledged by letter that he had sold his lands in Jackson County. His justification of his actions in selling his lands, or perhaps more accurately, a part of his rebuttal to the related doctrine of temporal obedience included in the fourth charge, was this:

> Now, sir, the lands in our country ... have not the least shadow of feudal tenures attached to them, consequently, they may be disposed of by deeds of conveyance without the consent or even approbation of a superior.[32]

In light of the high council's original concern about Oliver Cowdery's sale of his land in Jackson County, it is significant that Joseph insisted that, for each person who could rightfully claim it, clear title be given to his land, so that he could make any disposition of it he wished, as governed by his own conscience.

Cowdery goes on to observe that:

> If I were to be controlled by other than my own judgement, in a compulsory manner, in my temporal interests, of course, [I] could not buy or sell without the consent of some real or supposed authority."[33]

In his correspondence, Oliver gives a slightly different wording for the declaration on which the fourth charge is based:

> I will not be influenced, governed, or controlled, in my temporal interests by any ecclesiastical authority or pretended revelation whatever, contrary to my own judgement.[34]

With that restatement in mind, he continues his brief for the defense:

> Such being still my opinion [I] shall only remark that the three great principles of English liberty, as laid down in the books, are "the right of personal security, the right of personal liberty, and the right of private property." My venerable ancestor was among the little band, who landed on the rocks of Plymouth in 1620 - with him he brought those maxims, and a body of those laws which were the result and experience of many centuries, on the basis of which now stands our great and happy government; and they are so interwoven in my nature, have so long been inculcated into my mind by a liberal and intelligent ancestry that I am wholly unwilling to exchange them for anything less liberal, less benevolent, or less free.
>
> The very principle of which I conceive to be couched in an attempt to set up a kind of petty government, controlled and dictated by ecclesiastical influence, in the midst of the national and state government. You will, no doubt, say this is not correct; but the bare notice of these charges, over which you assume a right to decide, is, in my opinion, a direct attempt to make the secular power subservient to Church direction - to the correctness of which I cannot in conscience subscribe - I believe that principle never did fail to produce anarchy and confusion.
>
> This attempt to control me in my temporal interests, I conceive to be a disposition to take from me a portion of my

Constitutional privileges and inherent right - I only, respectfully, ask leave, therefore, to withdraw from a society assuming they have such right.[35]

The high council considering the charges against Oliver apparently agreed with his logic and deleted those two charges as inappropriate. The other charges they apparently felt were still sufficient to justify their action.

The significance of this transaction to the history of the united order firms may now be considered. Oliver Cowdery had been with the united order organization since its beginning. From the strength of his statements quoted above concerning constitutional and freedom issues, and the lack of any mention of previous conflicts of this sort, we may infer that this was the first time in Oliver's knowledge that an attempt had been made to establish control by a church organization over an individual's personal temporal affairs, on pain of loss of membership.[36] Apparently, such control was no part of the united order at least until just before its demise. In other words, the control features often attributed to the united order never existed during its healthy and productive life, and only arose at the time it was in a process of decline and disintegration. As discussed in the previous chapter, there is evidence that the brethren in Missouri had a tendency to overestimate their rightful authority. Their countenancing of certain economic endeavors by the brethren and forbidding of any economic associations with non-members shows a tendency of the sort resisted by Oliver Cowdery.[37]

Besides taking the excommunication action, the high council acting on Oliver Cowdery's case also voted that "Oliver Cowdery be no longer a committee to select locations for the gathering of the saints."[38] This action does not refer by name to Oliver Cowdery's membership in the united order, but one of its functions is clearly described. It is also interesting that the council realized that excommunication from the church did not necessarily separate him from the temporal organization assisting the gathering, and that function and office was addressed separately.

This action by the high council may highlight for us the problems of administration that arise when officers having temporal authority operate separately from those having ecclesiastical authority. To some extent there seems to have been an almost conscious competitive desire on the part of the ordinary and regularly constituted church organizations such as bishoprics and high councils, including the traveling high council or quorum of the twelve, to supplant the extraordinary or ad hoc united order, whose personnel had become entrenched in many important matters. This was probably a healthy and necessary tendency. The time for the ad hoc organizations was nearing its end, and the move was toward more permanent structures. The united order units were an important factor in the migration of the saints to Missouri, but by June 1838, the need for such organizations was largely past.

There is also another consideration: If the existence of the united order organization had become known to any significant number of people, much of its usefulness would be gone. The possible reference to it in Oliver's case, and the destruction of the press in Kirtland despite efforts to shield it by organizational changes, may be indicators that the previously secret nature of the order could not longer be maintained. On this point, see chapter 8 for an April 1837 account of a conflict between united order members and the Far West high council in which the existence and nature of the united order may have become known to a wider circle of members.

Chapter 9 Notes

1. HC 3:1. It is almost as though the Lord contrived to have Joseph moved west from Kirtland, despite the state in which he had to leave his affairs. This event was probably for the good of the saints, to overcome their reluctance to move to the next stage of necessary development, to hurry along the gathering and organization of the saints on the western frontiers.

2. Milton V. Backman, Jr., *The Heavens Resound: A History of the Latter-day Saints in Ohio, 1830 - 1838* (Salt Lake City, Utah: Deseret Book Co., 1983), p. 328.

3. *Heavens,* p. 328.

4. *Heavens,* p. 342. D&C 115 and 117 were invitations for the saints to leave Kirtland and move to the western settlements of the saints.

5. Edward Partridge was bishop at Quincy, Illinois, as of March 1839, HC 3:289. He died May 27, 1840, in Nauvoo, at the age of 46, HC 4:132. Newel K. Whitney, after some straying, (See D&C 117), went to Missouri and Illinois, was bishop of Commerce Middle ward in 1839, HC 4:12, and held the position of Presiding Bishop at least during the years of 1844 to 1848, HC 7:297, 462, 629. Born Feb. 5, 1795, he was 53 years of age in 1848. HC 1:145, biographical note mentioning his Indian trader experience.

6. D&C 115.

7. D&C 117.

8. HC 3:273, 347, 363, 377; 4:12. Newel K. Whitney died September 23, 1850, in Salt Lake City, Utah, at age 56. CHC 4:114.

His obituary in the *Deseret News* includes the following note: "He had long held the office of presiding bishop of the Church of Jesus Christ of Latter-day Saints - to receive from the rich by consecration and to distribute to the poor, the goods of this world."

9. HC 2:118, 120. Gilbert had been a successful merchant in Painesville, Ohio, and some time before 1830 had moved to Kirtland and taken as his junior partner Newel K. Whitney. He joined the church in Kirtland.

10. HC 2:509-510. See also *Heavens,* p. 327.

11. HC 2:522-523.

12. HC 3:284.

13. HC 3:232.

14. Born in 1779, HC 1:260n, John Johnson was 59 years at the time and may not have been able to move on to Missouri and Illinois. Several of his relatives in the Johnson family did apostatize at that time.

15. HC 2:511.

16. HC 3:17.

17. HC 2:483.

18. HC 2:511.

19. HC 3:3-5.

20. HC 3:6, 8, 284.

21. HC 3:48. It is not mentioned in what capacity he made the application concerning designating Far West as the county seat, but it is possible that he did so as a member of the corporation of Far West. See HC 2:521. It is interesting to note that Joseph Smith referred to him as "Brother Phelps."

22. HC 1:427-428.

23. D&C 117.

24. HC 3:11.

25. HC 2:491.

26. A committee store is mentioned in HC 2:491. At HC 2:505, a decision was made to have no store associated with the temple project, and to allow private enterprise to handle any needs.

27. HC 2:521.

28. HC 4:114. Sunday, April 12, 1840. The united order was often itself known as a "council." See chapter 9.

29. See chapter 11. The high council organizational form seemed to allow a great deal of flexibility. There are examples of both wide and narrow jurisdictional limits. Depending on conditions, including the existence of other church organizations, a high council's jurisdiction might range from local matters to general matters and from spiritual to temporal. The functions expanded and contracted as the needs of the moment changed.

But, at least during the first few years of the church's existence, the high councils were normally excluded from major temporal transactions, and were confined to spiritual and priesthood matters. See an incident, HC 2:481-483. On the other hand, we should recall that president Harold B. Lee's stake high council must have had significant temporal jurisdiction during the depression.

30. D&C 82.

31. HC 3:16. See *Heavens,* p. 327, for a discussion of other possible factors in Oliver Cowdery's apostasy.

32. HC 3:17.

33. HC 3:18.

34. HC 3:18.

35. HC 3:18. Perhaps Oliver Cowdery's overall argument may be summarized as follows: The church has no power to control his temporal activities; and if the church has no power to control his temporal activities, it also has no authority to excommunicate him for a failure to submit to that control.

36. This same question arose in Utah when the united order concepts taught there were under consideration. See talk by Orson Pratt on whether nonparticipants could retain their standing in the church. JD 17:35. The stated goal of central church ownership and control of all productive property was never actually achieved in practice, presumably because of objections of the same sort from the membership.

37. HC 2:491.

38. HC 3:18

CHAPTER 10

The United Order Firms are Replaced by the Corporate Trustee-in-Trust

Without attempting to directly answer the interesting question of why Joseph Smith wished to move from a partially decentralized technique for church property management to a centralized corporate form, it will still prove interesting to examine the evidence that he did so. Perhaps some clues as to the why of things will emerge after the information is assembled.

The first mention of the move to a corporate form occurred at a January 30, 1841, meeting in Nauvoo:

> Saturday, 30. -- At a special conference of the Church of Jesus Christ of Latter-day Saints, held at Nauvoo pursuant to public notice, I was unanimously elected sole Trustee-in-Trust of the Church of Jesus Christ of Latter-day Saints.[1]

Apparently this election was a necessary prerequisite to the formal incorporation process required by the Illinois legislation:

> City of Nauvoo, Hancock County, Illinois, Feb. 1, A.D. 1841
> To the County Recorder of the County of Hancock:
>
> Dear Sir: - At a meeting of the Church of Jesus Christ of Latter-day Saints, at this place on Saturday, the 30th day of January, A.D. 1841, I was elected sole Trustee for said Church, to hold my office during life (my successors to be the First Presidency of said Church) and vested with plenary powers, as

sole Trustee in Trust for the Church of Jesus Christ of Latter-day Saints, to receive, acquire, manage or convey property, real, personal, or mixed, for the sole use and benefit of said Church, agreeably to the provisions of an act entitled, "An Act Concerning Religious Societies," approved February 6, 1835.

Joseph Smith, (L.S.)[2]

The term "corporation" does not appear in these first quotes, but a later statement, dated April 1843, affirming the ascendancy of the new business unit, is more specific:

> The act of incorporation required of me securities which were lodged in the proper hands, as the law directs; and I am responsible for all that comes into my hands....
> So long as you consider me worthy to hold this office [Sole Trustee-in-Trust for the Church], it is your duty to attend to the legal forms belonging to the business; and if not, put some other one in my place.[3]

As the preceding quote intimates and as later events show, forming a corporation[4] and giving it the powers desired are two completely separate processes. There were still many vestiges of the previous decentralized and ad hoc arrangements that had to be gradually changed, discontinued, or absorbed. A year earlier, in March 1840,[5] while the first memorial to Congress was being prosecuted, there appears to have been a fear of the political effects of too much centralization; but by 1841 that fear was apparently overridden by other considerations.

The new corporation's first order of business, apparently, was to accomplish a clear break with its various more or less ad hoc predecessors:

Minutes of the General Conference of the Church held at Nauvoo.
[October 4, 1841]

... On motion, voted unanimously, that the trustee-in-trust be instructed not to appropriate Church property to liquidate old claims that may be brought forward from Kirtland and Missouri.[6]

Insulation from responsibility for debts of other business units is one of the inherent advantages of a corporate entity. The corporation was a new person and had no debts at the time of its beginning. It was a clean legal break from the debts of the prior partnership forms. The personal liabilities accrued by members of old and defunct partnerships would not be carried over to burden the new business unit, even though those persons may have management powers over the corporation.

During the greatest turmoil of the migration, when a corporate form was not available anyway, a partnership form was used. After things had settled down, a corporate form was adopted and a fresh start was made. The cancellation of old notes was probably very much a part of the demise of the old united order firm, burying the remains or tossing out the dregs.

The action by the conference could be considered as essentially a partial declaration of bankruptcy for a number of prior business units, a declaration on non-continuity with the past. Joseph Smith's own personal bankruptcy proceedings[7] may have been necessary to clear the air of old transactions, and to avoid constant attempts by creditors to prosecute claims against corporate assets based on old claims against Joseph Smith as an individual.

The Twelve had just returned in July from a two-year mission in England. They gained experience in church administration in the mission areas, and this was probably a good time for introducing the Twelve into the day-to-day workings of central church administrative affairs, with the new corporation as the mechanism. The Twelve were there to help enforce this idea of the disavowal of all old notes, and to back up the trustee-in-trust in phasing out the old and bad debts of the several partnerships.

However, canceling these old notes was not something one could do with the wave of a wand. Although the new corporation denied any liability for past individual or partnership debts, the church leaders and others were still subject to continuing claims. A large portion of the old notes and debts were held by church members against other church members, and thus might be considered "family" debts. These debts probably stemmed from the thousands of real estate and other transactions that occurred in the series of moves to Kirtland, various places in Missouri, and finally to Nauvoo. The saints had many troubles and needs for various resources, many acquired by loans evidenced by notes. Later events, including the loss of almost everything in Missouri, made those who signed the notes either unwilling or unable to pay the amounts promised.

In a move to clear away this overhang of debt, remove causes for friction, and perhaps even benefit the new church corporation financially, it was proposed, in an action dated April 12, 1842, that such notes be donated ("consecrated") to the Nauvoo temple, presumably via the trustee-in-trust:

> The Twelve ... appointed John Taylor, Brigham Young and Heber C. Kimball a committee to make arrangements for the payments due from President Smith as Trustee in Trust, to Mr. Wilkie .... Also voted that the Twelve unite their influence to persuade the brethren to *consecrate* all the old notes, deeds, and obligations which they hold against each other to the building of the Temple in Nauvoo, and that Willard Richards write an epistle in the name of the Twelve on that subject, and publish it in the *Times and Seasons,* which he did ....[8] (emphasis supplied)

A year and a half later, in February 1843, the notes were still showing up:

> Wednesday, 22. -- At nine this morning Brother Abel Owen presented a claim of considerable amount against Carter, Cahoon & Co., Kirtland, and notes of Oliver Granger of about $700 for payment. He said he was poor and unable to labor, and wanted something to live on. I told him to burn the papers, and I would help him. He gave me the papers, and I gave him an order on Mr. Cowan for fifteen dollars worth of provisions. This was a gift, as the Church was not obligated to pay those debts.[9]

The most interesting aspect of this incident is the fact that the bill was presented to the church at all, apparently based on the possibly widespread assumption that the new trustee-in-trust was for many purposes the direct successor of the united order firm. But Joseph took some pains to make sure that he did not appear to be accepting any responsibility for that prior organization's debts, so that others would not request payment on or sue on old notes of the united firms and their component and associated firms. He wished to make it clear that the money he did give the man was designated as a gift. It appears that Joseph is himself tacitly admitting that for many purposes the trustee-in-trust was a successor to (or more accurately, a replacement for) the old firms, but he did not wish to make it a successor as far as assumption of debts was concerned. Any moneys that were actually paid out would be within the discretion of the trustee rather than extracted by legal force.

There was at least one interesting and graphic confrontation in the process of rejecting the old and establishing the new administrative apparatus:

> Saturday, 11 [December 1841]. - Late this evening, while sitting in council with the Twelve in my new store on Water street, I directed Brigham Young, President of the Twelve Apostles, to go immediately and instruct the building committee in their duty, and forbid them receiving any more property for the building of the Temple, until they received it from the Trustee in Trust, ...[10]

> This morning [December 13, 1841] President Young delivered the message I gave him on Saturday evening to Reynolds Cahoon and Elias Higbee, the Temple Committee, in presence of Elders Kimball, Woodruff, and Richards.[11]

The assignment of this task to the Twelve by the Prophet probably served several purposes at once, including some important training. The Twelve were given the opportunity to begin to accept responsibility and authority for central church fiscal matters, and the temple committee were taught the nature of the new procedures and philosophy being established.

This event served notice that there was to be no more decentralization of collection and distribution of church funds as there had been in the past. The trustee was now to do it all in a centralized manner, either himself or through his agents, the Twelve.[12] Joseph used every available means to define and defend his new jurisdictional "turf."[13]

The announcement of the change in policy was followed up later with at least one accounting:

> Saturday, October 1. [1842] -- ....I had previously sent for the Temple Committee to balance their accounts and ascertain how the Temple business was going on. Some reports had been circulated that the committee was not making a righteous disposition of property consecrated for the building of the Temple, and there appeared to be some dissatisfaction among the laborers. After carefully examining the accounts and enquiring into the manner of the proceedings of the committee, I expressed myself perfectly satisfied with them and their works. The books were balanced between the trustee and committee, and the wages of all agreed upon.
>
> I said to the brethren that I was amenable to the state for the faithful discharge of my duties as trustee-in-trust, and that the Temple committee were accountable to me, and to no other authority; and they must not take notice of any complaints from any source, but let the complaints be made to me, if any were needed, and I would make things right.[14]

Notice that Joseph Smith did not miss this opportunity to lecture the brethren again on the importance of his position as trustee-in-trust and their duties to him. This indicates that more than one and one-half years after the announcement of the new corporate unit, there was still reason to worry that some did not perfectly understand and accept the new organizational arrangements.

Another series of events shows the transfer of real estate titles and transactions to the new corporation:

> A conference was held at Ramus on the 4th and 5th of December, 1841, ... It was unanimously resolved by the conference that the organization of the Church at Ramus as a Stake be discontinued ... and that William Wightman, the Bishop, transfer all the Church property in Ramus to the sole Trustee in Trust, Joseph Smith, President of the whole Church.[15]

> Tuesday, 16 [December 1841]. - William Wightman of Ramus, delivered to Joseph Smith, sole trustee-in-trust, the deed to the unsold and bonded lots of land in the town of Ramus [and various other specific land, notes, and bonds] after applying sufficient of said property to liquidate the claims of those from whom the town was purchased ....[16]

> Wednesday, 5 [January 1842]. - William Wightman signed over and delivered the town plat of Ramus to me, as sole Trustee in Trust for the Church of Jesus Christ of Latter-day Saints.[17]

Apparently the land at Ramus was actually held by the bishop of that area. This decentralized ownership of church property was apparently fairly common up until then, before the process began of consolidating control of both funds and land. Notice that only the unsold, mortgaged, or public lands were transferred to the trustee in trust. Lands privately held through completed purchases were not affected.

In the last quotes, lands already held by the church were transferred to the trustee in trust. In other kinds of transactions, new lands were also acquired by the trustee in trust for the purpose of stimulating and assisting the gathering process:

> Monday, 13 [December 1841]. -
> .....
> Some time in the fall of 1839, Daniel S. Witter, of the steam mill at Warsaw, solicited the First Presidency of the Church to make a settlement on the school section no. 16, one mile south of Warsaw, and the solicitations were continued by Daniel S. Witter, Mark Aldrich and others, from time to time, till the spring or summer of 1841, when articles of agreement were entered into between Calvin A. Warren, Esq., Witter, Aldrich and others, owners of the school section and the First Presidency, giving the Saints the privilege of settling on the school section ....[18]

Here the First Presidency, as trustee in trust, was doing the same things that had been previously done by the united order. A corporation had simply replaced the partnership in purchasing or otherwise providing land for the benefit of the migrating saints.

Having first worked at the "sending" end of the migration in England and the eastern states, the Twelve now became active in the receiving end of the gathering, as shown by the following epistle, dated October 12, 1841:

> An Epistle of the Twelve Apostles, to the
> Brethren Scattered Abroad on the Continent
> of America, Greeting
>
> .....
> In this city [Nauvoo], the church has succeeded in securing several extensive plats of land, which have been laid out in city lots, a part of which have been sold, a part has been distributed to the widow and orphan, and a part remains for sale. These lots are for the inheritance of the Saints, a resting place for the Church, a habitation for the God of Jacob....

> The town plat for the town of Warren, near Warsaw, is secured on such conditions that the brethren can be accommodated with lots on very reasonable terms; but the large plat in Nauvoo, purchased of Messrs. Hotchkiss, Tuttle, & Co., of New Haven, Connecticut, remains unpaid for....
>
> Let the brethren in the eastern states who have lands which they wish to dispose of, so that they may remove hither, and secure to themselves an inheritance among the Saints either in the cities or farms in the vicinity, and are willing to have their lands in the East made over to Messrs. Hotchkiss and Co. towards the payment of the foregoing notes, communicate with us immediately, at this place, stating to us the extent and value of their property.
>
> Then, as soon as we shall have received communications concerning property, sufficient to cancel the obligations, and the necessary preliminaries are understood with Messrs. Hotchkiss and Co., we will dispatch an agent to New Haven to complete the negotiation, transfer your property, take up the notes and secure a deed; and those whose property is thus transferred can have the value thereof here in city lots or lands in the vicinity; and thus your property will prove to you as good as money, inasmuch as you desire to emigrate; and you will no longer be obliged to tarry afar off because that money is so scarce you cannot sell and get your pay.[19]

The arrangements for the gathering of the saints in Nauvoo were the same in principle as those in Kirtland and Missouri, but had become much more sophisticated with growth and experience. Now the saints could execute a trade of their eastern lands for land in Nauvoo rather than go through the more difficult steps of selling one parcel of land to get money to buy another. This more convenient procedure was made possible by a more mature and centralized administrative mechanism. Hotchkiss & Co. would benefit by acquiring eastern land at relatively low prices and holding it for the most advantageous sale.

The above extract from the epistle of the Twelve is also interesting in that it provides more clues on the meaning of the word "inheritance" to the early brethren. It was land purchased in the normal way, but the transaction had spiritual significance because it was a part of fulfilling the commandment to gather.

Unfortunately, as before in Kirtland and Missouri, some members were not always willing to participate in the plans and commitments the brethren had made for the gathering. They preferred to circumvent the brethren and act on their own, causing the brethren financing and other difficulties. To help forestall those problems, Joseph Smith gave the Twelve an assignment, dated June 1842, to oversee the arrival of the immigrants:

> Also Joseph commanded the Twelve to organize the Church more according to the law of God; that is to require of those that come in to be settled according to their counsel, and also to appoint a committee to wait upon all who arrive, make them welcome and counsel them what to do. Brigham Young, Heber C. Kimball, George A. Smith and Hyrum Smith were the committee appointed to wait upon emigrants and settle them.[20]

The committee was apparently unable to persuade all the newcomers to cooperate fully as evidenced by Joseph's journal entry of February 13, 1843:

> ... I remarked that those brethren who came here having money, and purchased without the Church and without counsel, must be cut off.[21]

This comment by Joseph Smith epitomizes the circumstances of all the migrations of the saints in that era. The purchase of land was to be coordinated to avoid confusion and competition. In many cases the church (united firm, or later, the corporation) bought large tracts of land with the expectation that incoming saints would repurchase the land from the church unit. Where they didn't, but went their own way or even tried to make a profit at the expense of other church members, Joseph Smith considered them rebellious and selfish. Such behavior also left the church business unit with unsold land and no means to pay for it. There was no central control of property, but only the practical business concerns just mentioned.

The next entry, dated April 18, 1843, shows how land was made available to the incoming saints. They usually just bought it from Joseph Smith or someone else in the united firm, or, as here, a representative of the church corporation.

> Rode out on the prairie. Sold one hundred and thirty acres of land to the English brethren and took a bond from John T. Barnett for two lots.[22]

Another example of Joseph's many land transaction entries, dated November 9, 1842, will illustrate the way the land was first acquired:

> Wednesday, 9. - Paid E. Rhodes $436.93, it being the amount of three notes due for the north-west quarter of Sec. 9, 6 N. 8 W. ....[23]

This chapter concludes the detailed presentation of the development of the united order. By the time of Joseph's death, the initial gathering process had been completed, and a corporate mechanism put in place to handle central church business with the assistance of an experienced quorum of twelve. At this level of maturity, the central church business unit was in the proper form to continue fulfilling its role on through the future decades. To say that the united order ended with the phasing out of the partnership form would probably be inaccurate. The original intention that it be an "everlasting order," D&C 82:20, should lead us to conclude that the order has never ceased since its inception, although the outward legal forms have been adjusted as conditions required.

Chapter 10 Notes

1. HC 4:286. January 30, 1841. Nauvoo.

2. HC 4:287. February 1, 1841. Nauvoo.

3. HC 5:331. April 1843.

4. The church seems to have a strong tendency toward centralizing its functions, especially those having to do with control of money and property. There are some interesting exceptions such as the simultaneous existence of the two quorums of twelve overseeing separate church organizations during the first century A.D., but even then, although there could be no significant contact or coordination between the two bodies using normal means, a need was felt to establish a hierarchy or ranking relationship between the two quorums. 1 Ne. 12:9-10. There are probably a number of reasons for this tendency, but exploring those reasons in any depth is a separate study in itself, and beyond the scope of this study. What is important here is the fact that the tendency exists and manifested itself in Joseph's move to a corporate form for the central church business unit when conditions would permit.

5. HC 4:93, 98.

6. HC 4:427. October 4, 1841. A simply analogy may be useful here. To avoid trouble with stale claims related to payroll and other obligations, many firms today put a fixed amount into an account and pay a particular payroll or other obligation only from that account. If a check is presented after all the money is gone, it bounces and a separate procedure must then be started to collect it, if it can be collected at all.

7. The following quote mentions Joseph Smith's personal bankruptcy proceeding:

Monday, 7. - Spent the forenoon in council with Brother Hyrum Smith and some of the twelve, and in giving instructions concerning the contemplated journey to Springfield on the 15th of December next, and what course ought to be pursued in reference to the case of bankruptcy. HC 5:183-184. November 7, 1842. Nauvoo.

8. HC 4:589. April 12, 1842.

9. HC 5:287. February 22, 1843. Nauvoo. The firm of Carter, Cahoon & Co. probably consisted of Jared Carter, a member of and later President of the Kirtland high council, and also a member of the Kirtland Temple Building Committee, HC 2:28, 205, 511, and Reynolds Cahoon, also a member of the Kirtland Temple Building Committee, HC 2:205. Both of these men appear many times in the history in many situations. Oliver Granger also appears many times in the history as being active in church business dealings. HC 4:114.

10. HC 4:470, 472, 477, 491; 4:589; 5:184. December 11, 1841.

11. HC 4:472. December 13, 1841.

12. Note that this is more than three years after the tithing revelation of 1838, sections 119 and 120, showing that the tithing collection process had as yet changed little as a result of those two sections and was still decentralized to a significant degree.

13. The following quote mentions an apparent dispute over Joseph Smith's authority as trustee-in-trust to act in land transactions in the Warsaw area:

> Monday, 7.
> .... In the afternoon Calvin A. Warren, Esq., arrived, and I called upon some of the Twelve and others to testify before Squire Warren what they knew in reference to the appointment of trustee-in-trust, &c., showing also from the records that I was authorized by the Church to purchase and hold property in the name of the Church, and that I had acted in all things according to the counsel given to me. (HC 5:183-184. November 7, 1842. Nauvoo).

In March 1844 there is another attempt recorded by some unnamed person to challenge the propriety of the trustee's behavior in handling the donations to the temple, but this was obviously of no real significance and no serious challenge to the new organizational mechanism. HC 6:239.

In that same month, HC 6:259, a rather bizarre proposal was made, which, while probably unacceptable to Joseph, did recognize the position of the trustee-in-trust and the scope of the office. (Members from the southern states and Texas might turn over to the trustee-in-trust the proceeds from their slave-operated plantations.)

14. HC 5:166. October 1, 1842. Nauvoo.

15. HC 4:467, 468. December 4, 1841. Saturday. Ramus.

16. HC 4:477. December 16, 1841. Ramus.

17. HC 4:491. January 5, 1842.

18. HC 4:470-471. December 13, 1841.

19. HC 4:433-435. October 12, 1841.

20. HC 5:35. June 1842.

21. HC 5:272. Feb. 13, 1843. Joseph Smith. Nauvoo.

22. HC 5:365. April 18, 1843. Joseph Smith. Nauvoo.

23. HC 5:184. November 9, 1842.

CHAPTER 11

Relationships Among the United Order, the Quorum of the Twelve, the Kirtland High Council, and Other Early Administrative Bodies

We are so accustomed today to the Quorum of the Twelve taking a central role in all aspects of Church administration that it is hard to imagine that it was ever otherwise. And yet, although section 18, given in June 1829, directed the choosing of the Twelve, the first Quorum of the Twelve was not chosen in this dispensation until 1835, five years after the church was organized, four years after the first settlements were made in Missouri, and one and one-half years after the Saints were exiled from their properties in Jackson County. The Twelve did not begin to function in central church administrative roles until 1841. From 1835 to 1841 they were mostly on missions, and when not on missions, were restricted from displacing existing councils acting in central church matters. During the time from 1830 to 1841 there were many important matters of central church business to be dealt with, but the Twelve were mostly not available to accept those responsibilities. During the eleven year period that the Twelve were developing, that is, being chosen and organized, gaining experience, and receiving formal authority and specific church assignments, and otherwise becoming prepared for "bearing off the kingdom," the united order and other councils and units bore those central church administrative burdens.

It is interesting that the Savior was engaged in his ministry for some time[1] and had drawn to himself a number of disciples before the Jerusalem Twelve were formally called and ordained.[2] After a period of training, they were all sent out as witnesses to preach the Gospel[3] and returned with many spiritual experiences to relate.[4] Presumably Jesus had some assistants to help him while the Twelve were on their missions. Later the Seventy were called to perform similar missions and assist the Twelve. Only gradually did the Twelve begin to assume responsibility for the administration of the Church, and only fully accepted that role after the death and resurrection of Christ.

A similar sequence of events occurred in this dispensation. The Latter-day Twelve were called only after a goodly number of disciples had been assembled and tested in the fire of the Missouri conflicts and the Zion's camp episode. A few months after they were called they were sent on a mission to the East to hold conferences and act as special witnesses. Often called the traveling high council, they had few duties relating to the central administration of the Church in Missouri or Kirtland, but were to function mostly in areas where no church organization had previously existed.

For some administrative purposes, they were temporarily subservient to the high council in Kirtland. Their relationship to the high council organization went through various phases as the hierarchy of the new church was made clear. Later they reached equality with the high council and became more independent, and ultimately received authority over that and other similar bodies. After the death of Joseph Smith, the Twelve became the presiding council.

After they were called, the Twelve spent large amounts of time away from the central administrative activities of the Church in Kirtland, Missouri, and Nauvoo.

Some the Twelve left for England on June 13, 1837,[5] and the remainder left in August and September 1839,[6] and did not return until July 1841,[7] two years later. Apparently by then these men had accumulated most of the experience they needed so they could begin to accept the responsibility for directing all the affairs of the Church.

Even though was no Quorum of the Twelve existed during the first five years of the Church's existence, much central church administrative activity had to go on as the gathering gained momentum. The united order firm, with its eleven members, functioned in many ways as an interim Quorum of the Twelve in assisting Joseph Smith to carry out that early and important administrative responsibility, while the future Twelve were joining the church and gaining experience. For example, Brigham Young did not join the church until April 14, 1832, the same month that the united order was formed pursuant to sections 78 and 82, and did not see Joseph Smith for the first time until the fall of that year.[8]

Published historical records do not show that any of the original Twelve or the four replacements named in D&C 118:6 ever belonged to the united order, although the names of Orson Hyde and Willard Richards are shown as at least loosely linked to a few activities of the order. However, Oliver Cowdery and Martin Harris were members of the united order, who in their role as part of the Three Witnesses, chose and ordained the Twelve. This is one link showing that the united order prepared the way for the Twelve.

When the saints were thrown out of Missouri altogether in 1838, some of the Twelve assisted the saints in their travail, especially Brigham Young, but that quorum was still not formally assigned to handle central church administrative matters. They spent much of their time and effort in holding conferences and doing missionary work in the East and abroad.

Brigham Young's comments in Boston, September 11, 1843, summarize in two stages the acceptance of responsibility by the Twelve, first in missionary work, then in financial matters:

> Elder Brigham Young stated the object of the meeting. The first item of business is the spread of the Gospel of salvation. I want to state what devolves upon the Twelve. Nine years ago a revelation was given which was fulfilled in 1835; when fulfilled, the Prophet lifted up his head and rejoiced before the Lord. Previously, the responsibility of *spreading the Gospel* rested on him; now it is on the Twelve.
> ....
> Here are twelve men, and I defy all creation to bring a charge of dishonesty against them. We had to give security for the faithful performance of our duty as agents for the Nauvoo House and Temple. This has been heretofore unheard of in the Church. I glory in it. The *financial affairs* of the Church rest on our shoulders, and God is going to whip us into it. When men are in future called to do like Brigham, I will be one to bind them: this is a precedent. We are the only legally authorized agents of the Church to manage affairs, give counsel to emigrants how to dispose of goods, &c.[9] (emphasis supplied).

Although Brigham Young refers to a revelation given nine years previously, it is possible that he is referring to D&C section 18 given fourteen years earlier in 1829 which directed the Three Witnesses to seek out and ordain the Twelve who then became responsible for missionary work.[10] In the April 1843 conference, it was decided that the Twelve should be bonded and changes be made in the methods of collecting tithing and other offerings, specifically those for the Nauvoo House and Temple.[11] The Twelve had now become responsible for the administration of central church business affairs. They had been assigned joint responsibility for that role in 1838 along with the First Presidency and Presiding Bishopric in section 120, but did not really function in that role until five years later.

As the Twelve rose, the united order descended. By the time of the 1843 comment, the united order was apparently gone or all but gone and the corporate form of the Trustee-In-Trust with the Twelve as agents had absorbed its functions. The final death throes of the united order are seen in the efforts to clear away and burn all the old personal and partnership notes that still floated about from that early period. More abstractly, the order, in the sense of the central church administrative organ, did continue on, but its legal embodiment had changed drastically.

It's interesting to observe that the new institution of the Trustee-In-Trust, with the help of the Twelve, went through a process of establishing precedence over other previously existing organizations, such as the Nauvoo Temple Committee and the United Order, somewhat like the development process the Twelve passed through.

On February 14, 1835, most of the Twelve were ordained to their new calling as Apostles. On March 28, 1835, through the revelation of section 107, the Twelve were given some idea of the meaning of their new callings. They were called the "twelve traveling high councilors ... the Twelve Apostles, or special witnesses of the name of Christ in all the world,"[12] and were to "form a quorum, equal in authority and power to the quorum of the Presidency of the Church."[13]

However, that status of being next to the First Presidency in authority in all matters was apparently not to take practical effect for some time. Before their first mission, the Twelve were given the following instructions which imposed some administrative restrictions on them as far as authority over existing stakes:

> President Joseph Smith then stated that the Twelve will have no right to go into Zion, or any of its stakes, and there undertake to regulate the affairs thereof, where there is a standing high council; but it is their duty to go abroad and regulate all matters relative to the different branches of the Church.[14]

The Twelve left Kirtland on May 4, 1835, for a mission lasting about four months. One of their main messages[15] was that the members should send their money with wise men to purchase land in Missouri (from the bishop, an agent and partner of the united order firm) and make all other preparations to move there. Joseph Smith in one of his *Messenger and Advocate* editorials, dated September 1835, spoke at length on the topic of the gathering, including this interesting parable and application:

> But to illustrate more clearly this gathering: We have another parable - "Again, the Kingdom of heaven is like a treasure hid in a field, the which, when a man hath found, he hideth, and for joy thereof, goeth and selleth all that he hath, and buyeth that field!" The Saints work after this pattern. See the Church of the Latter-day Saints, selling all that they have, and gathering themselves together unto a place that they may purchase for an inheritance, that they may be together and bear each other's afflictions in the day of calamity.[16]

The Twelve sent the Saints west, and the united order settled them.

Even though much transpired after that time relating to the position of the Twelve in the Church hierarchy, still, two years later, at the beginning of the mission of the Twelve to England, a jurisdiction-limiting instruction was repeated to Thomas B. Marsh, then the president of that quorum:

> 27 Therefore, see to it that ye trouble not yourselves concerning the affairs of my church in this place [Kirtland], saith the Lord.
>
> 28 But purify your hearts before me; and then go ye into all the world, and preach my gospel unto every creature who has not received it;[17]

In June, speaking on the subject of governing the church in Missouri in the absence of the presiding authorities who had left there for a time, Joseph said, "The High Council has been expressly organized to administer in all her spiritual affairs; and the Bishop and his council are set over her temporal matters; so that the Elders' acts are null and void."[18] No mention is made of any role of the Twelve in the situation.

Four of the Twelve were drawn from the High Council of Kirtland,[19] indicating some kinship between the two bodies, but it was some time before the Twelve were considered to be on a practical par with that older administrative body. The Kirtland high council was a unique organization. D&C 102:9 makes the President of the Church the President of this first high council. That body did include Joseph Smith, Oliver Cowdery, Sidney Rigdon, and others. The authority of the Presidency of the Church was mingled with that of the high council and there may have been some confusion at times as to whose authority was being relied upon for any particular action. This unique high council might also be considered to be an interim body like the united order firm, organized to handle business until the Twelve could assume those functions. As the Twelve gained in authority, this body must necessarily lose some of its functions.

During their first mission, which lasted about four months, commencing in May 1835 and ending in September 1835, the High Council at Kirtland found fault with a number of actions by the Twelve. Because of the seeming smallness of the errors found, one might wonder if the Kirtland High Council were as much concerned about maintaining a position of administrative superiority to the Twelve as they were to correct wrongdoing.[20] In an action by the Kirtland High Council, two of the Twelve, Orson Hyde and William M'Lellin, were censured and disfellowshipped for their derogatory remarks concerning a school operated by Sidney Rigdon in Kirtland. The authority of the two was passed to the Seventy in some unspecified way. The source of the evidence against them was a letter from M'Lellin to his wife who had considered attending the school. By what means they acquired a copy of that presumably private communication is not mentioned. There is also a harsh word or two for Elder Marsh concerning his family. The words of the high council minutes will give the flavor of the transaction:

> The other item referred to is an extract from Elder William E. M'Lellin's letter to his wife as follows: -
> "You say that it will not be in your power to go to school this summer. I am glad that it is not, since Elder Hyde has returned and given me a description of the manner in which it is conducted; though we do not wish to cast any reflections."
> This the Council considered to be a libel on the face of it. Elder M'Lellin says, "We do not wish to cast any reflections," when the highest insult and reflections are cast by it upon the Church, the Presidency, and those who are held in much higher estimation in the sight of God and this Church than themselves.
> The vote of the council was: We hereby inform Elders M'Lellin and Hyde that we withdraw our fellowship from them until they return and make satisfaction face to face.
> We further inform the Twelve, that as far as we can learn from the churches through which we have traveled, you have set yourselves up as an independent council, subject to no authority of the Church, a kind of outlaws! This impression is wrong, and will, if persisted in, bring down the wrath and indignation of heaven upon your heads. The other ten are directed to proceed on and finish the conferences, and the two may act upon their own judgement whether to proceed or return.

> ....
> A letter was presented from Elder Thomas B. Marsh. The Council referred him to the commandment, which requires none to leave or bring his family without revelation or decision of the High Council.
> ....
> Let the hands of the ten be strengthened, and let them go forth in the name of the Lord, ... Let the power of the two be upon the Seventy until the two make full satisfaction;....[21]

On September 26, 1835, after the Twelve had returned from their mission,[22] the Council of the Presidency of the Church heard the matter and after confessions were heard, forgave the two brethren. The censoring body was denominated as the High Council of Kirtland, but the forgiving body was the Council of the Presidency. This may indicate that some looseness of practice and procedure was reviewed and modified in light of the new administrative force of the Quorum of the Twelve.

While on their mission, on August 7, 1835, nine of the traveling high council met at Bradford, Massachusetts to hear various cases and complaints.[23] An Elder Gladden Bishop had his license taken for various errors in spirit and doctrine. The case of Gladden Bishop was heard by the Kirtland High Council on September 27, and the results were as follows:

> After much instruction, the President decided that the counsel of the Twelve in this case was given in righteousness, also that Brother Bishop's confession be published in the *Messenger and Advocate,* and he be received in full fellowship, and receive his ordination and license as before; which the Council concurred in, and Brother Bishop was ordained by the Court an Elder.
> WARREN PARRISH, Clerk
>
> An attempt was made in the foregoing Council to criminate the Twelve before the High Council for cutting off Gladden Bishop at their Bradford conference, but their

attempt totally failed. I decided that the High Council had nothing to do with the Twelve, or the decisions of the Twelve. But if the Twelve erred they were accountable only to the General Council of the authorities of the whole Church, according to the revelations.[24]

The phrase "I decided" indicates that up to that point, it had not been clear to the Presidency and Kirtland High Council just how they were to interact with the new quorum. As other instances will indicate, it was still some time before all the relational questions were resolved.

When the Twelve were in Kirtland, the sequence of voting on priesthood matters and the seating arrangements of the different quorums were some indication of the Twelves' still uncertain location in the hierarchy of things. On January 13, 1836, a vote was taken concerning a new counselor to Bishop Newel K. Whitney.[25] The Presidency first approved the action, then the High Council of Zion (i.e., Missouri, not Kirtland), followed by the Twelve, the Seventy, and the Bishop of Zion. This procedure put the Twelve somewhere down the list of voting priorities.

On January 15, 1836, at what was apparently the first priesthood meeting or solemn assembly[26] held in the new Kirtland Temple, the quorums were all arranged, presumably according to their formal standing and precedence, and were called on to vote on various matters in the same sequence. The Twelve were placed below the High Councils of Kirtland and Zion.

The next day, January 16, in a special meeting, Thomas B. Marsh and all the other members of the Twelve addressed the matter of the seating arrangements and a number of other accumulated complaints and questions. Apparently, in some previous meetings, the Twelve had been placed next to the Presidency, but (perhaps because of objections from the high councils?) had not been on this most recent and important occasion. One continuing concern was that the decision of the Twelve in the Gladden Bishop case was appealed to the High Council of Kirtland, indicating perhaps that the High Council was a higher body that the Twelve.[27] The Twelve had been chastened based on a letter from Dr. Warren A. Cowdery, the presiding elder of the Freedom conference, and probably the equivalent of a district or stake president today, which seemed to be making the Twelve subject to the judgement of lesser administrative bodies. A charge by the Twelve against that same Dr. Cowdery had been ignored by the Presidency, again raising the question of the nature and extent of the authority of the Twelve.

In response to these concerns of the Twelve, President Smith apologized for using harsh words, re-acknowledged the place of the Twelve next to the Presidency, and covenanted not to heed any derogatory reports against the Twelve, except that which is infallible, without discussion with them on the matter. President Rigdon acknowledged his error in not prosecuting the action by the Twelve against Dr. Cowdery, and afterwards did so.[28] The next day, January 17, 1836,[29] at another meeting, the Twelve were seated next to the Presidency, followed by the Seventy, and the high councils of Kirtland and Zion. At a January 20 meeting, a similar seating sequence was followed.[30]

Many of the questions concerning the place of the Twelve had been settled, but the process was not yet over, and it had taken a year from the choosing of the Twelve to reach this state of things. The next question to be raised had to do with a general policy of Church government, the ordination and licensing of new church leaders. Joseph Smith proposed a resolution concerning the question.[31] The Twelve offered an amendment which raised both a substantive question and a procedural one concerning the authority of the Twelve. Because of the vagueness and generality of the resolution and the proposed amendment, the substantive question is difficult to grasp but appears to deal with just how "general" a conference needed to be to have the power to authorize the ordination of new leaders, and who was authorized to appoint, organize and convene such a conference. Was it only a conference of the whole Church in Kirtland, called by the Presidency in Kirtland, or could the Twelve see to that business by organizing smaller regional conferences while traveling?

The procedural questions had to do with the process of wording and passing resolutions of the sort proposed by President Smith. The two high councils of Kirtland and Zion felt free to reject the amendment of the Twelve, possibly feeling that they were to some extent protecting their prerogatives in the governance of the Church both at home and abroad.[32] Of course today, the high councils of stakes are far removed from any imagined authority over the Twelve.

The resolution was formally adopted by the Presidency of the church without the Twelve's amendment.[33] The Twelve later formally withdrew their amendment (three dissenting), but only after a much lengthier resolution on the topic had been considered and passed, which, by implication (article 3), gave the Twelve authority to call conferences abroad (without defining what "abroad" might mean), which conferences would have the authority to grant priesthood ordinations and give licenses to those ordained.[34]

On September 3, 1837,[35] three of the Twelve were disfellowshipped by a Committee of the Whole Church at Kirtland, including most leaders and many members, the proper body for such an action.[36] One week later, the three were restored to fellowship by a council of priesthood leaders.[37]

Some of the instructions that were given to the Twelve were much the same as those given earlier to the united order group. Their internal relationships and procedures were similar. The sharing of income as united order partners or members of the Quorum of the Twelve were alike for comparable reasons. These men were expected to spend a large part of their time in missionary and church administrative work and were "worthy of their hire:"

> The Twelve and the Seventy have particularly to depend upon their ministry for their support, and that of their families; and they have a right, by virtue of their offices, to call upon the churches to assist them.[38]

Among the Twelve themselves they were to aid each other temporally as necessary:

> Elder M'Lellin read the commandment given concerning the choosing of the Twelve; when it was voted that we each forgive one another every wrong that has existed among us, and that from henceforth each one of the Twelve love his brother as himself, in temporal as well as in spiritual things, always inquiring into each other's welfare.[39]

In a revelation to the Twelve after their return from their first mission, the Lord took them to task for not all dividing equally the money that came to them, and not being equal in other matters:

> Behold they are under condemnation, because they have not been sufficiently humble in my sight, and in consequence of their covetous desires, in that they have not dealt equally with each other in the division of the monies which came into their hands, nevertheless, some of them dealt equally, therefore they shall be rewarded; ....
> Behold the parable which I spake concerning a man (38:26) having twelve sons: for what man among you, having twelve sons, and is no respector of them, and they serve him obediently, and he saith unto one, Be thou clothed in robes, and sit thou here; and to the other, Be thou clothed in rags, and sit thou there, and looketh upon his sons, and saith, I am just? Ye will answer, and say, no man; and ye answer truly; therefore,

verily thus saith the Lord your God, I appoint these Twelve that they should be equal in their ministry, and in their portion, and in their evangelical rights; wherefore they have sinned a very grievous sin, inasmuch as they have made themselves unequal, and have not hearkened unto my voice; therefore, let them repent speedily, and prepare their hearts for the solemn assembly, and for the great day which is to come, verily thus saith the Lord. Amen.[40]

The question of equality discussed in the revelation came up again because of Orson Hyde's complaints[41] that William Smith had certain advantages at the temple committee store. After discussion and an admonition to the store operators, the matter was settled.

The instructions to the Twelve might be compared with a similar injunction to the members of the united order:

> And you are to be equal, or in other words, you are to have equal claims on the properties, for the benefit of managing the concerns of your stewardships, every man according to his wants and his needs, inasmuch as his wants are just.[42]

A few items indicating the rights or opportunities of support of the united order members may be useful here. The two bishops of Kirtland and Zion were members of the order and probably had claims upon both organizations for part of their living. For their help to the poor, they could claim under D&C 42:73, and for their help to the rest of the saints through the real estate development and merchandising operations, they could claim some support as a partner in the firm.

Sidney Rigdon was to rely on the operation of the tannery for his support, and hold himself subject to call:

> Let my servant Sidney Rigdon have appointed unto him the place where he now resides, and the lot of the tannery for his stewardship, for his

support while he is laboring in my vineyard, even as I will, when I shall command him.[43]

For a time, Joseph Smith supported himself by administering the land sales in Nauvoo, and then gave up that enterprise to be supported by the church while he completed his history and did other more spiritual things.[44]

In April 1835, the high council of Zion and others, including two of the Twelve, made an inquiry into the apparent profit-making operations of two members of the united order involved in real estate sales. The conflict ended with the brethren continuing to support the legitimacy of the united order members earning their livelihood through their efforts in conducting church business, and also is an instance where the united order members prevailed over the preferences of members of the Twelve.[45]

Chapter 11 Notes

1. James E. Talmage, *Jesus the Christ* (Salt Lake City: Deseret Book Company, 1961), p. 252.

2. *Jesus the Christ,* pp. 217, 228; Mark 3:13-19; Matt. 10:1-4; Luke 6:12-16.

3. *Jesus the Christ,* pp. 328, 331.

4. Mark 6:7-13; Luke 9:1-10.

5. HC 2:492.

6. HC 4:7-10.

7. HC 4:381.

8. HC 1:297.

9. HC 6:27-28.

10. HC 2:180-181. D&C 18:37.

11. HC 5:327-333.

12. D&C 107:23, 33, 34, 36, 38.

13. D&C 107:23-24. In section 18 (v. 27-32) the Twelves' calling was to be that of doing missionary work (v.28-29). No administrative functions are mentioned except the ordaining of priests and teachers (v. 32). Later in section 107, their role is described as much larger, being next in office to the Presidency (v. 24), and charged with setting in order all the other officers in the Church (v. 33, 58).

In D&C 107 (v. 23, 33, 34, 36, 38), given shortly after the calling of the Twelve, the uncapitalized term "traveling high council" is used more often than is the term Twelve Apostles. While their placement next to the Presidency is duly noted, their role as a traveling high council tends to downplay the administrative importance of the Twelve as far as central church matters are concerned, and tends more to focus on their missionary duties. They were to perform administrative functions only when there was no other body authorized to do so.

It is interesting to note that apparently, at that time, a standing high council within its geographic jurisdiction was equal in authority to the Twelve while operating in that same jurisdiction. (107:37). But the Twelve were told not to interfere with such standing councils. (D&C 112:27-28. HC 2:220).

14. HC 2:220. May 2, 1835.

15. HC 2:225.

16. HC 2:271-272.

17. D&C 112:27-28. HC 2:501. July 23, 1837.

18. HC 2:228.

19. HC 2:357, 366.

20. Actually this might be considered to be normal and healthy organizational behavior. Even though the Twelve were chartered by the scriptures, they might reasonably be required to prove themselves worthy and earn the respect that should go along with the calling. At first there may be a tendency for the old organizational unit to give up too little as they require the new group to "earn their spurs" while the new group may have a tendency to take too much as they explore their new role. At some point a workable compromise can be reached through experience, including some criticism back and forth. Later, in December 1835, Joseph made a comment related to this process when he said of the Twelve that "the burden is on them and is coming on them heavier and heavier." (HC 2:338)

21. HC 2:240-241. August 4, 1835. See HC 2:200 for a comment on the "Kirtland School."

22. HC 2:283.

23. HC 2:241.

24. HC 2:285. See also D&C 102:29-32.

25. HC 2:365.

26. HC 2:364, 370.

27. HC 2:372.

28. HC 2:372-375.

29. HC 2:376.

30. HC 2:377. See also HC 2:392, February 7 meeting; HC 2:402-403, March 3 meeting.

31. HC 2:394-395.

32. HC 2:396-397.

33. HC 2:398, February 22, 1836.

34. HC 2:402-405, March 3, 1836.

35. HC 2:509.

36. HC 2:285; D&C 102:29-32.

37. HC 2:512.

38. HC 2:221, May 2, 1835. Similarly, elders on missions were authorized to support self and family from contributions they received. D&C 84:103-4.

39. HC 2:219, April 28, 1835.

40. HC 2:300-301, November 3, 1835.

41. HC 2:333, 335-337.

42. D&C 82:17.

43. D&C 104:20.

44. HC 4:136-137, 141, 144. June 18, 1840.

45. HC 2:481-486. April 3-7, 1837.

CHAPTER 12

Communalism Was Not Present in The Ordinary Activities of the Joseph Smith Period

The prior chapters have shown that the united order was a small business organization created to assist the gathering of the saints. The unit involved no communalism except to the limited extent common ownership is involved in a partnership. Communalism is here defined as central or common ownership or control of property, especially when that centralization is doctrinally required. The term socialism is used here as a synonym for communalism.[1]

The purpose of this chapter is to show that not only was there no general communalism actually associated with the operation of the united order, or intended or required to be associated with the operation of the united order, there was also no evidence of communalism in the other more common temporal arrangements of the saints. There were a few cooperative business ventures organized by the saints, but they were instigated only for the reason that they promised practical economic benefits, not because there were any doctrinal requirements; one could join in the venture or not as his own interests or preferences dictated. Similarly, Joseph Smith's history mentions no "Ordervilles," or the communal kitchens, uniformity of clothing, etc., often characteristic of such societies, except to disapprove them.

Chapter 2 shows that the leading brethren actively combatted communalistic teachings or practices.

Although a thorough examination of the *History* shows there is no evidence of communalism during the Joseph Smith period, it is difficult to devise a graphic demonstration of the absence of such practices. Displaying a blank piece of paper entitled "Evidence of Communalism in the *History*" is one possibility, but not a very satisfactory one. It is easy to prove that a doughnut hole contains no edible material. It is much harder to quickly demonstrate that, within the six volumes of the history of the church assembled by Joseph Smith, there is no evidence of doctrinally required communalism. It would require a complete paragraph-by-paragraph review of the *History* to prove that there are no appropriate examples to be found there.[2] One easier option is to accept the word of someone who has been through the long review process and will testify to the absence of such material. Another option is to examine materials which *can* be found that are *inconsistent* with the communalism hypothesis. The reader is asked to consider both options for this chapter.

The most striking materials showing a rejection of communalism in common transactions come from the Nauvoo period, and they will be considered first. We will make the well-founded assumption that whatever Joseph Smith taught during that time, he would have taught earlier if the same circumstances had arisen. Chapter 2 shows Joseph combatting socialistic ideas from 1831 onward, while this chapter shows him achieving the same effect in the Nauvoo period by promoting positive ideas of economic freedom, and denouncing government impediments to such freedom. The difference between Nauvoo and other periods is that during most of the Nauvoo period the saints had almost complete control of their civil, military, religious, and economic activities. Elsewhere they had much less than complete control of their own society. In the Nauvoo period, Joseph

Smith was mayor, judge, prophet, real estate developer, and commander-in-chief of the city's militia. We could expect that the breadth of his authority in all these spheres would draw out and give substance to his true policy preferences, including his interpretations of the revelations he had received. The range of economic interests and activities within the church itself in Nauvoo would tend to bring responses from him that would never occur without that stimulus. This was the perfect time to institute a communalistic economic system if one had been desired, but Joseph Smith showed not the least interest in such a change. It was at a similar stage in Brigham Young's presidency that he proposed the most ambitious plans for economic centralization. The saints prospered in Nauvoo, and were instructed but not condemned concerning their economic behavior. In other words, the events of Nauvoo show that Joseph Smith's interpretation of the scriptures did not include a communalistic requirement, thus differing markedly from the commonly heard interpretations stemming from the Brigham Young period.

Other materials from the earlier Kirtland and Missouri periods are included in the second part of this chapter. The points made there are more subtle. Perhaps the discontinuance of the "family" mostly settled the communalism issue in Kirtland, and not until the socialism and government questions arose in Nauvoo did any serious public discussion of the question reoccur. In any event, during those early years we do not find examples of the unequivocal treatment of contending issues that arose in Nauvoo. We are left with only a few examples of common or characteristic behavior from which we may reach conclusions about the then-current teachings, beliefs and practices concerning economic matters. These examples may seem like minutiae when compared with the more forceful statements from the Nauvoo period and the disclaimers concerning statements by enemies discussed in chapter 2, but there is still a value in examining them, because that is all we have in the way of practical examples from that period.

Nauvoo

The next three quotations have to do with matters dealt with by the city government of Nauvoo while Joseph Smith was mayor. The first is dated May 14, 1842:

> ... Houses of infamy did exist, upon which a city ordinance concerning brothels and disorderly characters was passed, to prohibit such things. It was published in this day's *Wasp*.
> I also spoke at length for the repeal of the ordinance of the city licensing merchants, hawkers, taverns, and ordinaries, desiring that this might be a free people, and enjoy equal rights and privileges, and the ordinances were repealed.[3]

In this first quotation on Nauvoo, evil practices were condemned and eradicated, but no restriction was to be placed on legitimate activities, here the sale of goods.[4] The taxing of commerce through various "licensing" schemes has always been a favorite government pastime. Although the constitution does not directly restrict local taxes on commerce, the burdens that such taxation can place on interstate commerce has brought forth U.S. Supreme Court decisions condemning such taxes and restrictions. A similar attitude in local matters would likewise be beneficial to the growth of local commerce.

Joseph Smith's attitude of tolerance toward private enterprise is certainly inconsistent with the usual spirit of communalism or socialism which argues that the people are not wise enough to manage the important affairs of life, and the state or some other body must intervene in all important matters "for the good of the people". Joseph Smith's famous statement that "I teach people correct principles and they govern themselves" strongly supports the idea that individuals own and have complete control over the overwhelming bulk of property. The dictum would be reduced to meaninglessness if a central body made and enforced all significant economic decisions.

The second incident concerning Nauvoo city government is dated February 11, 1843:

> At ten o'clock attended the city council. I prophesied to James Sloan, city recorder, that it would be better for him ten years hence, not to say anything more about fees; and addressed the new council, urging the necessity of their acting upon the principle of liberality, and of relieving the city from all unnecessary expenses and burdens, and not attempt to improve the city, but enact such ordinances as would promote peace and good order; and the people would improve the city; capitalists would come in from all quarters and build mills, factories, and machinery of all kinds; new buildings would arise on every hand, and Nauvoo would become a great city. I prophesied that if the council would be liberal in their proceedings, they would become rich, and spoke against the principle of pay for every little service rendered, and especially of committees having extra pay for their services; ....[5]

In this second comment, the most significant item is Joseph's faith that if the city merely kept "peace and order," those with means would come to build up the city and make it great - "the people would improve the city." His trust in freedom and his patience to await the results are rare and remarkable traits.

His comment, counseling that no salaries or fees be charged by the city, is certainly antagonistic to the support of a central controlling body which may interfere with legitimate business. If the governing group is not allowed to receive a salary, or extract fees for various "services," they would naturally tend to keep their governing activity to a minimum. It would also be difficult for a clerical and professional bureaucracy to be built up as a continuing drain and restraint on economic activity.

An all-volunteer government, such as exists in the church today, means that it is almost impossible to operate a centrally controlled economy. With no full-time professional staff and associated bureaucracy, no one would expect that any significant economic planning could occur.[6]

The third incident concerning Nauvoo city government is also dated February 11, 1843:

> The council resolved that a market be established in the city. It was proposed to build two markets. But I told the council that if we began too large, we should do nothing; we had better build a small one at once, to be holden by the corporation; and if that would support itself, we could go on to build another on a larger scale; that the council should hold an influence over the prices of markets, so that the poor should not be oppressed, and that the mechanic should not oppress the farmer; that the upper part of the town had no right to rival those on the river.... We have been the making of the upper part of the town. ... We began here first; and let the market go out from this part of the city; let the upper part of the town be marketed by wagons, until they can build a market;....[7]

This third comment concerning a proposition that the city build a market appears somewhat inconsistent with the preceding comments in that it would involve the city government in some way with local business activity. There is no apparent reason why a private firm could not handle such a project. In fact it may well be that Joseph Smith would have preferred not to get involved at all in such a project. He did wish to keep it small to begin with. The city council may have overridden his counsel or preferences on this point. At least Joseph did not propose this project to the council.

But there may be another explanation for this deviation. The kind of market here considered may be somewhat akin to public facilities such as roads, highways, seaports, airports, etc., which do normally require some centralized coordination to be administered properly. The "market" contemplated may have been a facility like a farmers' market that could be rented out in sections for short terms so that produce or other goods could be sold by individuals. This kind of vegetable market is common in developing countries where packaging, storage, and transportation systems are not highly advanced, and vestiges are still seen occasionally in Pennsylvania and other eastern states. It might merely be a paved and sheltered area, perhaps having a loading dock for ease of handling goods. It may have been more of a wholesale market than a retail market and perhaps involved a more erratic trade than a local retail store.

The marginal nature of the project is indicated by Joseph's warning to start small and see if the facility prospers. Note the comment that in the other part of town, sales were successfully being made from wagons, presumably in the open air. With that sort of "low overhead" competition - essentially cost free - the market could probably not charge large fees for use of its shade and shelter.

Joseph apparently intended that the facility would be entirely supported by users fees and would not add any tax burden on the city residents. The initial investment might have been sought from local subscriptions, possibly from potential users, or from loans from outside sources. The legal difficulty of forming corporations to carry out large scale and risky undertakings of a quasi-public sort, plus the fact that the city already had the status of a corporation, may have been an argument for using the city as a vehicle to handle this particular project. There is also the possibility that outsiders would not wish to invest within the city until conditions were more settled. With the potential for more conflict with their neighbors as occurred in Missouri, investors, whether inside or outside the church, might be wary.

Joseph also seems to have felt a spirit of competition with another part of town and possibly wished to attract more business to his part of town through the market device. This is similar to the practices of many cities, states, and countries who try to make it attractive for businesses to locate there, often through various forms of inducements or subsidies, including the provision of various infrastructure items such as warehouses, grain elevators, ports, docks, roads, markets, etc. It appears that Joseph may have had this in mind.

The comment about influencing prices is a little startling, but it probably means only that by contracting to use publicly supplied space, the individual owed some duty to use reason in the prices he charged, at least so as not to embarrass the city government, and especially not to make it appear that the city supported him in his behavior. "Influencing" prices was probably meant to be a much milder effort than "setting" prices or otherwise controlling the flow of goods.

If the seller wished to charge high prices, he could go elsewhere, provide his own facilities and sell it as he wished. It is probable that the city's only control or remedy would be to deny him the use of the public facility. As landlord, the city could exercise some discretion as to whom they would rent the space. Normally, however, the behavior of the seller would have to be outrageous before the city could intervene, lest the city be charged with discrimination against particular persons in the use of public facilities.

At a meeting held Tuesday, March 12, 1844, in Nauvoo, a cooperative enterprise was proposed as a useful and practical program:

> A meeting of the inhabitants of the Tenth ward was held this evening at the schoolhouse on the hill, in Parley street, to take into consideration the propriety of establishing a store on the principle of cooperation or reciprocity. The subject was fully investigated, and the benefits of such an institution clearly pointed out.
>
> The plan proposed for carrying out the object of the meeting was by shares of five dollars each.
>
> The leading feature of the institution was to give employment to our own mechanics, by supplying the raw material, and manufacturing all sorts of domestic goods, and furnishing the necessaries and comforts of life on the lowest possible terms.
>
> A committee was appointed to draft a plan for the government of said institute, to be submitted for adoption or amendment at their next meeting; after which an adjournment took place till next Tuesday evening, at half-past six o'clock, at the same place.[8]

It is significant that this new organization was treated on a level with all other business enterprises, whether sponsored by the city or by an individual. (Only the temple was a directly church sponsored project). There was no doctrinal requirement for such an organization; people could enter into it or not as they chose, based on their own calculation of its merit and value to them. It was just one among a large number of business enterprises being built up in Nauvoo, and would compete with or complement the others according to existing and changing circumstances.

During a sermon delivered at the temple grounds, Sunday, October 15, 1843, Joseph gave some counsel as to the economic development of the city:

> I will now speak a little on the economy of this city. I think there are too many merchants among you. I would like to see more wool and raw materials instead of manufactured goods, and the money be brought here to pay the poor for manufacturing goods. Set our women to work,

and stop their spinning street yarns and talking about spiritual wives.

Instead of going abroad to buy goods, lay your money out in country, and buy grain, cattle, flax, wool, and work it up yourselves.

....

We cannot build up a city on merchandise. I would not run after the merchants. I would sow a little flax, if I had but a garden spot, and make clothing of it.

The temporal economy of the people should be to establish and encourage manufactures, and not to take usury for their money. I do not want to bind the poor here to starve. Go out into the country and into the neighboring cities, and get food, and gird up your loins, and be sober. When you get food, return, if you have a mind to.

Some say it is better to give to the poor than build the temple. The building of the temple has sustained the poor who were driven from Missouri, and kept them from starving; and it has been the best means for this object which could be devised.

Oh, all ye rich men of the Latter-day Saints from abroad, I would invite you to bring up some of your money - your gold, your silver, and your precious things, and give it to the temple. We want iron, steel, spades, and quarrying and mechanical tools.

It would be a good plan to get up a forge to manufacture iron, and bring in raw materials of every variety, and erect manufacturing establishments of all kinds, and surround the rapids with mills and machinery.[9]

Joseph makes a number of wise comments concerning the building up of Nauvoo, but of greatest significance is his refusal to use any compulsion in implementing any of his ideas. In the same sermon, he made the following comment:

It is one of the first principles of my life, and one that I have cultivated from my childhood, having been taught it by my father, to allow every one the liberty of conscience.[10]

He spoke on this topic several times as quoted below:

> February 13, 1844:
> ...Although I never feel to force my doctrine upon any person, I rejoice to see prejudice give way to truth, and the traditions of men dispersed by the pure principles of the Gospel of Jesus Christ.[11]

> March 24, 1844:
> President Joseph Smith again arose and said - In relation to the power over the minds of mankind which I hold, I would say, it is in consequence of the power of truth in the doctrines which I have been an instrument in the hands of God of presenting unto them, and not because of any compulsion on my part. I wish to ask if ever I got any of it unfairly? If I have not reproved you in the gate? I ask, did I ever exercise any compulsion over any man? Did I not give him the liberty of disbelieving any doctrine I have preached, if he saw fit? Why do not my enemies strike a blow at the doctrine? They cannot do it: it is the truth, and I defy all men to upset it.[12]

It is obvious that Joseph considered it very important to avoid the temptation to exercise inappropriate authority.[13] His faith in the benefits of freedom have been demonstrated in previous quotes. His philosophies, as shown in this and other chapters, were inconsistent with economic regimentation.

Kirtland and Missouri

One purpose of this study is to show that there were no communalistic or socialistic elements in the economic transactions that occurred in Joseph Smith's day and under his direction. Although we may not be able to say with perfect certainty that there never was any communalistic or socialistic transaction, we can say that if it did happen, it was inconsistent with all that was considered important by Joseph Smith and chosen by him to be reported in his history.

The transactions of the united order firm are of great interest, but just as interesting are other incidental transactions which serve to verify the consistency of the free market, personal independence principles practiced by Joseph Smith and his contemporaries.

The following comment, dated January 8, 1836, concerning the construction of the Kirtland Temple, gives an insight into business procedure used:

> The plastering and hard-finishing on the outside of the Lord's house was commenced on the 2nd of November, 1835, and finished this day. The job was let to Artemas Millet and Lorenzo Young, at one thousand dollars. Jacob Bump took the job of plastering the inside of the house throughout, at fifteen hundred dollars, and commenced the same on the 9th of November last. He is still continuing the work, notwithstanding the inclemency of the weather.[14]

The practice of subcontracting portions of the work on the temple for fixed dollar amounts was and is one of the most common and straightforward ways of getting a building constructed and rewarding those who do the work. There was nothing mysterious about the process. These men may have given the temple committee a good price and worked hard, but the operation was handled in the normal way. The workers were independent contractors, not servants of a central bureaucracy.[15]

Of course, ultimately, all the resources used to build the temple came from donations of some sort, either in money, in labor, or in kind; there was not enough money available to accomplish everything by contract. The following historical entry shows much about how the donation process was handled and rewarded, and also gives us some insight into the definition of some important words often used in Mormon economic literature:

> The Blessing of those who assisted in Building the
> House of the Lord at Kirtland
>
> March 7 [1835]. - This day a meeting of the Church of Latter-Day Saints was called for purpose of blessing, in the name of the Lord, those who have heretofore *assisted* in building, *by their labor and other means,* the House of the Lord in this place.
>
> The morning was occupied by President Joseph Smith, Jun., in teaching the Church the propriety and necessity of purifying itself. In the afternoon, the names of those who had assisted to build the House were taken, and further instructions received from President Smith. He said that those who had distinguished themselves thus far by *consecrating to the upbuilding* of the House of the Lord, *as well as laboring thereon,* were to be remembered; that those who build it should own it, and have the control of it.
>
> After further remarks, those who performed the labor on the building voted unanimously that they would continue to labor thereon, till the House should be completed.
>
> President Sidney Rigdon was appointed to lay hands on and bestow blessings in the name of the Lord.
>
> The Presidents were blessed; and Reynolds Cahoon, Hyrum Smith, and Jared Carter, the building committee, through the last two were not present, yet their rights in the House were preserved.
>
> The following are the names of *those* who were *blessed in consequence of their labor* on the house of the Lord in Kirtland, *and those who consecrated to its upbuilding:* [long list of names]
>
> ....
>
> The blessings and ordinations of particular individuals of the foregoing were as follows: - Reynolds Cahoon, Jacob Bump, and Artemus Millet, were blessed with the blessings of heaven and a right in the house of the Lord in Kirtland, agreeable to the *labor* they had *performed* thereon, *and* the *means* they had *contributed.*
>
> Alpheus Cutler ... received the same blessing. The blessing referred to was according to *each man's labor or donation* ....[16]

Some important phrases from this quotation will be repeated here for emphasis and discussion:

"Assisted ... by their labor and other means"
"Consecrating ... as well as laboring"
"Those ... blessed in consequence of their labor ... and those who consecrated to its upbuilding"
"Labor ... performed ... and ... means ... contributed"
"Each man's labor or donation"

The words and phrases just quoted show that, in the parlance of the time, the words "contribute," "donate," and "consecrate", were all used interchangeably and had the same meaning. The word "consecrate" did not imply a long-term absorption of self and property into a centralized organization. It simply meant the uncoerced, spontaneous donation of means as any church member might do today through the many programs available, including contributions for temple building.

Also of significance is the idea expressed here "that those who build it should own it, and have the control of it." That is an explicit recognition of the strict operation of private property, wherever, and to the extent, that concept can be reasonably applied. A protected or at least recognized stake in the outcome of a project is a strong incentive to work on that project, and may be the only fair way to reward the laborer. When something has been fairly determined to belong to a person, he may do with it as he wishes. His options include keeping it or donating it to a good cause.

Of course, in a practical sense, these men could not really exercise the perquisites of ownership in the usual way because the building was intended to be a community resource and could not really be sold or otherwise be translated into cash, at least for a long time. They could only make a donation of their share of the completed structure. However, they could rightfully feel pride in their accomplishments and could receive some "pay" in the form of thanks from the community much as a person might today who donates funds for a library or a hospital. The most important point is that Joseph recognized the legitimacy of the desire men have to personally own and control what they have created, and rewarded the men accordingly as best he could. This is the philosophical opposite of the common practice in the world of declaring and making the "state" the only legitimate owner and controller of property and the product of mens' labor.

In conjunction with the building of the Kirtland temple, and to simplify the transactions necessary to get the temple constructed, the temple committee operated a store. The evidence shows that the Kirtland temple committee store, which was probably separate from but allied with the united order, was run very much like any other store in the situation as far as purchases, sales, credits, etc., were concerned. There was no evidence of any formal communal practices operating or being doctrinally required.

A rather emotional episode shows that the store's sales and credit policies made it an institution which was a long way from a communal storehouse. Instead, its operation was generally consistent with ordinary retail marketing:

Orson Hyde's Letter of Complaint

DECEMBER 15th, 1835

President Smith: Sir -

....

After the [temple] committee [store] received their stock of fall and winter goods, I went to Elder Cahoon and told him I was destitute of a cloak, and wanted him to trust me, until spring, for materials to make one. He told me that he would trust me until January, but must then have his pay, as the payment for the goods became due at that time. I told him I knew not from whence the money would come, and I could not promise it so soon. But, in a few weeks after, I unexpectedly obtained the money to buy a cloak, and applied immediately to Elder Cahoon for one, and told him I had the cash to pay for it; but he said the materials for cloaks were all sold, and that he could not accommodate me; and I will here venture a guess, that he has not realized the cash for one cloak pattern.

A few weeks after this, I called on Elder Cahoon again, and told him that I wanted cloth for some shirts, to the amount of four or five dollars. I told him that I would pay him in the spring, and sooner if I could. He let me have it. Not long after, my school was established, and some of the hands who labored on the house, attended, and wished to pay me at the committee's store for their tuition. I called at the store to see if any negotiation could be made, and they take me off where I owed them; but no such negotiation could be made. These, with some other circumstances of a like character, called forth the following reflection:

In the first place, I gave the committee $275.00 in cash, besides some more, and during the last season, have traveled through the Middle and Eastern states to support and uphold the store; and in so doing, have reduced myself to nothing, in a pecuniary point. Under these circumstances, this establishment refused to render me that accommodation which a worldling's establishment gladly would have done; and one, too, which never received a donation from me, or in whose favor I never raised my voice, or exerted my influence. But after all this, thought I, it may be right, and I will be still - until, not long since, I ascertained that Elder William Smith [one of the Twelve] could go to the store and get whatever he pleased, and no one to say, why do ye so? until his account has amounted to seven hundred dollars, or thereabouts, and that he was a silent partner in the concern, but was not acknowledged as such, fearing that his creditors would make a haul upon the store.

While we [the Twelve] were abroad this last season, we strained every nerve to obtain a little something for our families, and regularly divided the monies equally for aught I know, not knowing that William had such a fountain at home, from whence he drew his support. I then called to mind the revelation in which myself, M'lellin, and Patten were chastened, and also the quotation in that revelation of the parable of the twelve sons, as if the original meaning referred directly to the Twelve Apostles of the Church of Latter-Day Saints. I would now ask if each one of the Twelve has not an equal right to the same accommodations from that store, provided they are alike faithful?

....

... Believing as I do, that I must sink or swim, or in other words, take care of myself, I have thought that I should take the most efficient means in my power to get out of debt; and to this end I propose taking the school; but if I am not thought competent to take the charge of it, or worthy to be placed in that station, I must devise some other means to help myself, although having been ordained to that office under your own hand, with a promise that it should not be taken from me.

The conclusion of the whole matter is: I am willing to continue and do all I can, provided we can share equal benefits, one with the other, and upon no other principle whatever. If one has his support from the "public crib," let them all have it; but if one is pinched, I am willing to be, provided we are all alike. If the principle of impartiality and equity can be observed by all, I think that I will not peep again. If I am damned, it will be for doing what I think is right. There have been two applications made to me to go into business since I talked of taking the school, but it is in the world, and I had rather remain in Kirtland, if I can consistently. All I ask is right.

I am, Sir, with respect,
Your obedient servant,
Orson Hyde.[17]

Joseph Smith noted the following response to the letter:

I told Elder Cahoon, of the Temple committee, that we must sustain the Twelve, and not let them go down; if we do not, they must go down, for the burden is on them and is coming on them heavier and heavier. If the Twelve go down, we must go down, but we must sustain them.[18]

The response is vague as to any practical changes in policy. It appears that he merely requested the store manager to be a little more willing to extend credit to the Twelve who had given so much of themselves and their means to the cause of the Kingdom.

There are a number of threads running through this letter that should receive comment. There is a hint here that

Orson might wish to receive back, through the temple store, part of the $275 he had earlier donated to the temple project. This illustrates the need for the "deed [of gift] that cannot be broken" language in the scriptures. Joseph Smith sympathized with him, but did not change the rule. There is mention of laborers, presumably laborers on the temple, who wished to pay their tuition at Orson Hyde's school by transferring their credits at the store to Orson. This transaction was refused. It may be that the laborers were trying to stretch their store credits further than they were supposed to go. The credits may have been established for subsistence needs of food and clothing for laborers and were not to be used for "luxuries" such as school tuition. There is even the possibility that the labor, when given, was really donated, and thus there was no basis for any transferable credits at the store.

Orson refers to the sharing of contributions received by the Twelve while traveling on church business, and seemed satisfied with the fairness of the procedure used. He alludes to other questions concerning economic relationships among the Twelve and between the Twelve and the institutional church represented here by the committee store. Besides sharing the income they receive while on ecclesiastical assignment, are the Twelve to share income they individually may have from other sources? (William Smith's other resources are mentioned.) Joseph Smith didn't specifically address that question; we can assume that his silence amounts to a "no." Orson also asks if the Twelve are to have a claim on the temple committee store (the "public crib"?) for their sustenance. Joseph Smith's silence on that question also amounts to a "no."

If an elite group such as the Twelve could not receive their support from a central fund, and did not share their personal income outside of direct donations to their quorum, then there can't have been much communalism being practiced within the church. A professional priesthood or paid ministry, is always a dangerous thing, and Joseph Smith went to extraordinary lengths to avoid it. In the related area of national government, there seems normally to be a close tie between the existence of an elite "priesthood" or party group and the practice of socialism or communism. If there is no elite controlling group supported by a central fund, it is very difficult to carry on a communal program of any magnitude.

Orson's letter is evidence of confusion in people's minds concerning economic relationships within church. Joseph's handling of the matter probably answered many questions and removed much confusion. He refused to require or sanction any "transfer payments" between elements of society, a common symptom of communalism, if not the *sine qua non*.

Examination of Orson Hyde's letter and of Joseph Smith's rather non-committal response leaves the general impression that, in Joseph Smith's mind, everyone in the whole LDS community including the Twelve and the united order members were responsible for themselves completely, and had no claim on anyone for support. This was true even while on missions, except to the extent people were willing to contribute to them during that time. Even those said to be receiving support from the "public crib" were merely those who had better credit terms than others - the debts still were expected to be paid. There was no storehouse to support the able. If a storehouse did exist, it was only for the poor who were without the means to care for themselves.

According to Orson Hyde's letter, the store refused to accept the responsibility to act as a bank in setting off accounts of one man against another. This may be one reason for the attempt in the next year (1836-37) to set up a bank in Kirtland.[19]

Another entry in Joseph Smith's history has to do with a unique meeting held in the temple on March 30, 1836:

Wednesday, 30. - At eight o'clock [A.M.], according to appointment, the Presidency, the Twelve, the Seventies, the High Council, the Bishops and their entire quorums, the Elders and all the official members in this stake of Zion, amounting to about three hundred, met in the Temple of the Lord to attend to the ordinance of washing of feet. I ascended the pulpit, and remarked to the congregation that we had passed through many trials and afflictions since the organization of the Church, and that this is a year of jubilee to us, and a time of rejoicing, and that it was expedient for us to prepare bread and wine sufficient to make our hearts glad, as we should not, probably, leave this house until morning; to this end we should call on the brethren to make a contribution. The stewards passed round and took up a liberal contribution, and messengers were dispatched for bread and wine.

[The meeting continued until seven o'clock in the evening.]

The bread and the wine were then brought in, and I observed that we had fasted all day, and lest we faint, as the Savior did so shall we do on this occasion; we shall bless the bread, and give it to the Twelve, and they to the multitude.

[The meeting then continued on and finally concluded at five o'clock in the morning.][20]

Here three hundred men met by appointment to spend 24 hours in the temple. It was known that at least one meal would be needed. If these men were bound together in an economic bond, wherein all surplus was kept in one location under the control of the bishop, and there was central economic planning, it would seem natural for the needs of these men to be met from that common fund. Note that it was 1836 and there had been plenty of time for such an arrangement to mature, if one had been intended.

Instead, what happened? The most informal and spontaneous means was used. After all were together and it was obvious that food and drink would be needed, a collection was taken up, and men sent out to purchase the needed supplies. It was group-oriented only in that there was probably some spontaneous sharing as some men contributed more than enough for themselves, so that some who had perhaps forgotten to bring money or who may have had little or none to bring, would be able to eat with the rest. Nonetheless, the intention would clearly be that each man was to pay for his own needs if at all possible because there was no other source of funds.

A letter, dated July 25, 1836, was sent by Joseph Smith and other church leaders in Kirtland to a citizens committee of Clay County, in response to a request by that committee for the saints to leave that county as they had left Jackson County. In Joseph Smith's letter there are some interesting comments relating to economics:

> It is said that our friends are poor; that they have but little or nothing to bind their feelings or wishes to Clay county, and that in consequence they have a less claim upon that county. We do not deny the fact that our friends are poor; but their persecutions have helped render them so....
>
> If a people, a community, or a society can accumulate wealth, increase in worldly fortune, improve in science and arts, rise to eminence in the eyes of the public, surmount these difficulties, so much as to bid defiance to poverty and wretchedness, it must be a new creation, a race of beings superhuman. But in all their poverty and wants we have yet to learn for the first time that our friends are not industrious and temperate.... We do not urge that there are no exceptions to be found; ... but this can be no just criterion by which to judge a whole society; and further still where a people are laboring under constant fear of being dispossessed; very little inducement is held out to excite them to be industrious.[21]

This comment indicates that Joseph Smith had an understanding of the principles of economics and human motivation. The fear of being dispossessed is a strong disincentive to work and to save, whether that fear is based on the expected behavior of mobbers or government controllers and tax collectors. Such a fear of personal loss will exist in a society where the central authority can take anything a person has. That fear, well justified by events, accounts for much of the sluggishness and inefficiency that characterize centrally controlled economies.[22] On the positive side, he also saw the important connection between undisturbed private ownership of productive property, and the strong incentives the owner has to make the best use of that property. The commonplace knowledge that the small "private" plots of land worked by peasants in communist countries produce at least thirty percent of the total agricultural output of the country is a strong continuing proof of this basic political/economic truth.[23]

Joseph's comments during May 1837 on the economic tides of the times, and the saints' participation in them, are instructive:

> At this time the spirit of speculation in lands and property of all kinds, which was so prevalent throughout the whole nation, was taking deep root in the Church. As the fruits of this spirit, evil surmisings, fault-finding, disunion, dissension, and apostasy followed in quick succession.... Other banking institutions refused the "Kirtland Safety Society's" notes. The enemy abroad, and the apostates in our midst, united in their schemes, flour and provisions were turned toward other markets, and many became disaffected toward me as though I were the sole cause of those very evils I was most strenuously striving against, and which were actually brought upon us by the brethren not giving heed to my counsel.[24]

We may assume that the speculation condemned here meant seeking high profits from trading in commodities rather than using available resources to further the gathering process. Although the reasons for the speculative spirit and the effects it had would be interesting to explore, the important point to be made in this chapter is that speculation could not occur without economic freedom and full individual ownership over land and goods. To speculate one must be able to buy and sell quickly and easily. To do that one must hold undisputed title. The quoted comment indicates that the church obviously had no more and claimed no more than "counseling" power over its members. There was no control over the buying and selling of flour or other provisions by a central storehouse or other institution. If that power had existed, it presumably would have been used, and no speculation could have occurred, at least by church members.

Land prices in Kirtland went up to many times their former level as the saints gathered there and the demand for land increased.[25] This indicates that there was full economic freedom and individualism. With no individually owned property, there is no market. With no market, there are no meaningful prices. The prices responded quickly to changes in market conditions, demonstrating that there was a market operating with property being bought and sold.

Joseph would presumably have tried to convince the saints to resist the temptation to take advantage of the rise in prices. The gathering process itself helped to raise the prices; the older land owners could benefit at the expense of newer converts. This profiteering would make the gathering process more expensive and would tend to slow it down, something Joseph would wish to avoid. Joseph also knew that the boom in Kirtland would be short-lived because the saints were programmed to move west soon. Unfortunately, keeping prices down in Kirtland would cause its own set of problems, because it would tend to entice goods to seek markets where prices were higher, and thus leave fewer goods available in Kirtland for use by the gathering saints. Apparently this was true even when church members were the sellers. They sought higher prices elsewhere rather than reserving their holdings to help the gathering process.[26] The fact that the church members could get into this situation shows that there was no control over their economic activities.

One irritating but slightly humorous situation which kept recurring concerned the economics of using the mails. Many people sent letters to the Prophet without prepaid postage, the sender expecting the Prophet to pay the postage upon receipt. He complained about it, paid some, and announced at various times that he would not pay postage on letters from anyone. Some of these incidents will be quoted here:

December 5, 1835:

I received a letter from Reuben McBride, Vilanova, New York; also another from Parley P. Pratt's mother-in-law, Herkimer County, New York, of no consequence as to what it contained, but it cost me twenty-five cents for postage. I mention this, as it is a common occurrence, and I am subjected to a great deal of expense by those whom I know nothing about, only that they are destitute of good manners; for if people wish to be benefitted with information from me, common respect and good breeding would dictate them to pay the postage on their letters.

I addressed the following letter to the editor of the *Messenger and Advocate:*

Dear Brother - I wish to inform my friends and all others abroad, that whenever they wish to address me through the post office, they will be kind enough to pay the postage on the same. My friends will excuse me in this matter, as I am willing to pay postage on letters to hear from them; but I am unwilling to pay for insults and menaces; consequently must refuse all unpaid.

Yours in the gospel,
Joseph Smith, Jun.[27]

January 1837:

Owing to the multiplicity of letters with which I was crowded from almost every quarter, I was compelled to decline all not postpaid, and gave notice of the same in the *Messenger and Advocate.*[28]

> April 10, 1843. (At a special conference of elders undertaking missions):
> The elders were reminded that they need not expect any attention would be given to unpaid letters directed to the Presidency.29

Joseph's reaction to the unpaid postage problem is an interesting example of his expectations that people ought to be independent, take care of their own business, and pay their own way, even as to such relatively small things as postage stamps. These comments also indicate in another way that Joseph was against any form of communalism. Obviously there was no central funds-collecting body that had the money to even pay postage on letters received. Many letters were coming from missionaries and others who might have some color of claim to a small amount of assistance from the central body. But even that was not approved. It would have meant placing a kind of tax or other levy on other saints to raise the needed money, and Joseph apparently did not want such a thing to occur.

Chapter 12 Notes

1. The use of the term socialism as a synonym for communalism may be explained as follows: Socialistic practices are usually justified and supported by a set of secular doctrines or beliefs which have many similarities to religious tenets. Operationally, the mechanisms may be almost identical and have similar effects. Although the intent may be different, the results are much the same. These assertions will not be further explained and documented in this book, but will receive further treatment in a study of the Brigham Young period.

For want of a better place, another definition is inserted here: This book presents a theory of LDS economic history more than it presents a theory of LDS economics. If asked to propose a theory of LDS economics, I would make a simple definition using three words: freedom, pragmatism, and expediency. People are normally left to their own devices economically. When conditions are such that there is serious reason to worry about the temporal welfare of the saints, the ecclesiastical leaders might counsel that some temporary economic changes be made. These would be practical suggestions to meet the perceived problems or threats. When the crisis was over, the "program" would go away as well. The crisis justifying significant economic changes would be one concerning survival of the church and its members, not just one concerning meeting higher goals of missionary or other performance.

2. Some of those who have written on the topic of the united order during the Joseph Smith times, and have argued for or assumed the communalistic nature of the united order, have perhaps inadvertently shown the weakness of their position by failing to cite examples from the *History* that confirm the communalistic interpretation. Geddes in his work *The United Order Among The Mormons,* in which he expounds on the social policies of the united order, cites no examples from the history, but uses only verses from the Doctrine and Covenants, extrapolating from there with the aid of works on economics that have no historical connection with the early church. The D&C verses are subject to other interpretations as shown in other chapters of this book.

Arrington in his work *The Great Basin Kingdom: Economic History of the Latter-day Saints, 1830-1900,* spends only about half of the first chapter, or about 15 pages, on the Joseph Smith period before going on to the Brigham Young period. Reference is made to agricultural companies organized in Far West and to the Nauvoo Agricultural and Manufacturing Society as examples of church-organized economic institutions. These units may have been made up mostly of church members, but otherwise they had no connection with the church either doctrinally or practically and were wholly voluntary. In his history, Joseph Smith took little note of these organizations, merely mentioning them once or twice. Other sources indicate that in Far West, the land to be used on the large farms was to be leased from the owners in normal business fashion, and that Joseph Smith commented it was a personal decision whether to join or not. See *Great Basin Kingdom,* p. 15.

It appears that these authors took ideas from the Brigham Young period and applied them to the Joseph Smith period without any particular effort to determine whether data from the Joseph Smith period supported those ideas or not. If they did find any conflicts or inconsistencies between the two periods, they were not mentioned. In this book on Joseph Smith's united order, rather than assuming that communalism was doctrinally required, the question was asked "Is communalism doctrinally required?" The answer was found to be "no," at least during Joseph Smith's time.

Some may contend that searching only the *History* is inadequate and that until every journal, newspaper article, or other piece of information from the era has been examined, it cannot be said that the search is conclusive. That extreme position may be countered by saying that it is most unlikely that obscure sources would be more accurate than the extensive materials assembled and reviewed by the church leaders who have considered that activity an important part of their calling. Of course, all historical materials can in some way improve our understanding of the conditions of a period, but on a question as important as the economic requirements of church membership, we should not need to seek sources out of the main stream. If no evidence of doctrinally required communalism appears in the main stream materials, we can safely assume that the omission was intentional and therefore conclusive. This is true regardless of the contrasting Brigham Young era materials. We should let Joseph Smith speak for himself and explain his own actions; we should not look to Brigham Young to do it for him. The Brigham Young period likewise needs to be dealt with on its own terms.

3. HC 5:8. May 14, 1842. Joseph Smith. Nauvoo.

4. Joseph's philosophy toward merchants and others is consistent with case law interpreting the interstate commerce clause in the U.S. Constitution.

5. HC 5:270. February 11, 1843. Joseph Smith. Nauvoo.

6. The experience at Brigham City, Utah, is the exception that proves the rule. Those who were willing to be volunteer managers of the city's many economic activities found themselves sorely overworked. Religious zeal alone was not enough to maintain the system indefinitely.

7. HC 5:271. February 11, 1843. Joseph Smith. Nauvoo.

8. HC 6:263. Tuesday, March 12, 1844. Nauvoo.

9. HC 6:58-60. Sunday, October 15, 1843. Nauvoo. Many of Joseph Smith's general recommendations sound very much like Brigham Young's. There was, however, a difference in the suggested means for implementing these ideas.

10. HC 6:56. October 15, 1843.

11. HC 6:213. February 13, 1844.

12. HC 6:273. March 24, 1844.

13. One might speculate as to whether his influence over the saints would have been greater or less if he had chosen to exercise a greater control over their temporal affairs. Such an attempt might increase his power for a short time, but it is likely that there would be a large net loss over time as the freedom-loving people he wished to attract moved elsewhere.

14. HC 2:363. January 8, 1836. Kirtland.

15. Note the contrast here with Brigham Young's government-style "public works" plan for doing major construction work. For example, see JD 5:19.

16. HC 2:205. March 7, 1835. Kirtland.

17. HC 2:335-336. December 15, 1835. Kirtland. There is little information in the history concerning the operation of the temple committee store, showing that it was not considered by Joseph Smith to have an important doctrinal or social effect. Other than the Orson Hyde letter, the only other reference found concerning its operation is an obscure entry, dated October 7, 1835, mentioning the ordinary process of stocking the store: "Bishop Whitney and Brother Hyrum Smith started by stage for Buffalo, New York, to purchase goods to replenish the committee's store." (HC 2:288. Oct. 7, 1835. Kirtland.)

18. HC 2:337-338.

19. Many communal groups have tried to create a central mechanism to do accounting for credits, rationing, etc., but here the store is resisting such a responsibility. The Kirtland bank could be viewed as a free market attempt to solve the accounting problem.

20. HC 2:430-431. March 30, 1836. Kirtland.

21. HC 2:459. July 25, 1836. Kirtland.

22. A similar fear can be experienced by nearly anyone today when we consider that even in supposedly free countries high tax rates are common. In communist countries conditions are even worse, and private property is rare or non-existent. Everything has already been taken from the people, and they

receive only a living allowance which can be stopped at any moment for any reason. A job there is a person's license to live. The state gave them their job if they have one, and the state could take it away.

23. See, for example, "Hungary's New Way," *National Geographic,* Vol. 163, No. 2, Feb. 1983, p. 245; Nicholas Donilof, "Who Says Free Enterprise is Dead in Soviet Union?" *U.S. News & World Report,* Vol. 96, No. 25, June 25, 1984, p. 36. This economic truth concerning the stimulating power of private property and its opposite, the weight of communal ownership, applies just as strongly in any setting.

24. HC 2:487-488. May 1837. Orson Hyde and Parley P. Pratt were two of the men taken up with this spirit of speculation. HC 2:488-491. No good account of Joseph Smith's counsel in this matter seems to be recorded, but we may assume that he was against the brethren's preoccupation with the effort to make a profit at the expense of others. He would have preferred that they focus their energies on furthering the gathering.

25. For more information on land prices and other economic matters, see Marvin J. Hill, *Kirtland Economy Revisited* (Provo, Utah: Brigham Young University Press, 1977).

26. During the early days in Utah, Heber C. Kimball, Orson Hyde, and others counseled the saints to store their grain rather than try to sell all the excess to outsiders at harvest time. They desired low and level prices so that newly arriving saints could acquire the food they needed at a reasonable price all through the year. The reasons for such counsel were probably the same as Joseph's -- promoting and supporting the gathering. A free market situation was assumed, modified only by what might be called "counsel control" of the market. JD 2:118-119; 4:108-109; 5:14-17, 20-23.

27. HC 2:325. December 5, 1835.

28. HC 2:475. January 1837.

29. HC 5:351. April 10, 1843. See HC 3:309 for an example of $30.00 postage on a letter.

Notes on the Doctrinal Treatment of Private Property and Individualism

All Gospel Principles are Individualistic
There is No Group Salvation

All the principles of the gospel have a similar characteristic: they apply only to individuals. There is no group salvation. Even though the scriptures may speak of groups of people receiving certain rewards, in fact those people are grouped by the individualized and objective criteria of understanding of and obedience to law, not by genealogy, social status, or group membership. Even marriage partners must be separately qualified before the highest reward can be given them.

Here is one of a myriad of examples of comments on the individualistic nature of Gospel principles:

> The foolish asked the others to share their oil, but spiritual preparedness cannot be shared in an instant. The wise had to go, else the bridegroom would have gone unwelcomed. They needed their oil for themselves; they could not save the foolish. The responsibility was each for himself. This was not selfishness or unkindness. The kind of oil that is needed to illuminate the way and light up the darkness is not shareable. How can one share obedience to the principle of tithing; a mind at peace from righteous living; an accumulation of knowledge? How can one share faith or testimony? How can one share attitudes or chastity, or the experience of a mission? How can one share temple privileges? Each must obtain that kind of oil

for himself .... *(Faith Precedes the Miracle,* pp. 253-256, quoted in Priesthood manual for 1983, pp. 212-213)

The freedom to control and direct one's own actions is necessary before one can be held responsible for one's spiritual status and growth. One cannot easily share the benefits and burdens of spiritual accumulations or preparedness. Individual freedom, control, and accountability are equally important in the realm of property and economic matters. It often happens that what is of great value in the hands of one person, is useless in the hands of another because of a lack of training or concern. For many types of property, a sharing of ownership or control means no one uses it well, and a loss to the individual and to society results. Individual control of an item of property normally leads to the highest and best use of that resource and both the individual and society benefit as a result.

*Undisturbed Ownership and Control
of Property is a Blessing*

Scriptural promises of peace and prosperity in the future often dwell on the undisturbed ownership and control of the products of ones labor, heralding that condition as a great and welcome change. Isaiah speaks of the millennial period and holds out one of these great promises concerning that era:

> 21 And they shall build houses, and inhabit them; and they shall plant vineyards, and eat the fruit of them.
> 22 They shall not build, and another inhabit; they shall not plant, and another eat: for as the days of a tree are the days of my people, and mine elect shall long enjoy the work of their hands.
> 23 They shall not labor in vain, nor bring forth for trouble; for they are the seed of the blessed of the Lord, and their offspring with them. Isaiah 65:21-23. See also *Articles of Faith,* p. 370.

Isaiah's prophecy that "they shall not plant, and another eat," is probably intended to be taken as a reassuring statement that true justice will prevail during the millennial time or in any other time in which the will of the Lord is practiced. This is a strong argument that the communalism some have imagined to be a part of the Gospel is indeed foreign to it.

In D&C 101 the Lord made a similar millennial promise concerning the land of Zion in Missouri:

> 96 And again, I say unto you, it is contrary to my commandment and my will that my servant Sidney Gilbert should sell my storehouse, which I have appointed unto my people, into the hands of mine enemies.
>
> 97 Let not that which I have appointed be polluted by mine enemies, by the consent of those who call themselves after my name;
>
> 98 For this is a very sore and grievous sin against me, and against my people, in consequence of those things which I have decreed and which are soon to befall the nations.
>
> 99 Therefore, it is my will that my people should claim, and hold claim upon that which I have appointed unto them, though they should not be permitted to dwell thereon.
>
> 100 Nevertheless, I do not say they shall not dwell thereon; for inasmuch as they bring forth fruit and works meet for my kingdom they shall dwell thereon.
>
> 101 They shall build, and another shall not inherit it; they shall plant vineyards, and they shall eat the fruit thereof. Even so. Amen.

In verse 101, the Lord again holds out an essentially millennial promise of peaceful enjoyment of the product of one's labors. The practicalities of things (v. 99) indicated that for the moment, long-term quiet use of the land was not possible. The Lord was and always has been vague on the topic of the timing of the second coming. Much like D&C 19:7, the concept of the millennium has been used to influence the behavior of the saints without ever getting "locked in" to any particular definition or promise of an exact time of fulfillment.

The Saints in Missouri had Individual Control of Land

The way the saints held land in Missouri is a topic of some importance. One insight appears in D&C 101:96-99 which counsels the saints, represented by Sidney Gilbert, that it is a sin for any to sell land to outsiders. Unless the saints had the legal power to sell the land to outsiders, or in other words they held clear title to the land, they would not have a choice in the matter, and therefore could not sin. This topic is considered further in other chapters in connection with section 85. It is assumed in the verses that Gilbert *did* have the legal power to sell the real estate in question. So did others hold similar power. The test was whether they would use their power against the Lord's will. For some related scriptures, see D&C 90:35 (35-37); 58:37; 72:10 (8-10).

The Saints Were Expected To Pay Their Own Way

During Joseph Smith's time, the saints were expected to pay their own expenses and to help others where possible. This applied even to those who spent time in the ministry. The Bishop was instructed:

> 11 To take an account of the elders as before has been commanded; and to administer to their wants, who shall pay for that which they receive, inasmuch as they have wherewith to pay; (D&C 72:11)

The rule that everyone is always expected to pay if they can, is inconsistent with any significant pooling or centralization of funds. If everyone must always place in a common fund everything beyond their minimum needs, then payments out of that common fund would have to be very regular occurrences because "uncommon" or unpredictable needs are a part of everyone's life, especially among people who are involved in a migration.

On the other hand, the rule is perfectly consistent with the expectation that all productive properties will be held and controlled by individuals, with the small exception of commonly owned meeting places and pooled welfare funds for the poor.

Consecration Was More an Inventory Than a Property Transfer

Another scripture on the "consecration" process:

> 15 Thus it cometh out of the church, for according to the law every man that cometh up to Zion must lay all things before the bishop in Zion. (D&C 72:15)

As evidenced by *Wilford Woodruff's Journal,* vol. 1, p. 16, this scripture does not mean that all was given to the bishop or that any "double-deeding" was going on, but rather that an inventory of both character and property was to be taken for the purpose of determining whether a person was worthy to join with the saints and whether he should be allowed to purchase land (or in a few instances be granted land based on extensive service to the church) and be allowed to occupy it in Zion, and if so, what price he should pay for the land. A worthiness and "ability to pay" determination was made by the bishop based on all the facts and circumstances of the individual's situation.

CHAPTER 13

Tithing and the United Order, Part 1:
Tithing Procedure is Adapted to Circumstances

The topics of "united order" and "consecration" are sometimes said to be "higher law" alternatives to the "lesser" law of tithing. The goal of chapters 13, 14, and 15 is to overcome and dissolve this false dichotomy by providing a better understanding of the history of tithing. There is a relationship between the change in tithing administration and the parallel events of replacing the united order partnership with a corporate form as the Twelve became involved in central administrative matters. The two series of changes leading toward administrative improvement support each other. Understanding one helps to understand the other.

Today we have come to assume that tithing is something that can only be handled by the central offices of the church. Here we wish to show that such an administrative procedure is really just one among many other administrative procedures which have been used in the past depending on conditions. This discussion will serve as a preparation for the question of the existence and nature of tithing in the early days of the church.

One of the difficulties of any historical study is that conditions today may be so different from those of the period under study, that the average person simply lacks the experiences that would enable him to understand the significance of events and practices in the earlier time. That is certainly the case for this study of the administrative practices of the Joseph Smith period. To begin to give the reader some reference points from which to evaluate and understand the Joseph Smith period, we must make a quick review of how tithing has been handled at various times in the history of the world. After establishing that there actually have been many different ways of handling tithing besides the way it is being handled at this moment in history, we will then be in a better position to understand the methods used in Joseph Smith's time.

Our first task is to differentiate between the policy or doctrine of tithing, on the one hand, and, on the other, the regulations, practices, or procedures for administering tithing. Everyone would admit that tithing means one-tenth, and that it is to be "given to the Lord" or "used for some Gospel purpose." That definition of tithing does not change with time. But what does "give to the Lord" or "use for some Gospel purpose" mean? The answer must change with the time and place. What makes sense in the 1830's or 2,000 B.C. would be impractical now, and vice versa. This chapter and the next concern themselves only with the "regulations" of tithing and not with its "policy" aspects. Some might say that the definition of tithing must be narrowed from "give one-tenth to the Lord" (policy) to "send by check one-tenth of current monthly income to the world-wide headquarters of the LDS Church in Salt Lake City, Utah" (regulations), and that no other behavior could be considered to be compliance with the law of tithing. This chapter will show that many other examples of tithing regulations and procedures have been acceptable in the past, and that variations are acceptable today.

Abraham's experience with tithing is the earliest recorded and should be considered here. The scriptures tell us of Abraham's rescue of Lot from his abductors, and of Abraham's control over many spoils as a result of the ensuing battle:

10 ... and the Kings of Sodom and Gomorrah fled ....

11 And they took all the goods of Sodom and Gomorrah, and all their victuals, and went their way.

12 And they took Lot, Abram's brother's son, who dwelt in Sodom, and his goods, and departed.

....

14 And when Abram heard that his brother was taken captive, he armed his trained servants, born in his own house, three hundred and eighteen, and pursued them unto Dan.

15 And he divided himself against them, he and his servants, by night, and smote them, and pursued them unto Hobah, which is on the left hand of Damascus.

16 And he brought back all the goods, and also brought again his brother Lot, and his goods, and the women also, and the people.

....

18 And Melchizedek King of Salem brought forth bread and wine: and he was the priest of the most high God.

19 And he blessed him, and said, Blessed be Abram of the most high God, possessor of heaven and earth:

20 And blessed be the most high God, which hath delivered thine enemies into thy hand. And he gave him tithes of all.

21 And the king of Sodom said unto Abram, give me the persons, and take the goods to thyself.

22 And Abram said to the king of Sodom, I have lift up mine hand unto the Lord, the most high God, the possessor of heaven and earth,

23 That I will not take from a thread even to a shoelatchet, and that I will not take anything that is thine, lest thou shouldest say, I have made Abram rich:

24 Save only that which the young men have eaten, and the portion of the men which went with me, Aner, Eshcol, and Mamre; let them take their portion.[1]

Note first that Abraham apparently kept back nothing for himself. He may have wished to be magnanimous, but there were also likely some practical reasons operating. For one, creating lifetime mortal enemies of the kings by keeping all their goods, while at the same time creating a temptation for them to attack Abraham in the future to reclaim the goods, would not be good politics. Also, nomads must be able to move freely with their flocks to new grazing areas and they keep their possessions to a minimum to facilitate those moves. To Abraham, keeping the goods could become a great burden or might even require a change of life style from that of a nomad to that of a stationary city dweller. Such a change would not appeal to him after his experience with the cities of Sodom and Gomorrah. A nomadic life allowed him the political and spiritual freedom to worship God as he wished. We might remember that Lehi left all his goods behind in Jerusalem. To have taken them would have meant the failure of his mission. He and his family could never have traveled as they did with such possessions to burden them.

The disposition of the goods was as follows: Abraham paid tithing to Melchizedek of all the goods recovered. Then Lot's goods were returned to him, minus the portion paid as tithing. The men who joined with Abraham for this military venture received their portions of the goods of Sodom that were taken at Hobah, those portions being somewhat reduced by the amount of tithing paid. Also, Abram's fighting men had eaten some of the food captured, and Abram did not replace it. All that remained was returned to the original owners.

That was a strange kind of tithing. It was paid out of the spoils of war, not out of the normal increase from farms or flocks. What he captured was simply a fortunate windfall from or byproduct of rescuing Lot. Abram would have attempted the rescue in any event. Hopefully war and the resulting tithing of spoils would not be a regular occurrence in Abram's life. There is no mention of any previous or subsequent regular payments to Melchizedek, but only this single and unusual transaction.

In other more normal times, what happened to resources designated by Abram to be used for Gospel purposes? It is likely that they were managed and distributed by Abram himself and used to help the poor or to meet other needs known to him. In today's money economy, tithing can be collected to a central place and then distributed to local areas based on need. But an effective money economy was probably not in existence in Abram's time, and it would probably not be useful to try to send animals and goods to Melchizedek on a regular basis only to have Melchizedek send a large portion of it back to care for the poor or for some other need in Abram's area, or to help some other independent patriarch care for his own.2

In Abram's time, unless some large centralized project such as a temple was under construction, it would be better and more efficient for each patriarch to use the resources he controlled to do good wherever he was with his nomadic family.

In summary then, the account of Abram's paying tithes to Melchizedek does not really support the proposition that tithing can only be tithing when it is paid to a central church authority and on a regular basis. For good reason, there appear to have been other procedures in effect in other periods of history.

Joseph Smith made a tithing covenant in 1834[3] and compared his covenant with that of Jacob of old. Here we will examine Jacob's experience. After having repeated to him in a dream the same promise that had been made by the Lord to Abraham, Jacob responded with the following promise:

> 20 And Jacob vowed a vow, saying, if God will be with me, and will keep me in this way that I go, and will give me bread to eat, and raiment to put on,
> 21 So that I come again to my father's house in peace; then shall the Lord be my god;

> 22 And this stone, which I have set for a pillar, shall be God's house: and of all that thou shalt give me I will surely give the tenth unto thee.[4]

The question at issue here is exactly what was the practical implementation of the promise to give a tenth to the Lord. Of course the Lord has no need of any material thing we might have. We might "give" something to him by destroying that something in a sacrifice by fire. Using the idea that "if ye do it unto them ye do it unto me," we can use it to benefit someone else such as a missionary or a poor person. We could use our resources to increase the spirituality of others by making printed revelations available to them or by providing a building in which to study and worship.

Personal resources can be used for Gospel purposes through individual contributions or through one or more cooperative organizations. These organizations might vary in size and scope from a small local group to a large centralized world-wide organization. By any of these methods, the same general results can be achieved, although in certain situations, one method may be more efficient than another.

Thus, the principle of tithing does not seem to necessarily require that contributions be made only to a central church authority. Although in this day it may sound like heresy to even suggest that any contribution that is not forwarded to the central church ever was or ever could be legitimately called tithing, purely practical considerations probably play a large role in day to day operation and often greatly modify the main rule of centralization. For example, a study of tithing-handling today would probably indicate that because of currency exchange controls and other political and practical problems, large amounts of funds, unquestionably tithing in nature, never reach Salt Lake City, but are kept and used within the country where the funds originate.

In these two instances, involving Joseph Smith and Jacob, it appears that the parties involved expected and assumed that they (and their children) would administer the funds, perhaps mostly in an alms-giving fashion. Joseph vowed to "give a tenth to be bestowed upon the poor in His church, or as He shall command."[5] It is highly questionable in both situations whether there was or could have been a centralized church organization suitable for and capable of handling efficiently ten percent of all the income of all the saints in the world.

In most cases the funds collected centrally today are ultimately distributed again locally in the far flung branches of the church. Doing that job well presupposes and requires very sophisticated communications, transportation, banking, management and similar systems. Otherwise, centralizing funds would in many cases be a less efficient use of them than could be accomplished locally. Anyone contemplating the nomadic or frontier settings of Jacob or Joseph Smith would have to conclude that efficient centralization of a world-wide church in their locality and time would require the daily intervention of angelic messengers, since the normal means available were so primitive.[6]

In contrast to these early primitive or scattered times, and as discussed in detail elsewhere, sections 119 and 120 seem more than anything to signal that a mature central organization had been achieved and that centralized collection and administration of tithing was on the way to becoming feasible. Nonetheless, it was still a long time after section 119 before anything like our present system was in existence.

The payment of tithing in kind as existed earlier in this dispensation is another example of a procedure that differs greatly from today's methods. Because of the problems of storage, perishability, and transportation, especially when there is no refrigeration or canning facility and no transportation except horse-drawn wagon, such a system must be administered on a local basis. Attempts to send all materials to a central regional location, let alone a world-wide center, would be pointless and wasteful. Without a thorough-going money economy, only a small portion of the means collected could be efficiently sent to a central site.

Another example of an unusual tithing procedure comes from the early Utah period. For a time, in a few locations such as Kanab and Orderville, Utah, many of the church members did not pay tithing individually. Instead, the economic organizations to which they belonged paid tithing to the central church for all employees.[7] Thus what we normally think of as an individual responsibility, was transformed into a corporate responsibility. In any other situation and location where all property and its produce were centralized, that might be an expected result.

One well-known example of a change in tithing procedure to adapt to circumstances was in the Pioneer Stake during the depression. Stake president Harold B. Lee received permission to hold all tithing funds in his stake for use in providing jobs and welfare assistance to the members within his stake.[8] That represents a significant departure from the usual procedure because of a change in the economic conditions of the time.

For our purposes here, this is an example of tithing funds raised locally and used locally, with those giving the funds having a good possibility of knowing personally how the funds are used. This avoids the impersonal corporate centralization and redistribution process and is probably more akin to the procedures used in the days of Abraham, Jacob, and Joseph Smith. But, it is doubted that anyone would challenge its status as tithing even though it was generated and used on a local level.

To broaden our discussion in another direction, we will consider the paying of tithing by those outside the church. Again the question is raised whether payment to any entity that is not the world-wide headquarters of the church will allow the act to be considered "paying tithing."

The late Ernest L. Wilkinson, for many years the president of the Brigham Young University, and therefore a prominent administrator of church assets, has described the benefits of paying tithing even by those who are not members of the LDS Church. His recorded discourse on the topic of tithing is interesting, but his later addendum to the discourse is even more interesting in the way it distinguishes between two basic tithing administrative procedures:

ADDENDUM BY THE AUTHOR

> On reading the foregoing address, which I am informed has been distributed by the public relations department of the university, I immediately noted one grave deficiency (undoubtedly there are many others). A number of the instances of the practice of tithing cited by me involved men who practiced this doctrine as a matter of personal conviction, even though the denominations of which they were members did not authoritatively preach that principle. Since they practiced this as a matter of personal conviction, apart from the doctrines of their particular church, they of course chose the particular charities which were the object of their bounty.
>
> To those of us who belong to the Church of Jesus Christ of Latter-day Saints, the practice of tithing by revelation means that we pay the amount to our respective bishops, who in turn transmit it to the general authorities of the church for proper use by the church. It is not for us as individuals to determine the particular purpose for which this tithing shall be spent.
>
> Ernest L Wilkinson[9]

In his discourse, he gave high praise to various non-LDS tithe-payers. In retrospect, he felt it wise to mute that praise and remove any possibility that a BYU employee or student, or other a church member, could use his discourse as a directive or excuse to "go thou and do likewise."

In a vein similar to Brother Wilkinson's statements is Elder Thomas S. Monson's address in April 1983 Conference,[10] in which he also speaks of non-LDS tithe-payers and those making charitable donations. Elder Monson compares large gifts such as additions to hospitals, which bear the names of their donors, with those gifts that are given anonymously. He declared that the anonymous gifts received a greater heavenly reward. For our purposes here, perhaps we may interpret his discourse as saying that there is a righteous way to pay tithing whether by those inside or outside the church, by choosing not to bask in any worldly acclaim the gift may bring. That principle applies to the various stages through which tithing has gone in this dispensation.

The administering of temporal goods or wealth is an inherently practical activity, and to fulfill its purpose, tithing administration must change as conditions in the world change. The tithing collection and distribution practices of today may be the best for the conditions of the majority of the saints today, but it is not necessarily the appropriate way for all times and all places. Even today there must be widely varying procedures in use at different locations in the world. As the church becomes even more international, the list of acceptable procedures will continue to grow. It is possible that, if not now, then sometime in the future, every procedure that has ever been used on the earth will be in simultaneous use in different locations.

Our current tithing administration system assumes that fast and reliable world-wide mail is one of the given conditions of today. Checks may be mailed from almost anywhere in the world to a central point. The sending of checks assumes that there is a world-wide banking system which allows the quick and safe transfer of monies between countries, and the exchange of multitudes of local currencies into a single currency for saving, "storing," or "stockpiling." This money must later be exchanged again into local currencies when it is expended. There is an assumption that communications with all parts of the world are good enough to allow a central body to direct events in far flung locations.

Of course, these conditions are not really true throughout the entire world. There are a number of countries today which do not maintain reliable mail, banking, telephone or telex systems, or do not allow the exchange of local currency or its transfer to foreign lands. Some peoples do not even have a money economy which would allow them to use such international facilities. It is also possible that major economic or political disruptions could make modern communications and financial facilities unavailable over large parts of the world and require at least temporary changes in procedure.

Even if it were possible to send money out of the country, in some countries it would not be wise to do so. Mail and banking transactions are often closely watched. Countries with a state religion or countries which forbid any religion would be likely to persecute someone who attempted to transfer money. Any of these and many other variations in circumstance may require a different procedure for handling tithing funds.

It may be useful here to suggest a method for describing and categorizing the complexity and sophistication of a tithing (or any other) administrative system. For this discussion let us define gospel funds as including every possible category of means transferred from one person to another for a gospel purpose. Gospel funds would include such general all-purpose terms as alms, tithing, and consecrations, which in turn include all the specific subcategories such as temple, missionary, building, budget, welfare, fast offerings, etc., etc.

We can begin to describe those many possible ways of handling gospel funds by using some pairs of descriptive words such as direct/indirect, local/central, known/unknown, and regular/irregular.

The most simple means of handling gospel funds would be to apply them (1) direct, that is from one person to another or from one person to a specific project without going through an intermediary, (2) locally, that is to some object or class of objects within the same geographic area as the giver, (3) to a known or visible person or project, and (4) on an irregular basis, that is, it is done as the need makes itself evident, rather than on the basis of some specific long term plan.

To describe the most sophisticated and complex mechanism for handling gospel funds, we would use the terms indirect, central (or remote), unknown and regular. Changing any of the four "simple" terms to its corresponding "complex" term means some additional administrative process or steps must be carried out between the first act of giving and the final step of actually putting the funds to use. In many charity programs, the administration of the funds uses up the bulk of the funds. This could happen in a church setting as well, if care is not taken.

The term "indirect" implies the need for an intermediary to at least collect and physically transfer the money or goods. A diagram showing levels of indirect transfer might include the following situations: (1) individual to individual, (2) individual to ward to individual, (3) individual to ward to central church to individual, (4) individual to ward to central church to ward to individual, etc.

If the funds are to go to a central (or remote) location, the transfer process is larger than if used locally. If the object of the funds is unknown or invisible to the giver, that implies the need for someone to make a decision as to how the funds should be used. If funds are given and/or applied regularly, that implies some planning, arrangements, and expectations on the part of the giver, the receiver, and the intermediary, if there is one. It may be necessary to anticipate both the need for and availability of funds, and to have some kind of a system to smooth out any anticipated mismatches between need and availability, using some buffering or warehousing mechanism.

In many cases the more complex mechanism is ultimately more efficient, but it requires effort and trust to organize and maintain it. An isolated frontiersman or desert nomad normally only has the most simple options for helping his immediate neighbors, although those options will be immediately gratifying. The city dweller in a twentieth century money economy has access to many complex administrative options which can be used for helping his "neighbor" anywhere in the world, although the very abstractness, impersonality, and uncertainty of the process may keep him from taking any action. In the two situations the principles of gospel giving are not any different, but the mechanisms for doing so are different.

The careful progression from the seen to the unseen, the known to the unknown, is a logical and reasonable process for introducing a powerful concept to those inexperienced in the gospel. In his April 1983 Conference address, President Ezra Taft Benson spoke of the revelation received February 27, 1833, called the Word of Wisdom. A portion of that address is quoted here for use as an analogy with the principle of tithing:

> At first the revelation was not given as a commandment. It was given as "a principle with promise, adapted to the capacity of the weak and the weakest of all saints, who are or can be called saints."

(D&C 89:3.) This allowed time for the saints to adjust to the principles contained in the revelation.

....

In 1851, President Brigham Young proposed to the general conference of the church that all saints formally covenant to keep the word of wisdom. This proposal was unanimously upheld by the membership of the church. Since that day, the revelation has been a binding commandment on all church members.[11]

As pointed out here, the Word of Wisdom was introduced by stages, not reaching its final implementation in the lives of the saints until years later. Although the principle was taken very seriously from the earliest days, as shown by many references to the need for compliance,[12] it seems at first to have had its strict application to a narrower group than the entire church population, usually being applied to a specific group of missionaries, or to a specific high council. etc. Would anyone be willing to say that, because it was not made generally mandatory for full fellowship in the Church until 1851, that the Word of Wisdom was not a principle of the gospel until that time? Probably not. It may be of some interest to note that the teaching of several aspects of the gospel was delayed in England until the time seemed appropriate. The Word of Wisdom was one of these topics. The doctrine of the gathering, and the revelation known as "the vision," D&C 76, concerning the three heavens, were also delayed for a time. Delaying those topics did not make them any less a part of the Gospel.

In a way similar to the Word of Wisdom, tithing was introduced by stages, first by way of counsel and request, "subscription," "loan," and "contribution," and then later by more strict commandment. At an early point in church history, a person could be considered a member in good standing who did not comply with the Word of Wisdom. Later that was not true. Tithing followed a similar pattern.

Perhaps these two most basic and significant of the "temporal" commandments are much alike in the difficulty of bringing the church up to a state of general obedience, and each requires a "warming up" or "milk before meat" period before strict obedience can be enforced.

Chapter 13 Notes

1. Genesis 14:10-24. See also, W. Cleon Skousen, *The First Two Thousand Years* (Salt Lake City, Utah: Bookcraft, 1980), p. 302.

2. At times during the Brigham Young period, this problem was dealt with by holding tithing receipts in Salt Lake City as evidence of central church ownership of tithing proceeds, but leaving the tithing in the form of goods and animals located in the various stakes from which they were contributed. In at least some cases, the ultimate disposition of the tithing was in the hands of the local authorities. *Great Basin Kingdom,* p. 363.

3. HC 2:174-175. November 29, 1834.

4. Genesis 28:20-22.

5. HC 2:175. November 29, 1834.

6. See HC 5:159 for Joseph Smith's comments on the insecurity and unreliability of the postal system in Nauvoo. See HC 7:610 for a note on pioneer mail-handling arrangements. See HC 3:309 for an example of $30.00 postage on a letter.

7. Leonard J. Arrington, *Building the City of God* (Salt Lake City, Utah: Deseret Book Co., 1976), pp. 238, 276, 288.

8. Ibid., p. 341.

9. Edwin J. Butterworth and David H. Yarn, ed., *Earnestly Yours* (Salt Lake City, Utah: Deseret Book Company, 1971), p. 177 (154-177).

10. Thomas S. Monson, "Anonymous," *Ensign,* May 1983, p.55.

11. Ezra Taft Benson, April Conference Address, *Ensign,* Vol. 13, No. 5, May 1983, p. 53.

12. See, for example HC 2:35, February 20, 1834; HC 2:482, May 28, 1837; HC 5:349, April 10, 1843.

CHAPTER 14

Tithing and the United Order, Part 2: Tithing was an Active Doctrine From the Beginning of This Dispensation

Tradition has it that tithing (1) was not introduced as a principle of the gospel in this dispensation until 1838 when Section 119 of the D&C was revealed, and then only (2) as a "lesser" law to temporarily fill the gap left by (3) the removal of the law of consecration from the gospel program. The purpose of this chapter is to show that none of the three elements of this tradition are supported by the history of the Joseph Smith period.

The topic of tithing is similar to the topic of the united order in that both are administrative or temporal in nature and both seem to have been interpreted at odds with the history of the Joseph Smith era. Because they both relate to temporal matters, additional information concerning one should contribute to a better understanding of the other. A major portion of the funds handled by the united order were tithing in nature. The end of the united order corresponds to the reorganization of tithing procedures represented by section 119 and the section 120 designation of a new administrative unit for tithing funds.

Joseph Smith must have become aware of the existence and nature of the law of tithing at an early stage in his calling as a prophet. The visits paid to him by Moroni do not specifically include a mention of the topic of tithing, but the references to chapters 3 and 4 of Malachi would surely have led Joseph to ponder those chapters, including the verses on tithing, as he reviewed his angelic instructions.

As he was translating the Book of Mormon, he could not have helped notice the comments at Alma 13:15 and 3 Nephi 24:8, 10 on the importance of tithing. The Alma account refers to Abraham's experience, and specifically mentions that the measure of tithing is one-tenth. The materials in 3 Nephi were reinserted into the Nephite scriptures by the Savior himself. It is unlikely that Joseph failed to notice that special emphasis on the book of Malachi.

Paying tithing, in the larger sense of the term as opposed to the more narrow procedural definition used in modern times, was a characteristic of the church members from the beginning of this dispensation. The Martin Harris financing feats are good examples of this behavior. Martin provided for at least two projects, one involving the first printing of the Book of Mormon in 1830, as directed by revelation:

> 26 And again, I command thee that thou shalt not covet thine own property, but impart it freely to the printing of the Book of Mormon, which contains the truth and the word of God -
>
> ....
>
> 34 Impart a portion of thy property, yea, even part of thy lands, and all save the support of thy family.
> 35 Pay the debt thou hast contracted with the printer. Release thyself from bondage.[1]

Martin Harris was also directed to be involved in the beginning of the land purchases in Missouri:

> 34 And now I give unto you further directions concerning this land.
> 35 It is wisdom in me that my servant Martin Harris should be an example unto the church, in laying his moneys before the bishop of the church.

36 And also, this is a law unto every man that cometh unto this land to receive an inheritance; and he shall do with his moneys according as the law directs.

37 And it is wisdom also that there should be lands purchased in Independence, for the place of the storehouse, and also for the house of the printing.

38 And other directions concerning my servant Martin Harris shall be given him of the Spirit, that he may receive his inheritance as seemeth him good.[2]

Publishing the scriptures and aiding the gathering certainly sound like tithing expenditure categories, regardless of the procedure used. This example may be compared to Abraham's experience where a very large amount was paid as tithing at one time, possibly representing the income of many years of work. Asking Martin Harris or all the other members of the church to pay in a few dollars a month as a fair tithing would not have been a useful way to get the Book of Mormon published, or to buy the Missouri land. The use of large, one-time transactions at the critical times, directly between the tithing payer and the seller, was the most expeditious way to accomplish the tasks at hand.

There are a number of references to and uses of tithing in the scriptures of this dispensation, the Doctrine and Covenants, that appear long before the 1838 pronouncement concerning tithing administration. At least as early as September, 1831, the concept of tithing was specifically mentioned in Kirtland, in D&C 64:23, as an aid to building up Zion:

> Behold, now it is called today until the coming of the Son of Man, and verily it is a day of sacrifice, and a day for the tithing of my people; for he that is tithed shall not be burned at his coming.[3]

This revelation was given for the benefit of a group of brethren who were preparing to begin their journey to

Missouri. They were acting in compliance with the Lord's directive that the saints gather to Zion, purchasing land there in the normal way so that they could settle and provide for themselves.[4]

The mention of tithing in D&C 64:23 thus comes in the context of commandments to the Saints to migrate to Missouri. It appears that the Lord expected that the myriad of administrative needs relating to the gathering to Kirtland and to the land of Zion in Missouri would require the contribution and use of the individual resources of the church members. That contribution and use of individual resources for gospel purposes is the essence of tithing. If the Lord labels as tithing the use of personal resources for the purpose of gathering oneself to an appointed place, who can say that it should not be called tithing?

This notion is strengthened by D&C 85:3, dated November 27, 1832, wherein the Lord makes it plain that the gathering to Zion under the proper procedure is a tithing operation, an expenditure of private funds for a gospel purpose:

> It is contrary to the will and commandment of God that those who receive not their inheritance by consecration, agreeable to his law, which he has given, that he may tithe his people, to prepare them against the day of vengeance and burning, should have their names enrolled with the people of God.[5]

Note here that the Lord essentially equates the idea of consecration with that of tithing. As explained elsewhere in greater detail, the consecration transaction spoken of here was simply a land purchase transaction with oversight and counsel from the church's agents, Bishop Partridge and others. These men were assigned to help the process and to see that things progressed consistent with the church's interests in having the saints gathered in an orderly way.

There was a contribution of money, in other words a tithing or consecration, and in return, the contributor received land. Those with more than enough money to purchase their own land were asked to donate to assist those who did not have sufficient.

The building committee for the Kirtland temple sent out a circular dated June 1, 1833, requesting subscriptions and donations for construction. The Saints are admonished to "exert yourselves with us, in raising the means to bring about the glorious work of the Lord ...."[6] The term "tithing" is not mentioned, but the purpose to be achieved is one normally assigned to tithing

In an extensive letter, dated July 1833, to those in the east, the brethren in Missouri gave many detailed and practical comments on the proper temporal and mental preparations to be made for the move to Zion. They especially warned members of the need to have adequate funds, plus, where possible, enough extra to help others, before beginning the journey, and specifically mentioned the law of tithing as it applied to that situation:

> ... All the tithes cannot be gathered into the storehouse of the Lord, that the windows of heaven may be opened, and a blessing be poured that there is not room enough to contain it, if all the means of the Saints are exhausted, before they reach the place where they can have the privilege of so doing.[7]

The letter demonstrates that the Missouri brethren had a good understanding of the concept of tithing as taught by Malachi 3:10 and its application to those early migrating saints.

On August 2, 1833, the Lord indicated that contributions for building a temple in Zion were to be considered tithing:

> 10 Verily I say unto you, that it is my will that a house should be built unto me in the land of Zion, like unto the pattern which I have given you.
>
> 11 Yea, let it be built speedily, by the tithing of my people.
>
> 12 Behold, this is the tithing and the sacrifice which I, the Lord, require at their hands, that there may be a house built unto me for the salvation of Zion--[8]

The temple in Missouri was never built, but the temple in Kirtland had been begun earlier that year. In fact, the corner stones of the Kirtland Temple were laid just 10 days before this revelation. Surely the mechanism for building either temple would be much the same. Both were apparently intended to be built during the same time period.

Even though the revelation apparently refers to the Missouri Temple, there is also the possibility that the phrases "built speedily" in verse 11 and "like unto the pattern which I have given you" in verse 10, could just as easily refer to the Kirtland Temple for which explicit plans had already been received and a temple committee appointed.[9] At a minimum, it seems fair to conclude that contributions to either temple could be considered tithing.

Another early instance of recognition and use of the tithing principle occurred at the time the Tippits group arrived in Kirtland in November 1834, and agreed to loan their land purchase money to Joseph Smith:

> On the evening of the 29th of November, I united in prayer with Brother Oliver for the continuance of blessings. After giving thanks for the relief which the Lord had lately sent us by opening the hearts of the brethren from the east, to loan us $430; after commencing and rejoicing before the Lord on this occasion, we agreed to enter into the following covenant with the Lord, viz.:
>
> That if the Lord will prosper us in our business and open the way before us that we may obtain means to pay our debts; that we be not troubled nor brought into disrepute

before the world, nor His people; after that, of all that He shall give unto us, we will give a tenth to be bestowed upon the poor in His Church, or as He shall command; and that we will be faithful over that which He has entrusted to our care, that we may obtain much; and that our children after us shall remember to observe this sacred and holy covenant; and that our children, and our children's children, may know of the same, we have subscribed our names with our own hands.
(Signed) Joseph Smith, Jun.
Oliver Cowdery

A Prayer

And now, O Father, as Thou didst prosper our Father Jacob, and bless him with protection and prosperity wherever he went, from the time he made a like covenant before and with Thee; as Thou didst even the same night, open the heavens unto him and manifest great mercy and power, and gave him promises, wilt Thou do so with us his sons; and as his blessings prevailed above his progenitors unto the utmost bounds of the everlasting hills, even so may our blessings prevail like his; and may Thy servants be preserved from the power and influence of wicked and unrighteous men; may every weapon formed against us fall upon the head of him who shall form it; may we be blessed with a name and a place among Thy saints here, and Thy sanctified when they shall rest. Amen.[10]

A rationale for this tithing covenant is given by the authors of a popular work on church history:

The principle of tithing was introduced when, in the late fall of 1834, Joseph and Oliver felt a strong personal need to set the proper example for the saints in their donations to the work of the Lord. They decided to pay a tenth part of their income for this purpose and to prepare a formal agreement to tithe. The brethren signed the following covenant:
[here the covenant quoted above is inserted]

> Although Joseph and Oliver chose to tithe at this time, the church as a whole did not practice the concept until after it was revealed by the word of the Lord, July 8, 1838.[11]

This comment by the author of the *Illustrated Stories* does seem to reflect the usual attitude that people today have toward the role of tithing in the early church. However it is incorrect to say either that "the principle of tithing was introduced ... in the late fall of 1834," or that "the church as a whole did not practice the concept until ... 1838." Large amounts of personal resources were devoted to gospel projects before that time, chiefly in the missionary and gathering process and building the Kirtland Temple. The use of funds for those activities was designated by the Lord as tithing. Even in the cases where extensive contributions occurred, but the word tithing is not connected with the event in the scriptures, the result is the same as if the contributions had been designated tithing.

In light of the rejoicing over receiving a loan of the small sum of $430, it is likely that Joseph had begun to despair that he could ever receive the money needed to accomplish the gathering through the tithing procedure. He may have felt much like President Lorenzo Snow who made a great effort to reemphasize tithing in Utah as a means to solve the church's financial problems.

In his prayer, Joseph compares his tithing covenant with that made by Jacob of old. Joseph declared that he would "give a tenth to be bestowed upon the poor in his church, or as he shall command," much as Jacob promised the Lord that he would "surely give the tenth unto thee." Both seem to assume that the tithing would be applied directly to projects of their choosing. This is similar to the method used today by those who are not LDS but wish to tithe, and who choose their own objects of charity. With that approach to tithing, then it is logical that buildings would be built or the poor helped using "subscriptions" and "donations." The money is tithing as it leaves the individual, but becomes "subscriptions" to the building committee or "donations" to the poor. In contrast, today's two-step process first accumulates funds carrying no stipulated use from the donor, calls the accumulation "tithing," and then "donates" or "subscribes" to projects considered appropriate by central funds managers.

Perhaps the clearest statement concerning the role of tithing in the early days of the church comes from a memorial, or circular letter, prepared by Bishop Newel K. Whitney and his counselors requesting funds for publications, the Kirtland Temple, and the poor:

> It is the fixed purpose of our God, and has been so from the beginning, as appears by the testimony of the ancient Prophets, that the great work of the last days was to be accomplished by the tithing of His Saints. The Saints were required to bring their tithes into the storehouse, and after that, not before, they were to look for a blessing that there should not be room enough to receive it. (See Malachi 3rd chapter, 10th verse). Our appeal, then, to the Saints is founded on the best of testimony, that which no Saint will feel to gainsay, but rejoice to obey.[12]

This memorial was circulated nearly a year before the Section 119 and 120 revelations, dated July 8, 1838, which deal with a procedural change in the method of collecting and administering tithing. The memorial is strong evidence that the principle of tithing was operational from the time the church was organized.

Chapter 14 Notes

1. D&C 19:26-27, 34-35. March 1830. Martin Harris.

2. D&C 58:34-38. August 1, 1831.

3. D&C 64:23. September 1831.

4. See D&C 63:24, 27, 36-39; HC 1:211.

5. D&C 85:3. November 27, 1832. HC 1:298-299.

6. HC 1:350.

7. HC 1:382. July 1833. A larger segment of the letter can be found quoted in chapter 5.

8. D&C 97:10-13. August 2, 1833. Kirtland.

9. The possible double meaning of the reference to temples is of interest. In D&C 94:1, Kirtland is known as "the city of the stake of Zion." D&C 109:2 mentions the commandment to build the Kirtland temple, and refers to D&C 88:119. D&C 94 and 95 also deal with sacred buildings.

10. HC 2:174-5. November 29, 1834.

11. Larry C. Porter, *Illustrated Stories from Church History* (Provo, Utah: Promised Land Publications, 1974), vol. 4, p. 14.

12. HC 2:516. September 18, 1837.

CHAPTER 15

Tithing and the United Order, Part 3: Sections 119 and 120 Improved Tithing Procedure

The materials in the preceding chapter indicate that tithing had an active role in church financing from the very beginning of this dispensation. Only the persons or organizations to which it was paid and the mechanics by which it was transmitted changed over time, while the doctrine remained the same.[1]

Sections 119 and 120 both represent significant steps in the development of the procedure and organization for administering tithing funds. Section 120 was given on the same day as section 119 (along with two other important administrative revelations, sections 117 and 118), and the two sections can be treated as practically a single revelation. The two sections are reproduced here, complete with the headnotes from the 1968 edition:[2]

Section 119

Revelation given through Joseph Smith the Prophet, at Far West, Missouri, July 8, 1838, in answer to the supplication: O Lord, show unto thy servants how much thou requirest of the properties of thy people for a tithing.

1 Verily, thus saith the Lord, I require all their surplus property to be put into the hands of the Bishop of my church in Zion,

2 For the building of mine house, and for the laying of the foundation of Zion and for the priesthood, and for the debts of the Presidency of my church.

3 And this shall be the beginning of the tithing of my people.

4 And after that, those who have thus been tithed shall pay one-tenth of all their interest annually and this shall be a standing law unto them forever, for my holy priesthood, saith the Lord.

5 Verily I say unto you, it shall come to pass that all those who gather unto the land of Zion shall be tithed of their surplus properties, and shall observe this law, or they shall not be found worthy to abide among you.

6 And I say unto you, if my people observe not this law, to keep it holy, and by this law sanctify the land of Zion unto me, that my statutes and my judgements may be kept thereon, that it may be most holy, behold, verily I say unto you, it shall not be a land of Zion unto you.

7 And this shall be an ensample unto all the stakes of Zion. Even so. Amen.

Section 120

Revelation given through Joseph Smith the Prophet, at Far West, Missouri, July 8, 1838, making known the disposition of the properties tithed as named in the preceding revelation, Section 119.

Verily, thus saith the Lord, the time is now come, that it shall be disposed of by a council, composed of the First Presidency of my Church, and of the bishop and his council, and by my high council; and by mine own voice unto them, saith the Lord. Even so. Amen.

Perhaps the first aspect of each revelation to be considered ought to be the question which brought it forth. For section 119, the question was "O Lord, show unto thy servants how much thou requirest of the properties of thy people for a tithing." Notice that the prayer does not ask "Is there such a thing as tithing or some other kind of church contribution?" Tithing is assumed to be an accepted and operating principle. The question was "How much tithing?" The question was mainly a procedural one, asking how things should be done at this stage of the church's development.[3]

At that time, large groups of saints, probably about thirteen hundred all together, were leaving Kirtland and migrating to Far West. A decision had to be made as to how to treat these new arrivals, and section 119 was apparently a result of such concerns. The saints who had moved to Missouri in earlier years had followed a rule similar to the one outlined in section 119. They had brought their monies to purchase land for themselves, and were asked to contribute any excess funds toward helping others who wished to migrate but did not have sufficient funds. Perhaps it was intended to maintain continuity and fairness by asking the newcomers to Far West to contribute as the earlier saints had done. The newcomers should not have the full benefit of the work, suffering, and loss of the earlier saints without some cost.

In earlier times, as when Martin Harris was asked to finance the printing of the Book of Mormon, "paying tithing" meant taking care of the Church's financial needs as they arose, even if that meant paying five years worth of "tithing" all at once for some specific item.[4] The regularized payment to a centrally managed fund implied in section 119 represents a level of procedural sophistication that the saints were barely ready for even in 1838. As we shall see, at least five years afterwards it was still an ideal rather than a fact for much of the Church.

Note that the term "tithed" as it is used in verse 5 is very general. The term "surplus properties" cannot be given any proportional figure such as one-tenth: it varies with the individual situation. So in this case, the "tithing" paid would not be one-tenth, but would simply be a contribution with the actual amount based on several practical considerations. And note that the "surplus" requirement was a one-time special procedure that was not to be repeated. The tithing paid by Abraham to Melchizedek was not from the normal increase from one month's or one year's labors, but was a windfall as a result of a battle to rescue a relative. It really represented a portion of the lifetime accumulations of many men. It was more of a "surplus property" contribution than a tenth of some recurring product of field, flock, or handicraft. These are indications that the term "tithing" is often used in a flexible way to refer to church contributions in general. We should not become overly concerned about the "one-tenthedness" of tithing. Even assuming that "tithing" means only one-tenth still leaves many important questions unanswered. One tenth of what? To whom? When? are all important procedural questions for which the right answers can vary a great deal, based on circumstance.

The tithing "how much" (one-tenth of what) question is an interesting and important one. If one has never paid tithing before, it might reasonably be requested of him that he pay one-tenth of all he has at the time of joining. That might be rather disruptive in some cases, so if it is modified to say all surplus property up to 1/10th, that might be reasonable. Again consider the difficulty or even impossibility of any regular collection of tithing. Where there were no banks, no storehouses, etc., the only choice is to ask for things as they are needed, and call the contribution tithing. There was only the general rule of gathering to Zion and caring for the poor. All the rest was left to on-the-spot creativity.

It is important for us to seek to understand the exact effect which section 119 was intended to have at the time it was given. There are several indicators that much of section 119 was intended to apply directly, in the form it was stated, only to those saints who were moving to Far West or other western church settlements, while other appropriate procedures, not discussed in the revelation, were to apply to other localities.

Verse 1 says that the surplus property is to be "put into the hands of the bishop of my church in Zion."[5] That would be a difficult accomplishment for anyone not living in or near Far West. Verse 4 says that "those who have thus been tithed," which logically can only be those in Zion, "shall pay one-tenth annually." Verse 5 states that "all those who *gather unto the land of Zion* shall be tithed of their surplus properties, ... or they shall not be found worthy to *abide among you.*" This language again localizes the immediate effect of the revelation. Verse 6 says that this law is to be used to "sanctify the land of Zion unto me," or "it shall not be a land of Zion unto you." This again is referring to a specific locality, Missouri, and leaves open the rule to be applied to those residing elsewhere.

Verse 7 appears to both widen and dilute the application of the prior verses. The use of the word "ensample," meaning example, may indicate that other areas of the world should follow the spirit of it, but not necessarily apply the identical procedure. In conjunction with the "ensample" term, the phrase "all the stakes of Zion," might be taken as a limiting term which might simply mean it applies to other organized stakes besides the Far West stake, for example, Kirtland, but in a less rigorous form. Perhaps the "one-tenth of all their interest annually" rule would be kept, but the "surplus property" rule would be delayed until actual migration to Missouri.

In other areas of the world, where stakes were not organized, it would not be required of every branch to accept surplus property or collect tithes regularly. Many of those scattered saints would be encouraged to gather to Missouri.

Transportation costs and the purchase of land required that large sums of money be acquired and spent by individuals. Would they who were directing all their resources toward their own gathering be required to send one-tenth to Far West? Probably not. The gathering process would tend to use up most of their means, including any "surplus." The tithing rules in section 119 most likely applied to those who had already completed the gathering process.

Application of section 119 may also have been limited because the practical administrative reach of the Twelve was limited to the western area - they could not administer a world-wide program. We can assume that in other localities individuals made donations, and that branch presidents and bishops accepted and disbursed some of these donations. These funds were tithing in every way except for the technical fact that the Council on the Disposition of the Tithes did not accept and disburse them.

In light of the above comments, verse 3 might be rewritten to read like this: "And this shall be the beginning of the tithing of my people as it relates to using the new more centralized and regularized plan, and it will begin with the people in Far West, and be spread as conditions permit."

Section 120 was received just after section 119, also presumably in response to a question of some sort. Unfortunately, the question which preceded the reception of section 120 is not mentioned in the history. However, from the nature of section 119 and other facts from the setting, we might surmise that the intervening question used in seeking clarification was something like this: "And who is to be appointed to administer the money and property collected by this new procedure?" The answer given describes what is known today as the Council on the Disposition of the Tithes.[6]

Since section 120 was given the same day as section 119, the statement "the time is now come" in 120 could not refer to tithing funds that had accumulated under section 119 and now needed to be administered. More likely the phrase means that the development of church ecclesiastical and administrative officers had now reached the appropriate level of experience and organization to be able to handle the new assignment related to tithing. The central collection, management, and expenditure of tithing funds was becoming feasible.

One might ask who was meant by the reference in section 120 to "my high council." It appears that the "twelve," the "high council," and the "traveling high council" were terms often used interchangeably in referring to the members of the Quorum of the Twelve. For example those terms have an identical meaning in the description of the area conferences of 1834:

> On the fifth of June, nine of the Twelve met in council at Rose, or Lyonstown, New York.
> ....
> On the 19th of June, nine of the traveling High Council met with the church in conference at Pillow Point, New York, ...[7]

The term "high council" as originally given was probably ambiguous enough to allow either the regular stake high council at Far West or the Twelve or some combination to serve as tithing administrators. Only gradually did the Twelve become *the* high council to the exclusion of all others.

The real doctrinal development contained in sections 119 and 120 is that finally there was a complete implementation of the leadership councils of the church which could be entrusted with the task of tithing administration. Before this revelation there was no fully functioning First Presidency, Quorum of the Twelve, and Presiding Bishop. After this revelation, these units gradually began to function properly.

The minutes of the general conference of April 1843 contain a wealth of insights into church financing procedures of the time. At that point, nearly five years after the Section 119 revelation concerning tithing and thirteen years after the organization of the church, there was still only a haphazard method of collecting moneys, as Joseph Smith bemoaned in his address to the saints. Notes and comments have been inserted in the following extended quotation to highlight significant points, and some words have been underlined for emphasis:

> *Minutes of the General Conference, beginning April 6th, 1843*
>
> ....
> He [Joseph Smith] next stated the object of the meeting, which was - ....
> Second. To take into consideration the expediency of sending out the Twelve, or some of them, amongst the branches of the Church, to obtain stock to build the Nauvoo House; for the time has come to build it.
> ....
> It is necessary that this conference give importance to the *Nauvoo House*. A prejudice exists against building it, in favor of the Temple; and the conference is required to give stress to the building of the Nauvoo House. This is the most important matter for the time being; for there is no place in this city where men of wealth, character, and influence from abroad can go to repose themselves, and it is necessary we should have such a place. The Church must build it or abide the result of not fulfilling the commandment.

Comment: Note that Joseph did not feel the saints had given him the power and choice of directing funds as he saw fit. He felt he could only request that they change the designated object or beneficiary of their gifts.

REMARKS OF THE PROPHET ON COLLECTING FUNDS.

President Joseph Smith said he did not know anything against the twelve. If he did, he would present them for trial. It is not right that all the burden of the Nauvoo House should rest on a few individuals; and we will now consider the propriety of sending the twelve to collect means for it. There has been too great a solicitude in individuals for the building of the temple to the exclusion of the Nauvoo House. Agents have had too great latitude to practice fraud by receiving donations, and never making report. The church has suffered loss, and I am opposed to that system of collecting funds when any elder may receive moneys. I am opposed to any man handling the public funds of the church who is not duly authorized. I advise that some *means be devised* for transacting business on a sure foundation.

Comment: No adequate means then existed to collect funds.

The Twelve are the most suitable persons to perform this business, and I want the conference to devise some means to bind them as firm as the pillars of heaven, if possible.

Comment: The twelve were not so automatically trusted in financial matters as they are today.

The Twelve are always honest, and it will do them no hurt to *bind them*. It has been reported that they receive wages at two dollars per day for their services. I have never heard this till recently, and I do not believe it. I know the Twelve have never had any wages at all. They have fulfilled their duties; they have always gone where they were sent, and have labored with their hands for their support when at home. If we send them into the world to collect funds, we want them to return those funds to this place, that they may be appropriated to the *very purpose* for which they were designed. I go in for binding up the Twelve solid, putting them under bonds; and let this conference institute an *order* to this end, and that the *traveling expenses* of the agents shall not be borne out of the funds collected for building these houses; and let no man pay money or stock into the hands of the Twelve, except he transmit an account of the same immediately to the Trustee-in-Trust; and let no man but the Twelve have authority to act as agent for the Temple and Nauvoo House.

Comment: See later discussion on this use of the word "order" in relation to a funds collection system.

I would suggest the propriety of *your saying* that no money should ever be sent by any man, except it be by some one whom *you have appointed* as agent, and stop every other man from receiving moneys.

Comment 1: Note the reliance ("your saying") on the democratic problem-solving and decision-making power of the saints. That is quite a different concept from today's practice of unanimously sustaining a finalized version of a proposal from the leaders. In a smaller organization a real and democratic consensus is more necessary and possible.

Comment 2: This suggestion about appointing an agent implies that in practice the central church was unable to know enough about the individual branches and their members to choose and appoint those agents for them as is done today.

It has been customary for any elder to receive moneys for the Temple when he is traveling. But this system of things opened a wide field for every kind of imposition, as any man can assume the name of a "Mormon" elder and gather his pockets full of money and go to Texas. Many complaints have come to me of money being sent that I have never received. I will mention one case. He is a good man: his name is Daniel Russell, from Akron, New York. His brother Samuel had been east on business for him, and there received twenty or twenty-five dollars as a donation to the Temple, which he put in Daniel Russell's bag, with his money, and forgot to take it out before he returned the bag. Two or three days after his return, he called on his brother for the money belonging to the Church; but Daniel thought Samuel had paid out too much of his money, and he would keep the Church's money to make good his own. I called to see Daniel Russell about the money, and he treated me so very politely, but did not give me to understand he ever meant to pay it. He said he did not know at the time that there was any church money in the bag, - that he had paid it out, and he had none now.

Samuel Russell, who brought the money from the east, stated to the conference that he did not think it was because his brother was short of funds that he kept it, for he had money enough. He had told him that he should not be out of funds again - that his brother had twenty dollars of the Church funds and some dried fruit for the President.

President Joseph resumed: I give this as a sample of a thousand instances. We cannot give an account to satisfy the people on the Church books unless something is done. I propose that you send your moneys for the Temple by the Twelve or some agent of your own choosing; and if you send by others and the money is lost, it is lost to yourselves; I cannot be responsible for it. Everything that falls into my hands shall be appropriated to the *very thing* it was designed for. It is wrong for the Church to make a bridge of my nose in appropriating funds for the Temple.

Comment: Here Joseph is defending the authority of the First Presidency and the associated temporal powers of the trustee-in-trust. He expects all funds to go through that channel rather than directly to the specific projects.

The act of incorporation required of me securities, which were lodged in the proper hands, as the law directs; and I am responsible for all that comes into my hands. The *Temple committee* are bound to me in the sum of $2,000, with good security. If they apply any property where they ought not, they are liable to me for it. *Individuals are running to them* with funds every day, and thus make a bridge over my nose. I am not responsible for it. If you put it into the hands of the Temple committee, neither I nor my clerk know anything of it. So long as you consider me worthy to hold this office [Sole Trustee-in-Trust For the Church] it is your duty to attend to the legal forms belonging to the business; and if not, put some other one in my place.

Comment: "This office" mentioned by Joseph refers to his position as sole trustee-in-trust for the church, the corporate property-holding entity.

My desire is that the conference minutes may go forth in some form that those abroad may learn the *order* of doing business, and that the Twelve be appointed to this special mission of collecting funds for the Nauvoo House, so that all may know how to send their funds safely, or bring them themselves, and deliver them to the Trustee-in-Trust or his clerk, who can always be found in the office. Who are the Temple committee, that they should receive the funds? They are *nobody*.... All property ought to go through the hands of the Trustee-in-Trust. There have been complaints against the Temple committee for appropriating Church funds more freely for the benefit of their own children than to others who need assistance more than they do; and the parties may have till Saturday to prepare for trial.

Comment: Harsh language and measures were apparently necessary to move more authority to from the temple committee to the First Presidency and Twelve. See later discussion.

It was then voted unanimously that the Twelve be appointed a committee to collect funds to build the Nauvoo House and receive moneys for the Temple, with this proviso - that the Twelve give bonds for the safe delivery of all funds coming into their hands belonging to the Nauvoo House and Temple to the Trustee-in-Trust; and that the payer also make immediate report to the Trustee-in-Trust of all moneys paid by him to the Twelve; and that the instructions of President Joseph Smith to the conference be carried into execution.

Elder W.W. Phelps proposed that the twelve sign triplicate *receipts* for moneys received, for the benefit of the parties concerned.

Elder Brigham Young objected, and said he should never give *receipts* for cash, except such as he put into his pocket for his own use; for it was calculated to make trouble hereafter, and there were *better methods* of transacting business and more safe for the parties concerned; that he wished this speculation to stop, and would do all in his power to put it down: to which the Twelve responded, Amen. Elder Young asked if any one knew anything against any one of the Twelve - any dishonesty. If they did, he wanted it exposed. He said he knew of one who was not dishonest. He also referred to muzzling the ox that treadeth out the corn, etc.

Comment: See discussion of receipts below.

President Joseph said, I will answer Brother Brigham. There is no necessity for the Twelve being abroad all the time preaching and gathering funds for the Temple. Spend the time that belongs to preaching abroad, and the rest of the time at home to support themselves. It is no more for the Twelve to go abroad and earn their living in this way than it is for others. The idea of not muzzling the ox is a good old Quaker song; but we will make the ox tread out the corn first, and then feed him. I am bold to declare that I have never taken the first farthing of Church funds for my own use, till I have first consulted the proper authorities. When there was no quorum of the Twelve or High Priests for me to consult, I have asked the Temple committee, who had no particular business with it; but I did it for the *sake of peace*. (Elder Cutler said it was so.)

Comment: Joseph is saying that he recognized more independent power on the part of the temple committee and local high councils before, as in Kirtland, but now wishes to change things.

Let the conference stop all agents from collecting funds, except the Twelve. When a man is sent to preach the first principles of the gospel, he should preach that, and let the rest alone.[8]

To a large extent, this episode concerning church finances occurred as a result of the need felt by Joseph Smith to follow the commandment to build the Nauvoo House.[9] It was proposed that the conference "institute an order" to deal with this and related problems. This is an interesting use of words, but no mystery. To Joseph Smith, an "order" was simply an arrangement for some specific administrative or business purpose, not some all-encompassing economic plan.[10] We still have this "order" today, because we have the First Presidency and Twelve handling the major church funds.

Joseph was asking the people to change the object of their donations more toward the Nauvoo House. Apparently, the funds being collected were usually earmarked for a certain, rather specific purpose. This meant that the donor retained a large amount of control over the donated funds. The general authorities exercised only limited control over the disposition of funds that were collected, and could not channel the funds as they thought best.[11]

Churches of other faiths today exhibit some of the same behavior. Members will often give to their own chapel and minister and city, but are not willing to send money off to some other distant management group for use in possibly unpredictable and unacceptable ways.

Joseph might have said that all donations to buildings are tithing, and he had all power over tithing. But he didn't say that, probably because the people would not support him in it.

Instead, Joseph took pains to make it clear that the First Presidency and Twelve, the General Authorities, would *not* redirect funds without the individual permission of the contributors. The funds collected by this new procedure were to be used for "the very purpose" for which they were designated by the contributor. Traveling expenses were not to come out of funds collected. No deductions were to be made for any reason. The honest behavior of the Twelve was not to be left to any uncertainty: they were to be bonded and held to account. These measures would assure people that the exact amounts they donated would be used as they directed. By removing the fear that their donations would prove ineffective by being consumed in the collection process itself, a common condition of charities today, the members were encouraged to make donations.

This plan was impractical in the sense that the Twelve could not be expected to pay all collection expenses from their own pockets, but the details of reimbursing them were not worked out at this time. Perhaps it was hoped that they could collect funds in conjunction with their "free" ecclesiastical or missionary trips.

Joseph called the temple committee "nobody" and threatened a court action for alleged misuse of funds. The result of these challenges to the committee was a reorganization giving the Council on the Disposition of the Tithes more authority. No misuse of funds was ever shown and the matter ended amicably. Note again that Joseph Smith was not asking (at this time) for the right to do whatever he wanted with the money that came in. If it were designated for the temple, it would go to the temple, but it would go through the trustee-in-trust, thus establishing the authority of that office. Later, when the reorganization had been accepted, the authority of the trustee-in-trust was established, and the habits and expectations of the members had changed, funds could more easily be funneled to meet current priorities.

Apparently there was no set system of giving money to local leaders and having them forward it to Nauvoo as is done today by the bishops. Individuals gave their money to whomever was going that way and hoped it would get there. This shows the primitive means of transferring funds then. The proposed solution was also a rather cumbersome one. The twelve were to travel around and physically collect it up - a wearisome task for that body. This emphasizes the distance they were from the finance-collecting, handling and disbursing mechanisms available to the church today. Like Abraham and Jacob, the saints of Joseph Smith's day could not pay their tithing by a monthly check mailed to a central office. Tithing could not be handled as it is today if one could not send money to a central place, or if the central place could not use it more effectively than the place of origin. The 1830's saints were better off than Abraham because they did have a postal system, but the money transfer system was not much better.

It would be interesting to know just what Brigham Young meant by his comments about there being a better way to handle funds than those proposed, by his disapproval of the use of receipts, and by his reference to speculation. His dislike of receipts must relate to some circumstance of the time. It appears that in that day (probably because of the inadequate supply of reliable money), receipts were closely associated with promissory notes or other negotiable instruments and were sometimes indistinguishable from them.[12] This may explain Brigham Young's concern about having multiple copies of receipts which might be used as commercial paper floating about the country. Even one copy seemed to be objectionable because of its potential use as a medium of exchange. The paper of a widely known person (such as Brigham Young was becoming, at least within the church) might easily be used as a kind of currency, and he did not like the idea of inadvertently becoming the proprietor of a one-man bank. Perhaps this fear of creating new money may be the basis for Brigham Young's comment about speculation.[13]

Even with this "speculation" concern, it still seems strange that Brigham Young would not be willing to sign a receipt as an agent of the church. He may really have been saying that he would not accept personal liability for the money he carried for the church. A courier of cash would have a large risk of losing it by theft. If it were lost he had no desire to be expected to replace it with his own. In such a traveling situation he did not wish to risk more than his own money, that which went "into his own pocket."

Brigham Young's "better way" apparently did not include the use of banks. Seeing today's world with easy, quick and safe international transfer of money through banks, one might wonder why the saints in Joseph Smith's day could not do the same, letting a bank take the risk of funds transfer. If it had been that easy, certainly the saints would have taken advantage of it instead of using agents who often proved unreliable. But the times apparently did not allow it. There was no national currency. Money was often not good except in the local area of the originating bank. The experience of the Kirtland bank gives some insight into this situation.[14] If the money itself from a distant bank was not acceptable, then a check for that money would be even less so. Sending cash money through the postal system was even riskier at that time than it is now, so that would not be a useful transmission method.[15]

From the history, we do not know the final arrangements that were made. But obviously something was worked out because the Twelve did begin to travel and collect funds. It appears that the money was collected and carried in the way Joseph had suggested, and that the Twelve were personally liable for at least a portion of any money lost.

About five months after the April 1843 conference, the twelve were in Boston to carry out the assignment given them in that conference. They confirmed that they had assumed a new role in church administration:

> We have a prospect of selling shares of the Nauvoo House, and of obtaining subscriptions for the Temple....
> Here are twelve men, and I defy all creation to bring a charge of dishonesty against them. We had to give security for the faithful performance of our duty as agents for the Nauvoo House and Temple. This has been heretofore unheard of in the Church. I glory in it. The financial affairs of the Church rest on our shoulders, and God is going to whip us into it. When men are in future called to do like Brigham, I will be one to bind them: this is a precedent. We are the only legally authorized agents of the Church to manage affairs, give counsel to emigrants how to dispose of goods, &c.[16]

On October 23, 1843, the twelve returned to Nauvoo and the funds collected were immediately used to purchase "groceries and different articles necessary for the Temple and the workmen thereon."[17] Another agent was later sent to England with a charge and authority similar to that given the twelve. He was "authorized to receive moneys for the Temple in Nauvoo, the poor, or for the Church."[18] The purposes for which the funds were collected covered all categories and were those always named and associated with consecration.

If we describe what came before 1838 as "consecration" and what came after as "tithing," then, by almost any objective performance standards, we should call the "consecration" period the lesser law and "tithing" the greater law. The earlier situation could better be described as a non-system rather than any kind of system. Temporal questions were handled on an ad hoc basis, the brethren and the Lord requesting funds as circumstances seemed to require and from whomever was at hand. Although a few made large contributions, the average amount collected from individual church members appears to have been rather small. Joseph Smith's large personal debts are some evidence of this.

One might observe that spontaneity is often associated with spirituality, and bureaucracy is often associated with the stifling letter of the law. However, spontaneous gestures will generally only solve small or short-lived problems; major or long-term problems require more planning and organization. For example, one does not produce a modern automobile without enormous preparation and investment. Providing for effective genealogy and temple work world-wide requires no less.

In contrast to the earlier "consecration," the later "tithing" system was on the way to becoming a regularized and dependable system which produced more revenue and could support a more extensive program. There was a clarification of the law rather than a replacement. Organization, procedure, and expectations all changed to higher levels. These structural changes made it a more consistent and evenly applied system. Today there is a distinction between tithing (any amount, normally less than ten percent), and a full tithing (ten percent or more). That is an example of the changes that have taken place.

Today the church is trying to limit its income and expenditures to tithing and avoid numerous other requests for funds. This movement toward almost total reliance on tithing is only possible if the tithing system is working well, thus making unnecessary the devising of other means to collect funds.

Tithing is a "higher" law because under it the members are asked to make a long term commitment of support and to have faith in their leaders concerning projects about which the members know very little. Under the pre-1838 program or so-called "consecration," only one-time or short term commitments had to be made, and only to specific visible projects. If a person were excited about a specific project he might contribute, but if he knew little about it or was doubtful of its worth, he would probably not contribute. It would be necessary for the bishops to be out stumping all the time for funds for specific projects just as Joseph Smith did.

It may come as a surprise to some that consecrations continued after Section 119, but by the definition of consecration used by the saints in the 1830's, there was no reason for any change. Consecrations are equivalent to donations. Tithing is a donation. So by definition, if tithing continues, donations continue, and therefore consecration continues. The two terms "tithing" and "consecrations" are not inconsistent or mutually exclusive but rather are part of the same program.

Tithing is an eternal doctrine and so is consecration, tithing being an element of the principle of consecration. Consecration was not removed nor was tithing a new doctrine. There was something that happened, something new in the 1838 revelations on tithing, but it amounted only to a modification of the procedure for collecting and administering tithing, not a basic change in any doctrine.

More precisely, consecration deals with how one uses all the resources one has, while tithes and offerings are that portion of a person's resources which are contributed to a church organization or directly to those in need. Everybody always does something with all the money and resources they have. Just what they do with it is an indication of their spirituality and concern for the good of others.

To summarize the history of funds collecting and management procedures, including tithing and "consecrations," it can be said that, rather than a decline from some higher standard or practice, there has been a long gradual improvement in organization and practice, and the 1838 revelations were part of that improvement.

Chapter 15 Notes.

1. Perhaps part of the reason for the controversy about the relationship of tithing and consecration arises out of Brigham Young's impatience with the rate of temporal progress of the saints and his arguments that tithing simply wasn't enough. He wanted to increase the church-controlled share of temporal activities and transactions. That share accomplished many things in Joseph Smith's day, but Brigham Young felt compelled by circumstances to seek more. There were many good reasons for his anxiety as will be described in a separate book.

Brigham Young seems to have desired to accelerate the accumulation of capital and general economic and social strength by promoting austerity measures. He did this by making maximum saving a religious duty and a requirement of salvation, and by creating a religious organization to enforce and administer that duty.

The real question even today is "What is the most efficient way to use the resources available?" Groups are more effective in some gospel-related activities, and individuals are more effective in others.

2. A printing error concerning the date of revelation of section 120 should be pointed out. The *History,* HC 3:44, gives July 8, 1838, as the date of revelation for both sections 119 and 120. However, the 1952, 1960, and 1968 editions of the Doctrine and Covenants show July 18, 1838, as the date of section 120. This was corrected to July 8, 1838, in the 1981 edition, and is corrected in the quotations of this book.

The headnotes from the 1981 edition are more lengthy than those in the 1968 edition. The additional commentary attributes to section 119 the traditional function of displacing a "higher" law with a "lesser." As shown in this and other chapters, that tradition appears to be counter to the facts of the Joseph Smith era.

An address by President Gordon B. Hinckley in General Conference, April 1984, May 1984 *Ensign,* pp. 46-48, contains several interesting and relevant points. He declares that "the Church has never taken a backward step since it was organized in 1830 - and it never will." This statement might be used in a general way* to counter the "backward step" tradition that a higher law was replaced by a lesser law in the 1838 revelation concerning tithing, sections 119 and 120.

President Hinckley also mentioned that "the demands upon the tithing funds are great" and that the construction of nearly 900 buildings in one year was "made possible by the *consecrations* of the Saints in obedience to the commandments of God." This equating of tithing and other contributions with the consecrations of the saints is consistent with Joseph Smith's use of those terms.

Pres. Hinckley mentioned the "Council on the Disposition of the Tithes, established by revelation and consisting of the First Presidency, the Council of the Twelve, and the Presiding Bishopric." We may assume that he was referring to section 120 where such a council was created. The term "First Presidency" was clearly used in section 120, but there may be some slight confusion as to the exact meaning of section 120 at the time it was given, since the term "my high council" and "the bishop and his council" were used rather than the more precise terms of "Council of the Twelve" and "Presiding Bishopric."

At the time of the revelations, the Twelve had yet to begin serious administrative duties in the headquarters of the Church, but there was a competent high council operating there. At the same time, the Twelve were also known as the "traveling high council," and because of their pre-eminent standing in the Church were surely intended to assume their duties concerning the tithes as soon as feasible, which did in fact begin to happen later that same year. The office of Presiding Bishop was just in the process of coming into being and is mentioned later in the history. Looking back, the Council on the Disposition of the Tithes is clearly foreshadowed and defined in general terms, if not precisely defined as it is today.

A comment from a period shortly after Brigham Young's time gives rise to an interesting question concerning the "displacing" tradition:

> The Lord revealed to his people in the incipiency of his work a law which was more perfect than the law of tithing. It comprehended larger things, greater power, and a more speedy accomplishment of the purposes of the Lord. But the people were unprepared to live by it, and the Lord, out of mercy to the people, suspended the more perfect law, and gave the law of tithing, in order that there might be means in the storehouse of

the Lord for the carrying out of the purposes he had in view; for the gathering of the poor, for the spreading of the gospel to the nations of the earth, for the maintenance of those who were required to give their constant attention, day in and day out, to the work of the Lord, and for whom it was necessary to make some provision. Without this law these things could not be done, neither could temples be built and maintained, nor the poor fed and clothed. Therefore the law of tithing is necessary for the church, so much so that the Lord has laid great stress upon it. Joseph F. Smith, *Gospel Doctrine* (Salt Lake City, Utah: Deseret Book, 1977) p. 225. (April Conference Report, 1900, p. 47).

One might wonder at the need for the "higher" law mentioned in this passage, since within the same passage, it appears that every legitimate temporal need of the church is shown to be accomplished by tithing. Today, the church is making ever effort to make tithing meet all of its needs for funds, and to avoid numerous other requests for contributions.

Actually, the amount of tithing paid may have gone up both temporarily and permanently for some people at the time of the Section 119 directive, at least for those moving from Kirtland to Nauvoo, rather than down as some have assumed happened under the so-called "lesser law".

*Considering the numerous apparent setbacks in the Church's past contacts with the world, one might be hesitant to accept the full long-term implications of this statement without further elaboration. Probably only President Hinckley knows the exact scope he intended for the statement. However, it is enough for our purposes if we merely take this statement as evidence of the opinion of someone deeply involved in the Church's growth process that, at least in doctrinal matters, the Church's development has been unidirectional. President Hinckley's comment is consistent with such scriptures as Acts 3:19-21 which speak of "the restitution of all things" which make it seem more likely that nothing would be lost, but rather that things would be added and improved and developed throughout this dispensation.

3. Verse 2 mentions the need to finance the temple at Far West. We might compare Section 119 with the earlier (1833) circular requesting funds for constructing the Kirtland Temple. HC 1:349-350. The circular requests subscriptions and donations without specifying any amount. Section 119 uses the word tithing which makes the amount more specific and also makes payment more of a duty.

4. Note Martin Harris's contributions. D&C 19:26; 58:35. HC 1:19, 76n.

5. This was a chance for the more well-to-do to help get the church established and assist the poorer members. Those coming from the East would be able to get land in the West much cheaper than in the East. It was claimed that the saints from England would find it only one-eighth as expensive in the West as in their home land. They could set themselves up there rather well and not suffer at all for the contribution of the surplus. To some extent, they could only get such a good deal because the other church members had made it possible by their previous pioneering.

6. See footnote 2.

7. HC 2:225. June 5, 1834.

8. HC 5:327-33. Bonding the 12. April 6, 1843. Apparently public preaching without any amplifying system was often quite a strenuous task. In more than one case, speaking in the open in windy conditions was said to have caused injury to lungs. HC 5:339; 6:431.

9. Perhaps if the Nauvoo House had been completed as Joseph desired, and emphasized at the conference, the saints might have entertained many men of influence who could have gained an accurate understanding of them and perhaps would have supported them against the outrages of the jealous mobbers and bandits of Missouri and Illinois.

Joseph's putting the Nauvoo House ahead of the temple for explicitly public relations reasons may sound like unpious religion, but probably was the only way ultimately to have finished and kept the temple in Nauvoo.

10. The very fact of having a "plan," whether 5-year or otherwise, almost by definition makes the system a socialistic one, because some central authority is controlling the use of property for centrally, and therefore "socially," determined goals. The contrasting situation is where economic planning is left to individual private citizens; there are millions of "plans" in that situation. The real-time summation of those "plans" is the only "plan" in effect. It is not under government control, and no one really knows exactly what it is until it happens.

"Jawboning" is the political term used to denote appeals to idealism, team spirit, nationalism, self-interest, etc., to convince people to accept a government recommendation. There is no Gospel objection to such methods, but governments normally go beyond that and use force of some kind to get compliance.

11. It is interesting that the president of the church had so little control over the flow and use of funds even for public purposes. He had great difficulty in directing funds away from building the temple and toward building the Nauvoo House. The question and problem would probably never even arise in the modern church. This shows how much the saints have come to have faith in their leaders. They have little to say about where their money is used, but they still continue to pay it in.

In 1843, the church still did not have "tithing" as we visualize it today. It was still much like the building of the Kirtland Temple - by subscription, more or less. They had not yet reached anything like our present rather abstract system.

12. For references to receipts, see HC 4:111; 6:28, 218, 230, 430.

13. The trouble that the church had recently experienced with old notes may have had some effect on Brigham Young's feelings on these questions. See chapter 10.

14. References on treatment of Kirtland money in other localities: See HC 2:487-488, 507-508; 6:429.

15. In some settings, centralization of administration is very difficult and may even be dangerous. Having assets concentrated in one location makes possible large losses in one fell swoop through the intervention of government or other force. In our day centralization seems easy, but only a small change in the affairs of nations would make it no longer possible.

16. HC 6:27-28.

17. HC 6:61.

18. HC 6:263-264.

CHAPTER 16

Joseph Smith's Definition of the Phrase "The Law of the Lord"

To begin this chapter we will quote again from Joseph Smith's history, February 1831, where he uses the phrase "the more perfect law of the Lord" in contrast to the "common stock" or communal society of the residents of Kirtland before their conversion to the Gospel:

> The branch of the Church in this part of the Lord's vineyard, which had increased to nearly one hundred members, were striving to do the will of God, so far as they knew it, though some *strange notions and false spirits* had crept in among them. With a little caution and some wisdom, I soon assisted the brethren and sisters to overcome them. The plan of *"common stock,"* which had existed in what was called *"the family,"** whose members generally had embraced the everlasting Gospel, was readily *abandoned for the more perfect law of the Lord;* and the *false spirits were easily discerned and rejected* by the light of revelation. [emphasis supplied]
>
> The Lord gave unto the Church the following: [section 41 follows].
>
> [The following footnote appearing in the documentary history text was added by its editor, B. H. Roberts]
>
> *This organization, called "the family," came into existence before the Gospel was preached in Kirtland, through an effort of the people of this neighborhood to live as the early Christians are said to have lived, viz., "and the multitude of them that believed were of one heart and of one soul: neither said any

of them that ought of the things which he possessed was his own; but they had all things common." (Acts IV:32.)[1]

In the foregoing quotation, Joseph Smith identifies the ideas of "common stock" or "family" communal living as being "strange notions and false spirits" which should be "discerned and rejected by the light of revelation." Joseph amplified these ideas in later statements (See Chapter 2).

The doctrines to which these people had been clinging consisted of the incomplete and confused sectarian ideas of the time. Perhaps in an attempt to give those vague and lifeless ideas some operational significance, they had also chosen to adopt what they supposed were some "straight and narrow" rules that would test their devotion to the Lord. Joseph probably appreciated their enthusiasm to find and live God's law, but found it necessary to replace almost their entire belief system with a new set of teachings, all together known as the law of the Lord. There was no room in the true and complete law of the Lord for the common ownership of property.

Joseph Smith rendered a new translation of large portions of the Bible very soon after the organization of the church, and as a result, was given many new gospel insights. For example, see the headnotes of section 76 which was given in February 1832 while Joseph Smith was translating the Gospel of John. By 1838, when Joseph Smith composed much of his history including this comment on the activities of the Kirtland saints, he had probably completed the bulk of his translation work. It was probably ready for publication in 1841 (D&C 124:89).

During his work on a new translation of the Bible, Joseph Smith made a few changes to the New Testament account of the "all things common" experience of the saints. (See Acts 4:32; 5:13) This indicates that he was quite aware of the existence of the passage, but, as illustrated in chapter 2, that he interpreted it differently than many do today.

In the scriptures received from the Lord through Joseph Smith, and in the entries of Joseph Smith in his historical journal, the term "law of the Lord" had a very broad meaning and encompassed the whole of the revealed Gospel rather than some narrow economic procedural specification. In the revelation given Joseph on the occasion of his visit to the saints at Kirtland (D&C 41), the term "my law," that is the law of the Lord to be given later in section 42, appears at least three times (v. 3, 4, 5). D&C 38:32 also foretells the revelation of section 42 containing "my law." A review of a portion of section 41 will be helpful here:

> 1 Hearken and hear, O ye my people, saith the Lord and your God, ye whom I delight to bless with the greatest of all blessings, ye that hear me; and ye that hear me not will I curse, that have professed my name, with the heaviest of all cursings.
> 2 Hearken, O ye elders of my church whom I have called, behold I give unto you a commandment, that ye shall assemble yourselves together to agree upon my word;
> 3 And by the prayer of your faith ye shall receive my law, that ye may know how to govern my church and have all things right before me.
> 4 And I will be your ruler when I come; and behold, I come quickly, and ye shall see that my law is kept.
> 5 He that receiveth my law and doeth it, the same is my disciple; and he that saith he receiveth it and doeth it not, the same is not my disciple, and shall be cast out from among you;
> 6 For it is not meet that the things which belong to the children of the kingdom should be given to them that are not worthy, or to dogs, or the pearls to be cast before swine.[2]

This February 4th revelation was given as direct preparation for the revelation which came five days later on February 9, 1831.

The February 9th revelation, D&C 42, "embracing the law of the church,"[3] contains commandments on a wide range of topics including missionary work, baptisms, the ten commandments, the healing of the sick, settlement of church disputes, the gathering, providing for the poor, etc. Part of the introduction, verse 2, directs the elders to "hear and obey the law which I shall give unto you."

In verse 3 of section 41, it states that "ye shall receive my law, that ye may know how to govern my church and have all things right before me." If the law is that comprehensive, then it must deal with much more than just a few economic matters.

In verse 4, the Lord speaks of being "your ruler," and when he comes we "shall see that my law is kept." This passage refers to all the laws that might be in existence during Christ's reign on earth. That is certainly a broad meaning for the word "law."

A portion of section 42 discusses care of the poor and in doing so employs the term "consecration." Because of the doctrines taught later during the Utah period, to some this may seem sufficient to conclude that "the law" equates to some all-encompassing economic system. However, the "consecration" aspect is only about ten percent of the entire revelation and can hardly be said to be more important than all the other important doctrines defined and stressed there. The "law" is the entire revelation, not just one segment of it. In the Joseph Smith setting, the term "consecrate" did not imply any centralized, bureaucratized property and income control mechanism.

Joseph composed the first part of his history in 1838. As he was preparing the 1831 portion, he placed the comment concerning "the more perfect law of the Lord" immediately before the two sections revealed to the new saints in Kirtland, sections 41 and 42. That physical contiguity in a history prepared at one time, itself tends strongly to indicate that the "law of the Lord" he had in mind was that which he placed next in the historical narrative. The implementation of that law is mentioned many places, such as D&C 44:6; 48; 51.

As further and powerful evidence of Joseph Smith's intent when using the phrase "the law of the Lord," his epistle dated January 22, 1834, at Kirtland takes a very expansive view of the phrase. Excerpts from that discourse may serve to brush away the narrow, confining, and mechanical connotations that some have associated with that phrase:

> All regularly organized and well established governments have certain laws by which, more or less, the innocent are protected and the guilty punished. The fact admitted that certain laws are good, equitable and just, ought to be binding upon the individual who admits this, and lead him to observe in the strictest manner an obedience to those laws. These laws when violated, or broken by the individual, must, in justice, convict his mind with a double force, if possible, of the extent and magnitude of his crime; because he could have no plea of ignorance to produce; and his act of transgression was openly committed against light and knowledge. But the individual who may be ignorant and imperceptibly transgresses or violates laws, though the voice of the country requires that he should suffer, yet he will never feel that remorse of conscience that the other will, and that keen, cutting reflection will never rise in his breast that otherwise would, had he done the deed, or committed the offense in full conviction that he was breaking the law of his country, and having previously acknowledged the same to be just.
>
> ....
>
> The laws of men may guarantee to a people a protection in the honorable pursuits of this life, and the temporal happiness arising from a protection against unjust insults and injuries; and when this is said, all is said, that can be in truth, of the power, extent, and influence of the laws of men, exclusive of the law of God, The law of heaven is presented to man, and as such guarantees to all who obey it a reward far beyond any earthly consideration; though it does not promise that the believer in every age should be exempt from the afflictions and troubles arising from different sources in consequence of the acts of wicked men on earth. Still in the midst of all this there is a

promise predicated upon the fact that it is the law of heaven, which transcends the law of man, as far as eternal life the temporal; and as the blessings which God is able to give, are greater than those which can be given by man. Then, certainly, if the law of man is binding upon man when acknowledged, how much more must the law of heaven be! And as much as the law of heaven is more perfect than the law of man, so much greater must be the reward if obeyed. The law of man promises safety in temporal life; but the law of God promises that life which is eternal, even an inheritance at God's own right hand, secure from all the powers of the wicked one.

....

It is necessary for men to receive an understanding concerning the laws of the heavenly kingdom, before they are permitted to enter it: we mean the celestial glory. So dissimilar are the governments of men, and so divers are their laws, from the government and laws of heaven, that a man, for instance, hearing that there was a country on this globe called the United States of North America, could take his journey to this place without first learning the laws of government; but the conditions of God's kingdom are such, that all who are made partakers of that glory, are under the necessity of learning something respecting it previous to their entering into it. But the foreigner can come to this country without knowing a syllable of its laws, or even subscribing to obey them after he arrives. Why? Because the government of the United States does not require it: it only requires an obedience to its laws after the individual has arrived within its jurisdiction.

....

When ... royal laws were issued, and promulgated throughout the vast dominion, every subject, when interrogated whether he believed them to be from his sovereign or not, answer, Yes; I know they are, I am acquainted with the signature, for it is as usual. *Thus saith the King!* This admitted, the subject is bound by every consideration of honor to his country, his king, and his own personal character, to observe in the strictest sense every requisition in the royal edict.

....

But for those who had heard, who had admitted, and who had promised obedience to these just laws no excuse could be urged; and when brought into the presence of the king, certainly, justice would require that they should suffer a penalty. Could that king be just in admitting these rebellious individuals

> into the full enjoyment and privileges with his son, and those who had been obedient to his commandments? Certainly not.
>
> We ask, again, would the king be just in admitting these rebels to all the privileges of his kingdom, with those who had served him with the strictest integrity? We again answer, no.
>
> We take the sacred writings into our hands, and admit that they were given by direct inspiration for the good of man. We believe that God condescended to speak from the heavens and declare His will concerning the human family, to give them just and holy laws, to regulate their conduct, and guide them in a direct way, that in due time He might take them to Himself, and make them joint heirs with His Son. But when this fact is admitted, that the immediate will of heaven is contained in the Scriptures, are we not bound as rational creatures to live in accordance to all its precepts? Will the mere admission, that this is the will of heaven ever benefit us if we do not comply with all its teachings? Do we not offer violence to the Supreme Intelligence of heaven, when we admit the truth of its teachings, and do not obey them?[4]

This sweeping treatment of the laws of God and a comparison of them with the laws of man shows the breadth of Joseph Smith's thinking on this topic. It seems fair to conclude that Joseph Smith regarded "the law of the Lord" as encompassing all revelations currently available, including the principle of continuous revelation of further laws. After releasing the Kirtland saints from the freedom-endangering coils of their communalistic "family," it seems most unlikely that he intended to present them with other doctrines which differed in name only.

Some have suggested that the "law of the Lord" may have been related to the united order. However, note that the united order was not revealed and organized until more than a year after Joseph Smith's February 1831 teachings to the new Kirtland members concerning "the more perfect law of the Lord."

It appears that after Joseph Smith's time the phrase "more perfect law of the Lord" was given a meaning exactly opposite to that intended by Joseph Smith in his admonitions to the Kirtland saints wherein he advised against communal living. Orson Pratt in his "Equality and Oneness of the Saints"[5] and in his discourses[6] uses the phrases "a more perfect law" and "this more perfect law of consecration," and gives them the most communal meaning imaginable - the total merger of all property under the control of the bishops. Brigham Young later taught this doctrine and made some efforts to put it into practice.[7] The materials presented in this chapter may serve to clarify what the term "Law of the Lord" meant to Joseph Smith.

Chapter 16 Notes

1. HC 1:146-147. February 1831. Joseph Smith. Kirtland. We may explain the seeming inconsistency between Joseph Smith's directions to the Kirtland saints and the footnote reference to Acts 4:32 by saying that during a crisis state of affairs, such as existed among the saints of Jerusalem who were being forced to leave the city by severe persecution, a lot of sharing may be necessary to assure survival. But during normal times, a general pooling of property of all kinds would cause confusion, inefficiency, irresponsibility, and ill will. This topic is discussed at greater length in note 15 of Chapter 2.

2. HC 1:147. February 4, 1831. Kirtland. D&C 41.

3. HC 1:148.

4. HC 2:7-8, 9, 10, 11.

5. Orson Pratt, "The New Jerusalem and the Equality and Oneness of the Saints" (Salt Lake City, Utah: Parker P. Robinson, Publisher, undated but possibly 1965), pp. 49-73, especially p. 57. From *The Seer,* pp. 289-300, July 1854.

6. See, for example, JD 2:97, 100. The following excerpt may give a clue about the relationship between Joseph Smith and Orson Pratt:

> Tuesday, 5 January, 1836. - Attended the Hebrew school divided into classes. Had some debate with Elder Orson Pratt concerning the pronunciation of a Hebrew letter. He manifested a stubborn spirit, at which I was much grieved. HC 2:356.

7. Brigham Young joined the Church April 14, 1832, more than a year after the Kirtland "family" episode, and probably had no direct experience with that episode. Later he promoted a version of the "family" idea in St. George and other Utah settlements.

CHAPTER 17

The Principles and Programs Described in D&C Section 42: The Meaning of the Word "Consecration"

The verb "to consecrate" and its many grammatical variations is nowhere explicitly defined in the scriptures, but a reliable definition of that word is vital to any understanding of the economic doctrines of the restored church. Because the word is not explicitly defined in the latter-day scriptures, one might reasonably assume that it was intended to have the meanings ordinarily attributed to it at the time and in the cultural context of the people receiving the revelations.

A dictionary should provide us with definitions that are widely if not universally accepted. Webster's Dictionary contains the following definitions:

> 1. "To make or declare sacred or holy;"
> 2. "To deliver up or give over, often with or as if with deep solemnity, dedication, or devotion;"
> 3. "Make memorable, significant, or consequential;"
> 4. "The solemn dedication in perpetuity of a church or of vessels used in the Eucharist esp. in the Roman Catholic Church."[1]

Let us review the scriptural occurrences of the word "consecration" and the meanings attributed to it by Joseph Smith and his contemporaries, and construct for ourselves a definition, or set of definitions. We will see that the Doctrine and Covenants does use the ordinary meanings of the word "consecrate," that is, meanings that are consistent with those in the dictionary, and does not establish any new meanings that deviate substantially from ordinary usage.

The two definitions of the word "consecrate" that will be considered here are represented by the words "dedicate" and "donate." We may begin a comparison of these two words by saying that a donation is normally an unconditional gift to another. The gift may be made based on an expectation that the property will be used for certain purposes, but after the procedure of giving is accomplished, the donor normally retains no control over its use. In contrast, dedicating something for a specific purpose is done with no change in title. The original owner still holds title and has the power to change the use of that property at some later time if he so chooses. Concepts of property and the effects, if any, of the idea of "consecration" on property ownership, use, management, transfer, and control are among the central issues addressed in this book.

The scriptures often use the word "consecrate" as the equivalent of the word "dedicate." The Lord sometimes designates or dedicates land, temples, anointing oil, and other resources for specific purposes. Here is one example from the Doctrine and Covenants:

> Hearken, O ye elders of my church, saith the Lord your God, who have assembled yourselves together, according to my commandments, in this land, which is the land of Missouri, which is the land which I have appointed and consecrated for the gathering of the saints.[2]

In this case, no change of ownership is implied; there is merely the forming of an intention or plan to use some resource in a certain way. When the Lord consecrates something, we would not imagine that he is giving up title or ownership to anything. He owns everything regardless of any earthly transaction. Thus this definition, a major one, does not imply a transfer of all property to another. Of a total of thirty-three scriptural references to the word "consecration" in the D&C concordance, sixteen are used in this sense.

There are also examples of individuals designating or dedicating property to a certain purpose, while still holding title. In fact, without owning the property, they probably could not ensure that it would be used for the purposes intended. One interesting example was given by President Heber C. Kimball, First Counselor to President Brigham Young from 1847 to 1868 and one of the original members of the Quorum of the Twelve, as he counseled the early Utah settlers on various practical matters:

> I will now make a few remarks in relation to building storehouses....
>
> ....
>
> When we have stored away our grain we are safe, independent of the world, in case of famine, are we not?
>
> ....
>
> I will advise every man in every settlement to build a storehouse; and if one cannot do so alone, let two or three build one between them. Store up and preserve your grain and then you will be safe.
>
> ....
>
> Let us go to work and cultivate the earth, and go into the fields, and bless the land, and dedicate and consecrate it to God; and then dedicate the seed, the implements, and the horses, and oxen. Do you suppose that that will have any effect? I know that it will. Nearly twenty years ago, I was in a place in England in which I felt very curious; but I did not know at the time what it meant. I went through a town called Chadburn, beyond Clithero. Before I went there, some persons told me that there was no use in my going, and asked me what I wanted to go to Chadburn for, saying it was the worst place in the country; for the sectarian priests had preached there faithfully thirty years without making any impression. Notwithstanding that, I went,

and preached once, and baptized twenty-five persons, where the priests had not been able to do a thing.

I went through the streets of that town feeling as I never before felt in my life. My hair would rise on my head as I walked through the streets, and I did not then know what was the matter with me. I pulled off my hat, and felt that I wanted to pull off my shoes, and I did not know what to think of it.

When I returned, I mentioned the circumstance to Brother Joseph, who said, "Did you not understand it? That is a place where some of the old prophets travelled and dedicated that land, and their blessing fell upon you." Then try it, and see if it will not leave a blessing for us to dedicate our lands. If you think that it will not, never bring another bottle of oil and ask us to dedicate and consecrate it for the benefit of the sick. I know that we can bless the land, and that through our blessing it will be filled with the spirit and power of God; and that, too, in great profusion, especially if we are filled with that spirit ourselves. Some may call me enthusiastic; but I am no more so than the old prophets were when they had the spirit of God upon them.[3]

When President Heber C. Kimball spoke of consecration, he was not referring at all to any transfers of property. He focused on the spiritual benefits of a certain way of seeking to bring the Lord closer to our lives, our lands, and our daily activities. One of the incidental consequences of an individual's use of priesthood power to make his lands more holy might be to make them more fruitful. If an individual's lands were more fruitful and he had an abundance for himself, he would then be in a position to contribute something to others, if he so chose, and thus, in that indirect way, the blessing of the land could contribute to the overall welfare of the saints. His reference to the building of storehouses makes it clear that he assumed than men would act independently in most cases, and would join together only for limited purposes based on economic realities and judgement.

Other examples of dedicating property will be discussed later in conjunction with section 85 and other materials and texts, but a short comment here may be helpful.

Section 85, especially verse 3, concerns land transactions in Missouri, and has both "dedicate" and "donate" aspects. The saints were to "donate" enough money to pay for their own land (purchased from what amounted to a church-affiliated real estate brokerage firm), and some extra, if possible, to help the poor acquire land. They were also expected to dedicate their newly acquired land to the Lord's purposes. The most significant practical aspect of this dedication was an agreement never to sell the land to anyone outside the Church, even if total loss of the land was the alternative. When the saints were forced to leave Missouri, a few did sell, but the bulk did not.

The second major definition for the word "consecration" is that of ordinary donations to the church. Today we have a long list of categories of donations, each with its own peculiar accounting procedure: tithing, fast offerings, welfare assessments, local and general missionary funds, special temple building funds, local and general building funds, ward budget, quorum dues, etc. This proliferation of categories might make it appear that the use of each fund is very narrow and specific. Actually, the number of specific things for which these funds are spent is almost infinite. Rent might be paid by tithing, fast offerings, missionary funds, etc. Food might be purchased with fast offerings, welfare assessments, missionary funds, ward budget, or quorum dues. Tithing might be used for any imaginable church purpose, two major
purposes being church publications and buildings. Tithing has been used for welfare purposes at times. Thus these categories are all rather broad operationally, and all are used to help along the Kingdom in general ways.

The early saints simply lumped all donations together and called them consecrations. The funds were used for essentially the same purposes as we have today.[4] They had a fund which we do not have today, a special gathering fund which was to help everyone move to Zion, including the poor.[5] This type of fund (the Perpetual Emigrating Fund) continued in Brigham Young's day as the gathering phase continued.

The following quotation illustrates the meaning attributed to the word "consecrate" in Joseph Smith's time:

> The Blessing of those who assisted in building
> the House of the Lord at Kirtland.
>
> March 7. - This day a meeting of the Church of Latter-Day Saints was called for purpose of blessing, in the name of the Lord, those who have heretofore assisted in building, by their labor and other means, the House of the Lord in this place.
>
> The morning was occupied by President Joseph Smith, Jun., in teaching the church the propriety and necessity of purifying itself. In the afternoon, the names of those who had assisted to build the House were taken, and further instructions received from President Smith. He said that those who had distinguished themselves thus far by consecrating to the upbuilding of the House of the Lord, as well as laboring thereon, were to be remembered; that those who build it should own it, and have the control of it.
>
> After further remarks, those who performed the labor on the building voted unanimously that they would continue to labor thereon, till the House should be completed.
>
> President Sidney Rigdon was appointed to lay hands on and bestow blessings in the name of the Lord.
>
> The Presidents were blessed; and Reynolds Cahoon, Hyrum Smith, and Jared Carter, the building committee, though the last two were not present, yet their rights in the House were preserved.
>
> The following are the names of those who were blessed in consequence of their labor on the House of the Lord in Kirtland, and those who consecrated to its upbuilding: ....
>
> The blessings and ordinations of particular individuals of the foregoing were as follows: - Reynolds Cahoon, Jacob Bump, and Artemus Millet, were blessed with the blessings of heaven and a right in the House of the Lord in Kirtland, agreeable to the labor they had performed thereon, and the means they had contributed.

Alpheus Cutler ... received the same blessing. The blessing referred to was according to each man's labor or donation ....[6]

Some excerpts from the foregoing quotation will help to make its significance more obvious:

1. "assisted ... by their labor and other means"
2. "consecrating ... as well as laboring"
3. "those ... blessed in consequence of their labor ... and those who consecrated to its upbuilding"
4. "labor ... performed ... and ... means ... contributed"
5. "each man's labor or donation"

The words and phrases just quoted show that, in the parlance of the time, the words "contribute," "donate," and "consecrate," and the phrase "assisted ... by ... means," were all used interchangeably and had the same meaning. The word "consecrate" did not imply a long term absorption of self and property into a centralized bureaucracy. It simply meant the spontaneous donation of means to a good cause as any church member might do today through the many programs available, including contributions for temple building.

We have been considering the two most important meanings of the word "consecration," that of "dedication" and "donation." Certain events which occurred during the early Utah period gave rise to a third definition of the word "consecration." It was used to describe an act involving the transfer of property as part of joining a communal order. That meaning did not exist at Joseph Smith's time, and the attempts to give that definition a practical implementation during Brigham Young's time were often abortive. Perhaps that is some indication that the word was never meant to carry that meaning. There has been a tendency to take that definition and apply it retroactively to the time of Joseph Smith to the exclusion of all other meanings. This has been detrimental to an accurate understanding of the use of the word in various contexts.

Some of the confusion concerning the proper meaning of the word consecration has come from a loose reading of portions of D&C 42. This section was called the law of the Church by the Lord himself and it contains many commandments. One of them has to do with church contributions in general, including welfare aid to the poor. This revelation was given in the special circumstances of the gathering of the saints to Kirtland in preparation for the move to Missouri. The welfare needs were large because many saints arrived in Kirtland with all their means expended. They had no money to acquire property so they could grow food, provide housing, and otherwise care for themselves. But the procedure for handling the problem was not anything unusual by today's standards. The people in Kirtland were asked to donate food and land to the poor newcomers through the Bishop. In our urban society, we might pay someone's rent to provide them a place to stay rather than give them some land. Those people who donated or sold land, gave or sold only what they felt they could spare in the circumstances and kept the remainder.

It is difficult to portray in a few words the true setting and economic circumstances of those early saints. But an understanding of the practical problems that faced them would help us to understand the actions taken to solve those problems. It is hoped that insights into this process can be gradually accumulated from the various historical materials that are scattered throughout this entire book. A few observations here may help to begin that process:

1. The Bishop did not become the controller of all economic activity as some have imagined. He merely performed a series of one-time transactions to get the new people settled. To the extent they could buy land themselves, they were expected to do so. The church leaders bought

large tracts of land in advance so that the incoming saints could purchase the land at the most reasonable rates.

2. Some of the incoming saints moved as organized companies and shared some resources for the duration of their trip simply because that was the most efficient way to make the journey. These arrangements normally did not continue beyond the accomplishment of the short-term objective for which they were formed.

3. We should be aware that the Lord told the people gathering to Kirtland that they would be moving on to other locations further west as soon as arrangements could be made, and that within about five years, Kirtland would have completed its role as an interim gathering and staging location for the westward migration.[7] These expectations for the future may have caused them to have a different attitude about holding and using land than if they were planning for themselves and their families to remain there the rest of their days.

4. There were both "carrot" and "stick" incentives operating as well as the more idealistic and spiritual ones. The saints were encouraged to migrate by the cheap land out west: land was selling for $1.25 an acre in Missouri. They were also given reason to fear remaining in the East because of the predictions concerning wars and other difficulties (D&C 38:28-30; 42:64).

With this very short introduction to the economic setting of the time in mind, let us consider the parts of section 42 that deal with the idea of consecration:

> 30 And behold, thou wilt remember the poor, and consecrate of thy properties for their support that which thou hast to impart unto them, with a covenant and a deed which cannot be broken.
>
> 31 And inasmuch as ye impart of your substance unto the poor, ye will do it unto me; and they shall be laid before the bishop of my church and his counselors, two of the elders, or high priests, such as he shall appoint or has appointed and set apart for that purpose.

32 And it shall come to pass, that after they are laid before the bishop of my church, and after that he has received these testimonies concerning the consecration of the properties of my church, that they cannot be taken from the church, agreeable to my commandments, every man shall be made accountable unto me, a steward over his own property, or that which he has received by consecration, as much as is sufficient for himself and family.

33 And again, if there shall be properties in the hands of the church, or any individuals of it, more than is necessary for their support after this first consecration, which is a residue to be consecrated unto the bishop, it shall be kept to administer to those who have not, from time to time, that every man who has need may be amply supplied and receive according to his wants.

34 Therefore, the residue shall be kept in my storehouse, to administer to the poor and the needy, as shall be appointed by the high council of the church, and the bishop and his council;

35 And for the purpose of purchasing lands for the public benefit of the church, and building houses of worship, and building up of the New Jerusalem which is hereafter to be revealed -

36 That my covenant people may be gathered in one in that day when I shall come to my temple. And this I do for the salvation of my people.

37 And it shall come to pass, that he that sinneth and repenteth not shall be cast out of the Church, and shall not receive again that which he has consecrated unto the poor and needy of my church, or in other words, unto me -

38 For inasmuch as ye do it unto the least of these, ye do it unto me.

39 For it shall come to pass, that which I spake by the mouths of my prophets shall be fulfilled: for I will consecrate of the riches of those who embrace my gospel among the Gentiles unto the poor of my people who are of the house of Israel.

40 And again, thou shalt not be proud in thy heart; let all thy garments be plain, and their beauty the beauty of the work of thine own hands;

41 And let all things be done in cleanliness before me.

42 Thou shalt not be idle; for he that is idle shall not eat the bread nor wear the garments of the laborer.

....

53 Thou shalt stand in the place of thy stewardship.

> 54 Thou shalt not take thy brother's garment; thou shalt pay for that which thou shalt receive of thy brother.
> 55 And if thou obtainest more than that which would be for thy support, thou shalt give it into my storehouse, that all things may be done according to that which I have said.
> ....
> 62 Thou shalt ask, and it shall be revealed unto you in mine own due time where the New Jerusalem shall be built.
> 63 And behold, it shall come to pass that my servants shall be sent forth to the east and to the west, to the north and to the south.
> 64 And even now, let him that goeth to the east teach them that shall be converted to flee to the west, and this in consequence of that which is coming on the earth, and of secret combinations.
> ....
> 70 The priests and teachers shall have their stewardships, even as the members.
> 71 And the elders or high priests who are appointed to assist the bishop as counselors in all things, are to have their families supported out of the property which is consecrated to the bishop, for the good of the poor, and for other purposes, as before mentioned;
> 72 Or they are to receive a just remuneration for all their services, either a stewardship or otherwise, as may be thought best or decided by the counselors and bishop.
> 73 And the bishop, also, shall receive his support, or a just remuneration for all his services in the church.[8]

Verses 30 and 31 of Section 42 contain the phrases "consecrate of thy properties" and "impart of your substance." These phrases mean the same thing, that is, contribute to the poor as much as you feel you can or ought, according to your circumstances. There is no implication here, as some have thought, that some complicated centralization of property ownership and control is intended or required. There is only a simple mechanism for collecting donations to help the poor. The spirit of this whole procedure, found in many places in the scriptures, is repeated in verse 38, "For inasmuch as ye do it unto the least of these, ye do it unto me." Alms should be done in secret, if possible, even if done by an organization (3 Nephi 13: 1-3).

Verse 30 also contains the phrase "that which thou hast to impart" which states a very simple and uncomplicated rule. To the extent that the poor are in need and to the extent you have some to spare, a gift is appropriate. This is the same law that was given to the Nephites in the Book of Mormon, and the same law and standard that applies today. The following Book of Mormon scripture describes the process of giving gifts between individuals as the occasion presents itself:

> 27 And again Alma commanded that the people of the church should impart of their substance, everyone according to that which he had; if he have more abundantly he should impart more abundantly; and of him that had but little, but little should be required; and to him that had not should be given.
>
> 28 And thus they should impart of their substance of their own free will and good desires toward God, and to those priests that stood in need, yea, and to every needy, naked soul.
>
> 29 And this he said unto them, having been commanded of God; and they did walk uprightly before God, imparting to one another both temporally and spiritually according to their needs and their wants.[9]

One of President Marion G. Romney's conference addresses makes it clear that any "consecration" transfer is a gift of part of one's substance, not a mandatory transfer of all. The process of humbling the rich and exalting the poor through gifts is to be done as a free and individual process and not through centralized control or coercion:

> Can we see how critical self-reliance becomes when looked upon as the prerequisite to service, when we also know service is what godhood is all about? Without self-reliance one cannot exercise those innate desires to

serve. How can we give if there is nothing there? Food for the hungry cannot come from empty shelves. Money to assist the needy cannot come from an empty purse. Support and understanding cannot come from the emotionally starved. Teaching cannot come from the unlearned. And most important of all, spiritual guidance cannot come from the spiritually weak.

There is an interdependence between those who have and those who have not. The process of giving exalts the poor and humbles the rich. In the process, both are sanctified. The poor, released from the bondage and limitations of poverty, are enabled as free men to rise to their full potential, both temporally and spiritually. The rich, by imparting of their surplus, participate in the eternal principle of giving. Once a person has been made whole or self-reliant, he reaches out to aid others, and the cycle repeats itself.[10]

The law of consecration as outlined in the D&C Section 42 is essentially the equivalent of today's welfare plan. Its purpose was to provide for the poor rather than to fulfill some abstract leveling purpose. Only the portions necessary to assist the really poor need be given to the bishop to administer.

In at least nine verses in Section 42, known to us as the "Law of the Church," it is made clear that the object of the consecrating process is the assistance of the poor. In some verses it is made clear which poor are to be assisted - those that are not idle (v. 42), those that are not proud (v. 40), and those that are clean (v. 41). Other general church purposes are mentioned (v. 35) including the "purchasing of lands for the public benefit of the church, building houses of worship, and building up the New Jerusalem" to be revealed. These functions are all now done by the regular payment of tithing, welfare, and other donations.

The advantage of these present-day methods, of course, is their consistency and predictability, making long-term planning possible. The suggested payment levels are based upon estimates of the need for funds for the various functions. As will be discussed elsewhere, this is in striking contrast to the ad hoc and uneven financing methods that were the only methods available while the church was in constant turmoil.

The idea that the "consecration" process is a partial one for the limited purpose of caring for the poor and other legitimate general church-related programs is emphasized several times in Section 42. The phrases "of thy properties (v. 30)," "of your substance (v. 31)," and "of the riches (v. 39)" indicate that only a portion of one's properties need be donated, but would mean something quite different if the word "of" were removed. "Consecrating of thy properties" is different from "consecrating thy properties." Without the word " of," the word "all" is implied.

It is interesting to note that there is some room for historians to debate whether the text of verse 30 has always been exactly as it is rendered in our modern publication.[11] Apparently, some documents from various sources before the 1835 publication of the first edition of the Doctrine and Covenants show verse 30 containing the phrase "all thy properties." This is quite a different meaning from the present phrase "of thy properties." Actually, the possibility that it may have been consciously changed from "all" to "of" would only strengthen the argument here. After some experience, it may have been clarified that "of" was indeed the correct policy. That old controversy may explain some of the confusion today.

Leaving the historical question, we may find some benefit in focusing on the text. To be internally consistent, the remainder of Section 42 seems to require the "of" interpretation. This makes it doubtful that there ever was a legitimate "all" version.

The stewardship concept is closely bound to the law of consecration. Note how the comments on stewardship in

D&C 42:32 strengthen the conclusion that consecrations are limited. Every man was to be "a steward on his (a propertied person's) own property (never consecrated), or that which he (a poor person) has received by consecration." Some people read the second phrase ("that which he has received by consecration") as being merely another way of saying, or a redefinition of, the first phrase ("his own property"). They read this portion of verse 32 so that the two categories of final ownership are the same, that is, all land was once owned individually, then all given to the Church and a portion received back. But this is not correct. Actually, there are two categories of property, one purchased and held in the normal way, and one received as a gift from another's "consecration" or gift of a portion of his property.

This concept of two ways of acquiring title to property is important and it is worth another attempt to make it more clear. The phrase "his own property, or that which he has received by consecration (somebody else's gift)" refers to (1) property never given away ("non-surplus"), and (2) property received through the bishop as the result of someone's gift ("surplus").

Verse 32 mentions that "every man shall be made accountable unto me, a steward over his own property." Actually, there is no change in status here, because every man is always accountable to the Lord. However, there is a recognition that by involvement in a welfare activity, we are acknowledging the Lord's hand in all things. The phrase "a steward over his own property" again acknowledges that the man does in fact own and control his property and is not merely the employee of one of the Lord's agents such as a bishop. As a separate but related point, all men could reasonably be held to the same standard of accountability before the Lord, because after the receipt of the gift through the bishop, the man who was poor would then hold his property just as absolutely as the man who had made the gift continued to hold his non-surplus property (property he chose not to consecrate).

In further support of the limited consecration or donation idea, verse 33 mentions that other consecrations from "properties in the hands of ... any individuals" might be necessary in the future "to administer to those who have not." This implies either that all was not consecrated the first time, or that consecration is a repetitive and on-going process, just like our normal present-day contributions. Either situation argues against the rigid double-deeding mechanism imagined by some. Verse 33 also says that "this ... consecration ... is a residue," an amount over and above the needs of the original owner. The amount of the surplus or residue was completely determined by the donor.

A definition of "residue" or "surplus" can be extracted from examples appearing in the scriptures. In one example of this idea of a residue, missionaries were instructed to use donations to support themselves and their families, with any excess to be sent to the bishop to be used for printing revelations and for other purposes.[12] In another example, excess literary firm income was to go into the storehouse for general church use, but only after the needs and wants of the firm's proprietors were satisfied.[13] In a third example, excess travel funds were to be returned to the church after the completion of the journey for which they were advanced.[14]

There are other more general examples of the idea of a residue that may apply here also. In a tribal, peasant, or pioneer subsistence economy where there may be no efficient means of preserving and storing food or transporting certain properties, a person's "residue" often must be shared or it is lost and no one benefits from it.

Money, whether in the form of coins or in the even more esoteric form of a bank account, is only useful as a store of value when there is a reasonable opportunity to exchange some of that rather abstract substance for real and useful goods. The gathering and migrating saints were often unable to use money as a means of making their properties portable. Their unconvertible and nontransportable properties, particularly lands, would tend to become "residue" merely because they were of no use to the owners, but might be of use to other church members. This would be akin to the situation described in the New Testament (Acts 4-5) where the saints were all forced to leave Jerusalem because of persecution. Selling their homes and lands and sharing the proceeds was not a very remarkable action because failure to sell their land would mean a total loss of it anyway. Many probably could not sell their land at all, and so those who could trade their land for money might well count themselves blessed and be willing to share with others less fortunate.

Brigham Young was requested to collect "surplus" property during 1838 in response to the revelation in D&C 119. He reported Joseph Smith's instructions to him as follows:

> The brethren wished me to go among the churches, and find out what surplus property the people had, with which to forward the building of the temple we were commencing at Far West. I accordingly went from place to place through the country. Before I started, I asked Brother Joseph, "Who shall be the judge of what is surplus property?" Said he, "Let them be the judges themselves, for I care not if they do not give a single dime. So far as I am concerned, I do not want anything they have."[15]

This comment indicates that all transmissions of property to the Church are to be done on the same basis, that is, as a result of the operation of untrammeled individual agency.

Verses 30, 32, and 37 of section 42 mention that the consecration or "gift" (D&C 51:5) is to be made with a covenant and deed that cannot be broken. This is a bit of practical wisdom rather than some deep and mysterious doctrine. There should be order and predictability in the process of administering the property made available to the poor. It would be most embarrassing and disruptive to have later claims made on the property by the original owner. Whether the original owner remains faithful in the church or not, the property flow should be undisturbed. Of course, under normal circumstances, only those who become disenchanted with the church or apostatize from it would make a request to have a gift returned. That would be like our asking to get our last ten years of tithing back all at once. Attempting to fulfill such a request would cause some trouble no matter what the circumstances, but things would be at their worst if real estate titles were affected.

In more legalistic language, an irrevocable deed of gift was to be used in land transfers to avoid title disputes later on. Joseph Smith expressed concern that these formal steps be handled correctly for this very reason. He instructed Bishop Partridge on the matter in a letter:

> ... We wrote to Brother W. W. Phelps, and others in Zion, from Kirtland, as follows: (Sidney Rigdon actually penned the letter)
>
> Brethren: --
> ....
> We would again say to Alam [Edward Partridge], be sure to get a form according to law for securing a gift. We have found by examining the law, that a gift cannot be retained without this.[16]

Section 83 is closely related to section 42 and will be inserted here for comment:

> 1. Verily, thus sayeth the Lord, in addition to the laws of the church concerning women and children, those who belong to the church, who have lost their husbands or fathers:

> 2. Women have claim on their husbands for their maintenance, until their husbands are taken; and if they are not found transgressors they shall have fellowship in the church.
> 3. And if they are not faithful they shall not have fellowship in the church; yet they may remain upon their inheritances according to the laws of the land.
> 4. All children have claim on their parents for their maintenance until they are of age.
> 5. And after that, they have claim upon the church, or in other words upon the Lord's storehouse, if their parents have not wherewith to give them inheritances.
> 6. And the storehouse shall be kept by the consecrations of the church; and widows and orphans shall be provided for, as also the poor. Amen.[17]

Note that within section 83 it is assumed, as always, that people are first to rely on themselves, then on their families, and only then on the church. The parents are to provide for their children in all ways, including assisting them to acquire land or other productive property if needed. The church assists only in unusual cases (v. 5).

The widows, orphans, and poor are to be cared for from consecrations or donations. This implies a constant and even flow of resources rather than one-time or spasmodic contributions. This again sets the limit on the needs for contributions, and argues against any large scale centralization of properties. The properties producing the funds needed to support the poor would be most efficiently operated by private owners, with a small portion of the income donated to the support system for the poor. Those assisted by the church are the very ones least able to use productive property efficiently, so allocation of any large amount of productive property to them directly would usually be unwise.

Another insight into individual property and welfare situations was recorded in the history in conjunction with instructions to brethren leaving on missions. These men were to provide for themselves, and especially, their families from their own resources. Except for really unusual cases, there was to be no communalistic merging of properties or debts, even for the important function of missionary work. The charity of others was not to be relied on if there were means to prevent it:

> President Young instructed the elders not to go from church to church for the purpose of living themselves or begging for their families or for preaching, but to go to their places of destination, journeying among the world and preaching by the way as they have opportunity; and if they get anything for themselves, they must do it in those churches they shall build up or from the world, and not enter into other men's labors.
> ....
> Let not the elders go on their missions until they have provided for their families. No man need say again, "I have a call to travel and preach," while he has not a comfortable house for his family, a lot fenced, and one year's provisions in store, or sufficient to last his family during his mission or means to provide it.
> ....
> When the Twelve went to England, they went on a special mission, by special commandment, and they left their families sick and destitute, God having promised that they should be provided for. But God does not require the same thing of the elders now, neither does he promise to provide for their families when they leave them contrary to counsel. The elders must provide for their families.
> I wish to give a word of advice to the sisters, and I will give it to my wife. I have known elders who by some means had got in debt, but had provided well for their families during their contemplated mission; and after they had taken their departure, their creditors would teaze (sic) their wives for the pay due from their husbands, till they would give them the last provision they had left them, and they were obliged to subsist on charity or starve till their husbands returned. Such a course of conduct on the part of the creditor is anti-Christian and criminal; and I forbid my wife from paying one cent of my debts while I am absent attending to the things of the kingdom; and I want the sisters to act on the same principle.[18]

The fact that it was Brigham Young teaching these principles of self-reliance might be tucked away for recall during our examination of the Brigham Young period.

Joseph Smith warned that some would complain about the contributions they had made. The following excerpt indicates both that people were only asked to give part of their property, and only then to assist the poor, and that there would be those who would later change their minds and want those gifts back:

> I also cautioned the Saints against men who came amongst them whining and growling about their money, because they had kept the Saints, and borne some of the burden with others, and thus thinking that others, who are still poorer, and have borne greater burdens than they themselves, ought to make up their losses. I cautioned the Saints to beware of such, for they were throwing out insinuations here and there, to level a dart at the best interests of the Church, and if possible destroy the character of its Presidency.[19]

This is the down side or dark side of "consecration." Some made donations for the support of needy saints, and then later wished to have their contributions back. This was when the "deed that cannot be broken" clause came into effect to prevent chaos, confusion, hardship, and even further ill will.

An important summarizing thought for this portion of the chapter is that at least as far as section 42 is concerned, there is no mention of a need to have the two-way deeding of all property which has come to be associated in the public mind with the term "consecration." Only the "residue" is consecrated in a one-way transaction. This theme appears in other chapters.

There is one last important topic to be considered before we finish up our look at section 42. The normal mode of economic interaction between the saints is buying and selling, not gifts or "consecrations." Verse 54 states that "Thou shalt not take thy brother's garment; thou shalt pay for that which thou shalt receive of thy brother." This verse makes it clear that normal business rules are to govern transactions between saints. The donations or "consecrations" are only for the benefit of the poor and are only a small portion of the economic transactions in normal times. We may extend the effect of this verse a little by reading it to mean that what cannot be done directly (getting goods from another without paying for them), cannot be done indirectly through some centralized organization performing a "take from the rich and give to the poor" Robin Hood function. The next step of logic is to say that if no such function can legitimately be performed, then we may conclude that no such Robin Hood organization could exist. Beyond providing appropriate meeting places, and similar facilities so that the church may perform its ecclesiastical functions adequately, the only required economic function, whether centralized or not, is care of the poor. Only an organization appropriate to accomplish those goals should exist.

Referring back to President Romney's comments quoted earlier in this chapter, it is important to understand the relationship between the poor and the rich. The principle of justice does not give the poor any enforceable claim on the property of the rich. However, mercy operates such that if the rich do not recognize the needs of the poor and attempt to fulfill them, the rich, in turn, can expect no mercy and help in their own case when the Lord judges them. They may be denied exaltation. But of course, if they did not desire to help others during their mortal life, they would be out of place and would make serious mistakes in a state of exaltation, because helping others is what exaltation is all about.

Verse 55 should also be examined. It says "and if thou obtainest more than that which would be for thy support, thou shalt give it into my storehouse, that all things may be done according to that which I have said." Note that this is a command direct from the Lord to each individual, and that each is admonished to "give" to support the various purposes mentioned earlier. This command from the Lord is not to be enforced by local administrators. It is more like the "Be ye therefore perfect" kind of command which can only be carried out by individuals, each in his own way and at his own pace.

There is a great contrast between this meaning and other possible meanings. For example, if the command had been made to the bishop or some other central authority, and the word "take" was used, we would have the opposite meaning, the philosophy which is always associated with socialism, communism, or any other form of centralized control employing force.

Some who have accepted the philosophies of force would imagine that without an enforceable taxing power, no important organization can continue to exist. However, the church is and ought to be denied that power, and yet it continues to flourish. In the same way, any other organization which itself is righteous and is performing a righteous purpose will be supported by righteous people. If it ceases to be supported spontaneously by righteous people, then it ought to collapse.[20] In a purely civil setting, it may be necessary for a righteous majority to use force to protect itself against a criminal or irresponsible minority or an outside threat, but even that use of force should be kept to a minimum.

We may conclude then that verse 55 should be read as a request for donations based on (1) the observed needs of the poor for food and land, (2) the needs of the church, that is the whole group, for buildings, etc., and (3) the ability of each member to contribute to these worthy causes. The bishop may request a certain donation from a member, but he has no administrative power to do more than make the request and thus indicate his judgement as to the needs of the poor or of the group. Asking for contributions that go beyond that needed to aid the poor would tend to remove capital from productive use and would lower the overall efficiency of the economy. The member controls his property absolutely and is responsible for the final choices he makes as to the amounts and kinds of gifts given.

Chapter 17 Notes

1. "Consecrate," *Webster's Third New International Dictionary* (Chicago: Encyclopedia Britannica, Inc., 1976)

2. D&C 57:1. For other statements concerning land, see also D&C 51:16; 52:2; 58:57; 82:13; 84:31; 85:3; 94:3; 103:22, 24, 35; 105:15, 29; 115:7; 124:44. Concerning temples, see D&C 109:12. Concerning other things, see D&C 42:39; 104:60, 66.

3. JD 5:18; address by Heber C. Kimball, April 6, 1857 in Salt Lake City.

4. General donations, 124:21. Church publications, 84:104. Missionary funds, 72:13 (9-13); 84:103. Building fund, 42:35. Welfare, 42:30, 33, 37, 39, 71; 51:5; 83:6; 90:28.

5. Migration or gathering fund, 42:35; 85:1-3; 103:22; 105:29. 6. HC 2:205; entry dated March 7, 1835, at Kirtland.

7. D&C 64:21-22. Revelation dated September 11, 1831, at Kirtland. HC 1:211-214.

8. HC 1:148; Feb., 1831, at Kirtland.

9. Mosiah 18:27-29. Other Book of Mormon scriptures dealing with assistance to the poor, or alms, are summarized here: Mosiah 4:16-26 give if you have; Mosiah

18:27-29 give if you have, receive if not; Alma 16:16 no inequality; 4 Ne. 1:3 all things common among them; Alma 5:55 help poor; 3 Ne 13:1 secret alms; Jacob 2:17-19 be free with your substance; Mosiah 21:17 gave to widows; Alma 35:9 help to poor; Alma 1:26-27 gave to poor; Alma 4:13 succoring; 3 Ne. 12:42 give to him that asketh.

10. President Marion G. Romney, "The Celestial Nature of Self-Reliance," *Ensign*, Vol. 12, No. 11, Nov. 1982 (Oct. 1982 conference), p. 91, 93. Also see lesson entitled "Personal Responsibility," 1983 Relief Society manual, p. 98, for additional current comments on individual versus group (Church) responsibility. It contains the following quote: "There is no ultimate safety in programmed security where others assume accountability for our direction and performance." Address by Elder Dean L. Larsen, *Ensign*, May 1980, p. 78.

11. See Leonard J. Arrington, *Building the City of God* (Salt Lake City, Utah: Deseret Book Company, 1976), p. 427-28.

12. D&C 84:103-104.

13. D&C 70:5-8.

14. D&C 90:29. See also D&C 119 (surplus property to be given to pay various church expenses), and D&C 42:30-34 (funds to care for poor to be raised by donation from excess property).

15. JD 2:306.

16. HC 1:362-363. June 25, 1833. Kirtland.

17. D&C 83; April 30, 1832; Independence.

18. HC 5:350-351; April 10, 1843; Brigham Young; Nauvoo.

19. HC 3:27; May 6, 1838; Joseph Smith; Far West.

20. Mosiah 29:25; Hela. 5:2; 6:40; 10:11; Alma 10:19; 4 Ne. 1:40; Hela. 1:5; (3-5, 13); 3 Ne. 7:2, 6; D&C 18:6; 61:31.

CHAPTER 18

Summary

The Riddle of the Secret Names:
A Clue to Understanding the United Order

In the new 1981 edition of the Doctrine and Covenants, many of the secret names appearing in section 82, revealed April 26, 1832, have been removed as unimportant relics of the past.[1] But how did they come into being in the first place? This intriguing riddle seems never to have been solved. As the clues to the riddle and thus the riddle itself begins to fade, it is a good time to put forth a solution.

The answer to the riddle is not a mere curiosity, for it changes dramatically some of the traditional meanings associated with such gospel terms as the united order and the law of consecration. The united order of Joseph Smith's time has been described by some as a program intended to be a church-wide experiment in Christian communism, but which, because of various shortcomings of the saints, fell short of that goal. A cursory reading of parts of the Doctrine and Covenants might lead one to that conclusion. However, it should be remembered that, like most of the sections in the Doctrine and Covenants, the revelations that deal with economic matters were given to specific people for specific purposes. Generalizing from these individual situations must be done very carefully to avoid reading in more than is there.

Actually, a careful study of the publicly available *Documentary History of the Church* shows that the united order was a small group of hand picked men given specific assignments at the beginning of the gathering and organizing of the saints. And contrary to the traditional idea of failure, the united order of Joseph Smith's time performed its mission brilliantly. This group was chosen before the Twelve Apostles were even called,[2] and long before the Twelve assumed any significant administrative functions. It combined the functions of today's Corporation of the President, the First Presidency, the Quorum of the Twelve, and the Presiding Bishopric in carrying out the business affairs of the church. After the Quorum of the Twelve became a mature and stable body, the highest two quorums assumed all the duties of the united order, and the original ad hoc administrative body ceased to have any existence separate from those two quorums.

The united order was composed of the church leaders in Kirtland (Joseph Smith, Sidney Rigdon, Oliver Cowdery, Newel K. Whitney, and Martin Harris), and those who had recently been sent to Missouri (Bishop Edward Partridge, William W. Phelps, John Whitmer, and Algernon Sidney Gilbert).[3] Later, two other men were added by specific revelations, Frederick G. Williams, D&C 92, and John Johnson, D&C 96.

The united order was organized as a general partnership, with a branch in Kirtland and one in Missouri. A basic feature of a business partnership is that the law considers all the partners to be fully liable for the business agreements made by any one of the partners. In that sense, all the partners hold all business and personal assets in common. Their business gains are placed in one account before each person's share of the total is calculated. The properties or monies that are held in common are available for the use of the individual partners.[4]

The men at the head of the church often had both public and secret callings. A letter dated June 25, 1833 from Joseph Smith and Sidney Rigdon in Kirtland to various brethren in Missouri illustrates a number of relationships:

> Let Brother Edward Partridge choose as counselors . . ., Brother Parley P. Pratt and Brother Titus Billings . . . .
>
> Zombre [John Johnson] has been received as a member of the firm, by commandment, and has just come to Kirtland to live; as soon as we get a power of attorney signed agreeably to law, for Alam [Edward Partridge] we will forward it to him, and will immediately expect one from that part of the firm . . [5]

Here Bishop Partridge is addressed by his normal name for public ecclesiastical topics, and separately by his secret name for united order business. The passage concerning John Johnson serves to equate the "order" mentioned in the commandment or revelation, D&C 96, with the "firm" used to conduct various items of central church business. The power of attorney mentioned is an instrument closely associated with the law of agency and partnership. The word "firm" implies a small and closely knit group, not something general and public.

From the group of eleven partners, subgroups were formed as specific transactions or functions needed to be carried out.[6] These subgroups were kept insulated from each other.[7] In today's world where liability-limiting corporations can be formed almost at will, the myriad of general partner/silent partner[8] arrangements of Joseph Smith's order would likely be recast into a system of subsidiary corporations under the control of a parent corporation. However, that was not possible in Joseph Smith's day,[9] and the united order partnership system was a legal and creative solution to the needs of the time. If two or three men operate one store under a normal business name, and two or three other men operate another store under a different business name, and a third group operates a printing establishment under a third business name,[10] no one would have reason to suspect that all were really manifestations of the same underlying group.[11]

This separation and secrecy had an important and legitimate business purpose. It allowed the united order brethren to control their business credit, risks, and liabilities. If a creditor of one enterprise realized that he could claim payment from several other enterprises because they were all parts of the same organization, that creditor might severely disrupt the plans and programs of the gathering and settlement of the saints. As it was, the creditors contracted with a limited set of men, and looked only to them for repayment.

The brethren contracted some large debts in their business dealings with the trade and finance institutions of their time.[12] These large lines of credit were necessary to sustain extensive purchases of land in Kirtland and Missouri.[13] Church control of this land made the "gathering" a practical possibility. Saints could move to those areas with assurance that they could purchase land at a reasonable price and begin to improve it for their use.[14] The same process occurred with supplies. Wholesale purchases of goods were made by church-controlled firms and resold to the saints.[15] This provided a reliable source of supplies and precluded price gouging by outside traders.

It was necessary that some of the early plans for migration be carried on in secret.[16] If anyone, church member or not, were to know where and when the church was planning to move, they might attempt to profit at the expense of the faithful saints by first purchasing the land from the government and then reselling it at a large profit to the saints.[17] Instead, the church-controlled united order entity made those first purchases and thus prevented damaging price escalations.

Thus the existence, true nature, and mission of the united order was known to very few, whether in the church or out. The world was only able to see those manifestations of the united order that the church leaders (and the Lord) wished them to see. That may explain the fact that the riddle of the secret names has remained so long unsolved.

As conditions changed and the center of gravity of the church's migrating population moved further west, it became appropriate to have two separate general partnerships.[18] After the initial thrust into Missouri, communication between the east and west branches probably was too slow to allow the bulk of the decisions to still be made in Kirtland. Men on the spot had to be given that authority. The single firm became two firms, and each probably added extra personnel.[19] They continued to have business dealings with each other, loaning money back and forth, but the eastern branch relinquished control of the western branch's operating decisions. Finally, sometime in the period after 1838, the functions of the united order were absorbed by the First Presidency, the Quorum of the Twelve, and the Presiding Bishopric,[20] culminating with the move to a corporate form in 1841.[21]

Chapter 18 Notes

1. Code names also appeared in sections 78, 92, 96 and 104 of earlier editions. Note that another secret name could have been removed from the 1981 edition: "Alam" was the secret name given to Bishop Edward Partridge, see HC 1:363.

2. The Twelve Apostles were called February 14, 1835, HC 2:180-200.

3. For assignments see D&C 57; HC 1:191. For secret names see David J. Whittaker, "Substituted Names in the Published Revelations of Joseph Smith," BYU Studies 1983, Vol. 23, pp. 103-112. Although not named as formal members of the first united order partnership, two of Bishop Partridge's counselors, John Corrill and Isaac Morley, appear to have been closely associated with its transactions (for example see HC 1:318, 394n, 395n, 399, 411), and later, as bishops themselves (HC 1:363, June 1833), may have become members of the separate united order firm in Zion. HC 2:434, 436.

4. D&C 82:11-20; 104:67-77.

5. HC 1:363.

6. HC 2:433-4.

7. HC 2:287, 324, 475.

8. HC 2:335-6.

9. See note 2 at end of chapter 1 for background on the availability of the corporate form.

10. HC 1:365; 2:273, 482-3.

11. HC 1:270.

12. D&C 82:22; 104:78-81. See Marvin S. Hill, et al, *Kirtland Economy Revisited* (Provo, Utah: BYU Press, 1977), pp. 26, 36. HC 1:365; 2:44-9, 492.

13. The same pattern of block land purchases by a central church body for resale to the saints was continued in Far West (HC 2:468, 496, 521; 3:63-4), and Nauvoo (HC 4:7-8).

14. HC 2:478-80.

15. HC 1:365; 2:288.

16. D&C 28:9; 42:35.

17. For example, Ezra Thayre probably had this in mind when he gave funds to the church to purchase lands, but wished to take title and control the disposition of the lands purchased with his money, D&C 56:8-10. D&C 85 is also aimed at those who wished to circumvent the church land development plans with plans of their own, HC 1:298.

18. D&C 104.

19. For example, John Whitmer in Missouri, HC 2:434, and Willard Richards in Kirtland, HC 2:492.

20. See D&C 119; 120.

21. The end of the united order partnerships and the beginning of the corporate form in 1841 (where the term "Trustee-in-Trust" was used), also saw the nonrecognition of old debts and notes of the partnership forms. Perhaps after losing many hundreds of thousands of dollars because of mob violence there really was no other alternative. This was a kind of informal bankruptcy proceeding, with an accompanying change of business form. The personal bankruptcy of Joseph Smith was apparently a part of this whole pattern of making a new beginning.

CHAPTER 19

Conclusion

In the preceding chapters we have described Joseph Smith's united order as a partnership designed to carry out general church business matters, especially those related to the gathering of the saints to Missouri. We have noted its replacement by a corporation. We have explored its relationships to other church organizations of its day, and to the collection and disbursing of church funds.

There are a few major points to be extracted from this survey of the united order firm's existence. First, it should be clear that the united order firm and its members performed their assigned roles brilliantly in spite of the great difficulties to be overcome, and were in no way the failures tradition seems to have labeled them. The saints were gathered in large numbers to western areas and ultimately reached a safe destination. These men made a great contribution by performing many of the tasks that were later absorbed by the Quorum of the Twelve as it assumed its proper role in the church hierarchy. Through this transfer of function, the united order became "an everlasting order" as appointed by revelation. (D&C 64:28)

We should also be able to learn something from this historical case study about the relationships between economic principles and the gospel. During the life of the united order firm and thereafter, in fact during the entire Joseph Smith period, the normal use of the term consecration simply meant contributions to the church for general purposes such as public buildings and printing, and for the care of the poor. It had no connotations of required communal joinder of property or centralized direction of labor. There was an additional more general and spiritual meaning for the term consecration: a willingness to use one's property in a way consistent with the current gospel program. In Joseph Smith's day, that often meant resisting mob action and helping destitute immigrants. In our day it might mean supporting missionary and genealogy work or resisting pornography or attacks on the institution of the family. Each person makes a choice as to how all his property and effort are used. In the broadest sense, consecration simply means that gospel purposes underlie the decisions that are made by each individual.

This study helps show that there is no predetermined detailed formula for righteous economic and social action defined in the scriptures or elsewhere in the gospel. Gospel principles tell us in general terms how we should do our duty and relate to others, but do not provide the details. Often the most effective use of resources can be made under individual control. In other cases, group cooperation, coordination and pooling of resources is more effective in reaching the objective.

We have many different examples since the church was organized. In the Joseph Smith era we saw committed people constructing and changing a program of mutual helpfulness as the need arose. A thorough study of the Brigham Young era would probably show that the unique requirements of time and place determined the programs proposed, without necessarily setting a pattern for future circumstances. The church program today differs from each of these two earlier periods, and the setting in which it operates is also much different.

From these observations we might conclude that every era has its own social, technological, economic and political setting and that the church program will vary accordingly. The shape of future programs will depend on the future needs and environment.

Philosophical writers have constructed various stories or parables to illustrate their utopian concepts of individual and societal behavior. Perhaps we can describe a utopia of our own. In it each person would know and understand all the facts and circumstances of the time and situation, would be motivated by the same righteous goals, and thus would tend to reach similar conclusions about the proper course to take in the future. Only minimal coordination, "a word to the wise," would be necessary. This equal understanding and spontaneous cooperation would make possible the fully enlightened unity that is expected of celestial beings.

There is another question this study may help resolve. Tradition has it that the saints of Joseph Smith's time were directed to join in societies having centralized ownership and control of property. This supposed centralization directive created the paradox of having some gospel teachings which support the individual freedoms symbolized by the Constitution, including the right to private property and the separation of church and state, while other teachings suggest that all property should be bound together and placed under church control. The communal traditions and the freedom philosophy both make fundamental statements about the way society should be organized. It is difficult for both paradigms to be in full effect at the same time and place.

In an attempt to resolve the paradox, this study has presented evidence that the traditions are incorrect: Joseph Smith did nothing to compromise individual freedom through any agency of church or government, and maintained individual ownership and control of property as one of the keys of that freedom. In this way, the policies of Joseph Smith's time are consistent with those of our own.

INDEX

Abraham	31, 150, 271-274, 277, 287, 288, 299, 310, 311
Abram	272-274
Ahashdah	85, 89, 103, 104
Alam	89, 91, 104, 106, 108, 222, 348, 360, 362
Aldrich, Mark	209
Annanias	43
Arrington, Leonard	17, 260, 285
Avard, Dr.	21
Babbitt, Alson W.	48
Baldwin, Wheeler	31
Bardsley	135
Barnett, John T.	212
Barzillai	144
Bates	123, 128
Beebee, Calvin	183
Benjamin, King	22
Benson, Ezra Taft	282, 285
Billings, Titus	14, 103, 139, 140, 360
Bishop, Gladden	225, 227
Brewster, Collins	38, 39
Bump, Jacob	246, 247, 336
Burkett	103
Cahoon, Reynolds	207, 214, 247, 336
Campbell, Alexander	28
Campbellite	27
Carlin, Thomas	142, 183, 206, 214, 247
Carter, Jared	214, 247, 336
Carter, Phebe W.	142
Carter, Simeon	183
Clapp, Matthew	27
Clark, J. Reuben	1, 13-15, 118, 119, 139
Coltrin, Zebedee	147
Copley, Lyman	82
Corrill, John	103, 107, 166, 179, 180, 183, 184, 362
Coville, James	74
Cowan	206

370   INDEX

Cowdery, Oliver	72, 73, 76, 89, 91, 97, 99, 104, 111, 112, 134, 135, 137, 147, 157, 164, 167, 170, 171, 191, 194-196, 201, 219, 223, 227, 292, 359
Cutler, Alpheus	247
Enoch	45, 84, 85, 87, 90, 113, 148
Enoch(Joseph Smith)	2, 4-7, 14, 16-18, 20-23, 27-29, 31, 34-40, 42
Evans	26, 187
Finch, John	28, 29
Fordham, Elijah	31
Gause, Jesse	16, 87, 118
Gazelam	85, 89, 90
Geddes	143, 260
Gilbert, Sidney	75-77, 79, 91, 98, 99, 107, 112, 113, 118, 122, 131, 174, 191, 199, 267, 268, 359
Gilbert, Whitney & Co.	98, 100
Granger, Oliver	192, 193, 206, 214
Hagen, Everett E.	41
Harris, Martin	77-79, 89, 91, 167, 168, 177, 191, 219, 287, 288, 294, 298, 319, 359
Higbee, Elias	183, 207
Hinckley, Gordon B.	316
Horah	89, 91
Hotchkiss	210
Hurlburt	137
Hutterites	125
Hyde, Orson	134, 137, 138, 162, 163, 219, 224, 230, 249, 251-253, 263, 264
Johnson, John	103, 104, 106, 107, 133, 134, 147, 160, 162, 191, 199, 359, 360
Jones	135
Joses	43
Kimball, Heber C.	40, 136, 137, 205, 207, 211, 264, 333, 334, 354
Knight, Vinson	161, 162
Lee, Harold B.	200, 277
Lewis, J.	162
Lyman	31, 135, 139, 142, 143, 183
Lyon, Father	167, 302
M'Lellin, William E.	136, 224, 229, 250
Mahalaleel	89, 91

Mahemson	89
Marks, William	1, 13, 28, 44, 171, 224, 247, 304
Marsh, Thomas B.	183, 222, 224-226
McWithy, Isaac	167, 168, 170, 177
McBride, Reuben	258
McKay, David O.	1
Melchizedek	272-274, 299
Mennonites	125
Millet, Artemus	246, 247, 336
Monson, Thomas	279, 285
Morley, Isaac	103, 107, 118, 166, 179, 180, 183, 362
Myres, Jacob	147
Norris	38, 39
Olihah	89
Owen, Able	206
Partridge, Edward	9, 14, 24, 42, 62, 64, 65, 71-73, 75, 78, 80, 88, 91, 103, 104, 106-109, 112, 117, 118, 121-123, 128, 140, 166, 179-181, 191, 198, 289, 348, 359, 360, 362
Patten, David W.	180, 182-185, 250
Patten, John M.	181
Pelagoram	84, 88, 103
Phelps, William W.	76, 78, 91, 97-100, 103, 104, 107, 110, 112, 117, 118, 120, 150, 160, 164-167, 179-181, 183, 185, 186, 191, 193, 200, 307, 348, 359
Porter, Francis	25, 161, 295
Pratt, Orson	17, 18, 103, 201, 258, 264, 330, 360
Pratt, Parley P.	103, 258, 264, 360
Pulsipher, Zerah	139
Richards, Willard	173, 205, 207, 219, 364
Rigdon, Sidney	22, 25-28, 72, 73, 78, 79, 84, 85, 88, 89, 91, 102, 103, 111, 147, 157, 164, 167, 171, 172, 184, 190, 223, 224, 227, 230, 247, 336, 342, 348, 359, 360
Roberts, B.H.	15
Romney, Marion G.	342, 352, 355
Russell, Samuel	305, 306
Russell, Daniel	209, 305, 306
Sawyer	38
Shalemanasseh	89, 91
Shederlaomach	102
Sloan, James	239

Smith, Eden	34, 135, 193, 220, 221, 226, 312
Smith, Emma	97
Smith, O.A.	28, 242
Smith, George A.	40, 211
Smith, Hyrum	162, 172, 192, 193, 211, 214, 247, 263, 336
Smith, Joseph F.	318
Smith, Samuel	160, 305, 306
Smith, William	15, 76, 78, 91, 97, 102, 103, 109, 111, 112, 117, 121, 133, 135-137, 147, 150, 157, 161-164, 167, 171, 191, 208, 224, 230, 250, 252, 359
Smith, Abraham O.	31
Snow, Erastus	17
Snow, Lorenzo	246, 293
Sophira	43
Stevens	161
Stokes, Alfred Edward	26
Alfred Edward	26
Taylor, John	205
Thayre, Ezra	139, 363
Tippits	159, 291
Van Buren	337
Warren, Calvin	171, 209, 210, 215, 225, 227
Whitmer, David	160, 164, 166, 180, 183, 185
Whitmer, John	82, 91, 97, 99, 104, 107, 139, 150, 160, 164-166, 179, 180, 183, 185, 191, 193, 359, 360, 364
Whitmer, Peter	88, 139
Whitney, Newel K.	76, 82, 84, 85, 88, 89, 91, 98-100, 103, 104, 106, 111, 112, 117, 133, 137, 147, 162, 191, 198, 199, 226, 263, 294, 359
Wight, Lyman	31, 139, 142, 143, 183
Wightman, William	208
Wilkie, John	36, 37, 205
Wilkinson, Ernest L.	278
Williams, Frederick G.	102, 103, 133, 135, 137, 147, 157, 161, 162, 164, 167, 191, 359
Witter, Daniel S.	209
Woodruff, Wilford	40, 139, 141, 142, 207, 269
Young, Brigham	333, 336, 337, 347, 350, 355, 365
Zombre	102, 103, 105, 359

About the Author

KENT W. HUFF is an attorney and computer consultant with experience in economic regulation and related data collection and analysis. He has worked for nine years in Saudi Arabia with the Saudi Ministry of Finance in association with the United States and Saudi Arabian Joint Commission on Economic Cooperation. He was born in Utah Valley, attended BYU, married Suzanne Snow from Los Angeles, and has six children. He has two law degrees from George Washington University in Washington, D.C., and worked for ten years there, mostly for various U.S. government agencies, before the move to Saudi Arabia.

www.ingramcontent.com/pod-product-compliance
Lightning Source LLC
LaVergne TN
LVHW091246080426
835510LV00007B/138